12.40

The Canadian Imagination

The Canadian Imagination

Dimensions of a
Literary Culture

Margaret Atwood	Marine Leland
Peter Buitenhuis	Marshall McLuhan
Douglas Bush	Brian Parker
Northrop Frye	George Woodcock

Edited with an introductory essay by

David Staines

Harvard University Press
Cambridge, Massachusetts,
and London, England
1977

Library of Congress Cataloging in Publication Data
Main entry under title:
The Canadian imagination.

Includes index.

1. Canadian literature—History and criticism—Addresses, es-
says, lectures. I. Staines, David, 1946–
PR9184.6.C35   810'.9   77-9587
ISBN 0-674-09355-0

Contents

Acknowledgments

MARGARET ATWOOD: "Backdrop Addresses Cowboy," from *The Animals in That Country* (1968), by permission of Oxford University Press (Canada) in association with The Atlantic Monthly Press; "Thoughts from Underground," from *The Journals of Susanna Moodie* (1970), by permission of Oxford University Press (Canada).

MARGARET AVISON: "Identity," from *Winter Sun* (University of Toronto Press, 1960), by permission of the author.

EARLE BIRNEY: "Can. Lit.," from *The Collected Poems of Earle Birney* (1975), by permission of The Canadian Publishers, McClelland and Stewart Limited, Toronto.

HERMIA FRASER: "Song to the Wanderer," from *The Book of Canadian Poetry* (1943), by permission of Gage Publishing Limited.

A. M. KLEIN: "Portrait of the Poet as Landscape," from *The Collected Poems of A. M. Klein* (1974), by permission of McGraw-Hill Ryerson Limited.

IRVING LAYTON: "From Colony to Nation," from *Music on a Kazoo* (1956), by permission of The Canadian Publishers, McClelland and Stewart Limited, Toronto.

DENNIS LEE: "1838," from *Nicholas Knock and Other People* (1974), by permission of the Macmillan Company of Canada Limited and Houghton Mifflin Company.

DOUGLAS LEPAN: "A Country without a Mythology," from *The Wounded Prince and Other Poems* (Chatto and Windus, 1948), by permission of the author.

Susan Musgrave: "Witchery Way," from *Selected Strawberries: Poems 1969–1973* (Sono Nis Press, 1977), by permission of the author.

John Newlove: "The Pride," from *Black Night Window* (1968), by permission of The Canadian Publishers, McClelland and Stewart Limited, Toronto.

Alden Nowlan: "Genealogy of Morals," from *The Things Which Are* (Contact Press, 1962), by permission of the author.

E. J. Pratt: "Behind the Log," "Brébeuf and His Brethren," "The Cachalot," "The Deed," "Dunkirk," "From Stone to Steel," "The Iron Door," "Like Mother, Like Daughter," "The Prize Cat," "The Roosevelt and the Antinoe," "The Titanic," and "The Truant," from the second edition of *Collected Poems* (1958), by permission of the Macmillan Company of Canada Limited.

James Reaney: "Winnipeg Seen as a Body of Time and Space," from *Selected Shorter Poems* (1975), by permission of Press Porcepic Limited.

F. R. Scott: "W. L. M. K.," from *The Eye of the Needle* (Contact Press, 1957), by permission of the author.

Francis Sparshott: "Episode in Frederick, Md.," from *A Cardboard Garage* (1969), by permission of Clarke, Irwin and Company Limited.

Wilfred Watson: "Emily Carr," from *Friday's Child* (1955), by permission of Faber and Faber Limited.

The Canadian Imagination

Introduction

Canada Observed

David Staines

Canada is both young and old. It is young as a nation, only slightly more than one hundred years old. When the four original provinces of Lower Canada (Quebec), Upper Canada (Ontario), Nova Scotia, and New Brunswick united to form the Dominion of Canada under the British North America Act of 1867, their southern neighbor, the United States, was already approaching the celebration of its centennial. The tenth and last province, Newfoundland, joined the dominion in 1949; the country as presently constituted is scarcely a quarter-century old. At the same time, however, Canada is old as a place of European settlement. Near the end of the tenth century the Vikings arrived on Canada's Atlantic coast, and about five centuries before Christopher Columbus discovered America, Leif Ericson created a short-lived colony in Newfoundland.

Canadian history is the record of a colony paying allegiance to several mother countries; to follow Canada's historical development is to trace its time as a colony of France and of England and, finally and most elusively, as an economic colony of the United States. Part of the history of Canada is an account of the slow realization of its own independence, an acceptance of its importance within an international framework, and, most significant, a discarding of the colonial mentality which had characterized the country and its actions for many years.

Canadian history shows a series of attempts to unify a land so vast as to defy unity. Canada is a country of distinct regions oriented along an east-west axis imposed upon the north-south axis of the geography of North America. The continent's natural economic flow is north-south, and the physical border between Canada and the United States is both arbitrary and nondifferentiating. The Maritime Provinces share so many features with New England that they are often called the Boston States. The prairie farmer feels more kinship with his counterpart just south of the border than he does with a farmer on Prince Edward Island or even in Ontario. Southwestern British Columbia has many affinities with the temper of the Pacific Coast states. The Canadian landscape partakes of the geographical north-south flow of the continent, while it tries to attain a tentative unity through an imposed east-west axis first based on the waterways of the country, the Saint Lawrence River and the Great Lakes, and later developed in the network of railways which span the nation.

Canada's motto, "A mari usque ad mare" [From sea unto sea], might easily apply to an island, yet Canada is a sprawling giant, a land of nearly four million square miles, with the longest coastline in the world and the Atlantic and Pacific oceans as the eastern and western borders. The cold and remote Arctic territories serve as the northern border, and the United States is the southern border. Within these borders lies not merely one country, but a series of regional units. Like their southern neighbors, Canadians find their home within particular regions of their country; Canada is a federation, not only of ten provinces, the Yukon, and the Northwest Territories, but also of geographical and psychological units. Whether these regions be the Maritimes on the East Coast or British Columbia on the West Coast, they provide centers of identity for Canadians. The sheer size of the country will always deny a sense of unity to all its citizens, a unity which was the dream of the architects of confederation. The Canadian preference for a mosaic structure in which all the ethnic and social regions retain their distinctness is central to an understanding of the nation. As a country Canada is not only a mosaic of ethnic cultures but also a mosaic of regions, each with its own sense of identity; the nation, therefore, exists in a dialectic of regional and ethnic tensions. The tension of the French and the English, the two founding peoples of the country, is at the center of this dialectic, and such tensions, always dynamic and demanding, have given Canada its uniqueness. And the mosaic pattern becomes a further element operating against national unity. Canadian history follows a pattern of attempts to impose order and political unity, but not cultural homogeneity, on the whole country.

The development of the literature of Canada has been complicated and tentative. In a sparsely populated country the nineteenth-century artist found himself isolated and alone without an audience. From the earliest period of Canadian literary history, the problem of an audience has been a continual and trying dilemma for both writers and critics. In the "Introductory Essay" to the first anthology of native Canadian poetry, *Selections from Canadian Poets* (1864), Edward Hartley Dewart lamented: "There is probably no country in the world, making equal pretensions to intelligence and progress, where the claims of native literature are so little felt, and where every effort in poetry has been met with so much coldness and indifference, as in Canada. And what is more to be deprecated than neglect of our most meritorious authors, is the almost universal absence of interest and faith in all indigenous literary productions." Such indifference was a reflection of the country's colonial mentality; Canada would turn instinctively to England, France, and the United States for its reading material. As late as 1938 the novelist Frederick Philip Grove complained that "Canadians are at bottom not interested in their own country; I honestly believe they prefer to read about dukes and lords, or about the civil war in the United States." When Hugh MacLennan looked back on the period before the Second World War, he saw the writer's bewilderment in finding his proper audience: "When I first thought of writing this novel [*Barometer Rising*, published in 1941] Canada was virtually an uncharacterized country. It seemed to me then that if our literature was to be anything but purely regional, it must be directed to at least two audiences. One was the Canadian public, which took the Canadian scene for granted but never defined its particular essence. The other was the international public, which had never thought about Canada at all, and knew nothing whatever about us."

The attitude of the Canadian audience has changed. The new growth and vitality of Canadian literature have altered the reading habits of a once-colonial audience. No longer does the reading public turn instinctively and solely to other countries; Canadian literature has come of age, and a verification of its maturity is its informed and interested audience. In 1972 the novelist Margaret Laurence offered a happy contrast to Grove's disgruntled comment: "At one time it was extremely difficult to be a Canadian writer. We still had for many, many years a kind of colonial mentality, a great many people felt that a book written by a Canadian couldn't possibly be good. It had to come from either New York or the other side of the Atlantic to be any good. This whole cultural climate has changed incredibly, and particularly in the last decade. My first book was published in 1960, and the change in those twelve years in the whole cultural situation has been enormous. Canadian writers are probably in a better situation now than they have ever been. Very few Canadian writers of any seriousness or worth do not find a considerable readership in their own country."

The attitude of the international audience has also changed. In the early part of this century Stephen Leacock wrote most of his shorter pieces for publication abroad, in either England or the United States, and he consequently avoided creating unmistakably Canadian settings. When Morley Callaghan began his literary career in the twenties, he avoided specifically Canadian backgrounds in order to write primarily for an American audience. Now, however, Canadian literature commands international respect and attention. The writer need no longer fear his own Canadian world. Writing with distinctive Canadian voices, Margaret Atwood, Marie-Claire Blais, Robertson Davies, Margaret Laurence, Mordecai Richler, and Gabrielle Roy are only a few of the contemporary authors who have loyal international audiences.

The Canadian Imagination is a testimony to the vitality and complexity of Canadian literature and culture. In the spring of 1976 I had the opportunity of introducing a course on Canadian literature in the Department of English and American Literature and Language at Harvard University. Through the financial assistance of the Canadian Consulate General in Boston, I was able to invite distinguished authorities on Canada to visit the university; to supplement the course, the visitors offered a lecture series of coordinated perspectives on Canadian literary culture. Their observations and insights became the force behind the creation of this volume. Developing and expanding the ideas they expressed in Cambridge, they have contributed five of the accompanying studies; at the same time I invited Peter Buitenhuis, Douglas Bush, and George Woodcock to write complementary studies. These eight critics here offer a series of distinct outlooks on important aspects of the Canadian scene.

It is significant that the observations presented in *The Canadian Imagination* are made not by travelers to that foreign world but by knowledgeable commentators of that world. Although the reflections are of importance to Canadians, they are addressed primarily to a foreign audience. Only one volume of criticism of Canadian literature, Edmund Wilson's *O Canada* (1965), has been published in the United States. Even though the growing excitement in Canadian cultural life is signaled by the fact that a critic of Wilson's eminence should seek to know Canada, his volume remains ultimately unsatisfying; it is, as the subtitle states, *An American's Notes on Canadian Culture*. Edmund Wilson remained an outsider trying to synthesize the complexity of a culture he was only beginning to comprehend.

The eight chapters of this volume form a distinct shape. The vigor and maturity of recent developments in English Canadian poetry and fiction are the center of the first four chapters. In the fifth essay, "Stephen Leacock," Douglas Bush explores an earlier period of Canadian literature; Leacock's era was a time when Canada was slowly emerging as a nation in both the political and literary sense. The sixth chapter turns to the most recent development in English and French Canadian literature, a strong indigenous drama. The seventh chapter focuses solely on Quebec literature, an important component of the Canadian literary character. And the final chapter looks at the frequently debated question of the Canadian identity.

Like Canadian history, the growth of Canadian literature has been cautious and slow. Its earliest phase consists of eighteenth-century accounts of native industries—fishing, furs, and forestry; the journals that recount these activities reveal the successes and hardships of the pioneers. Such early writings, generally by visitors to the country who were using or exploiting the land's resources for their own and their homeland's benefit, offer little more than a description of the natural wealth of a new-found land.

In the nineteenth century Canadians began to explore the land that was their home. Whereas the politicians sought to impose some form of unity on a seemingly impossible terrain, authors wanted to understand the landscape that thwarted the politicians' dream. An interesting writer of this period is Susanna Moodie, who came to Canada from England with her husband and family in 1832. In her two major books, *Roughing It in the Bush* (1852) and *Life in the Clearings versus the Bush* (1853), she examined the Canadian frontier. The first book is harshly critical, written, as she confesses, by one whose "love for Canada was a feeling very nearly allied to that which the condemned criminal entertains for his cell—his only hope of escape being through the portals of the grave." Her hard existence in the forest gives way, after eight years, to a more civilized life in Belleville, Ontario, and this life forms the subject matter of her second book. Now she forsakes her position as disenchanted exile from the warmth of England and becomes a prophet of Canada's future. "An English lady, writing to me not long ago," Mrs. Moodie recounts, "expressed her weariness of my long stories about the country of my adoption, in the following terms:—'Don't fill your letters to me with descriptions of Canada. Who, *in England*, thinks anything of *Canada*!'" Who in the mother country cared about the life of the colony? Yet Mrs. Moodie saw that the colonial status was temporary:

> Be not discouraged, brave emigrant! Let Canada still remain the bright future in your mind, and hasten to convert your present day-dream into reality. The time is not far distant when she shall be the theme of many tongues, and the old nations of the world will speak of her progress with respect and admiration. Her infancy is past, she begins to feel her feet, to know her own strength, and see her way clearly through the wilderness. Child as you may deem her, she has already battled bravely for her own rights, and obtained the management of her own affairs. Her onward progress is

certain. There is no *if* in her case. She possesses within her own territory all the elements of future prosperity, and *she must be great!*

Susanna Moodie's prophecy was valid, although time was necessary for the colony to accept its destiny.

Like Canadian history, Canadian literature reflects the struggle of a young country to assert itself against the pressures of a mother country and a neighboring giant to the south. As early as 1858, Thomas D'Arcy McGee, the most persuasive spokesman for confederation, was declaring the path open to a truly Canadian literature: "We have the materials—our position is favourable—northern latitudes like ours have been famed for the strength, variety and beauty of their literature, all we demand is, that free scope be allowed to the talent and enterprise of the country, instead of allowing an unhealthy foreign substitute to be presented to our people." Despite Canada's position as a colony, young writers, McGee exhorted, should rise above the imitation of foreign models. Canadians stand in need of a distinctive literature, he realized, which speaks directly to their own world:

> The books that are made elsewhere, even in England, are not always the best fitted for us; they do not always run on the same mental gauge, nor connect with our trains of thought; they do not take us up at the by-stages of cultivation at which we have arrived, and where we are emptied forth as on a barren, pathless, habitationless heath. They are books of another state of society, bearing traces of controversies, or directed against errors or evils which for us hardly exist, except in the pages of these exotic books. Observe, I do not object to such books, especially when truthfully written; but it seems to me we do much need several other books calculated to our own meridian, and hitting home to our own society, either where it is sluggish

or priggish, or wholly defective in its present style of culture.

It would be many years before Canadian writers realized completely that foreign models were "books of another state of society."

Nineteenth- and early twentieth-century Canadian literature attempts to respond to the Canadian scene in a manner too reminiscent of other countries. Early Canadian poetry in English, for example, is dominated by the inheritances of English Romantic and Victorian poetry, although the poets who clung to the clichés of English romanticism were trying to describe the unique landscape of the New World. Such geographical delineation was a necessary prelude to the development of a distinctive Canadian literature. The immensity and power of the unpopulated land long remained a dominant theme of Canada's art; only after a confrontation with the landscape have artists moved to a confrontation with the inhabitants of the land.

McGee was right in his assertion that Canada could never develop a literature and culture of high excellence by imitating other countries. But Canada's colonial mentality seemed to favor and demand fidelity to foreign models. Moreover, as a colony Canada retained the moral facade of the mother country, be it the rigid Catholicism of French Canada or the narrow Protestantism of English Canada, and this facade became a further hindrance to the development of a distinctive art. If the early writings did attempt the important task of defining the landscape, they also refrained from confronting life. Douglas Bush told readers of the *Canadian Forum* in 1922 that the major drawback of the Canadian literary scene was sententious moralism:

No one reads a Canadian novel unless by mistake. Canadian fiction never comes to grips with life, but remains weak and timid; it has nothing to say. A mass of Canadian poetry consists of apostrophes to dancing rivulets that no doubt give considerable pleasure to the author's relatives. Robert Service has recently revived the glories of the once wicked and popular (and fictitious) Montmartre, but when Canadians try to sing of sin and sinful places, the effect is indescribably sad; their efforts have the same vivid realism that one finds in romances about the House of Hapsburg written by elderly American ladies in the Western states who have saturated themselves with the wickedest memoirs the local librarian could supply.

One can see no future for Canadian letters until Canadians learn to obey the fine injunction to "sin gladly." When we sin we do it in such a sneaking, hugger-mugger way, emoting moral platitudes until we are out of sight. An Englishman, Shaw said, thinks he is moral when he is merely uncomfortable. In this respect as in others Canada is steadfastly loyal to English tradition.

Proclaiming sentimentalism and insipidity as the twin muses of Canadian literature, he asserted: "We have in Canada more than enough books which tell us of the virtuousness of virtue and the viciousness of vice; if our morals are worth keeping they will not be damaged by books which attempt to do neither, but merely give an honest picture of human life."

In the *Commonweal* of November 6, 1929, Bush raised the question, "Is There a Canadian Literature?" in an essay of that title which charted the increasingly populated road to a truly distinctive and mature Canadian literature. Observing the contemporary excitement in literary circles on the appearance of Mazo de la Roche's *Jalna*, the short stories of Morley Callaghan, and the pioneer novels of Frederick Philip Grove, he concluded: "Creative and critical work has quickened its pace in the last few years. While only a few of the older writers were in touch with the modern mind, the newer ones are not provincial in outlook; yet they are in general dealing more and more with the material they know, which is as it should be. The best Canadian writing is moving away from the local and parochial to the local and universal, and it can increasingly be judged by other than domestic standards." For so long Canadians had struggled with the immense and often hostile nature which confronted them everywhere. Now they would find their literary home in the immediate land around them; the local need not be parochial. And the local seemed the only way for the Canadian to obtain a tenable position in his land. Working with his own familiar region within Canada, the artist explored more easily the universal truths of which art and life are made.

E. J. Pratt, deeply conscious of his Newfoundland upbringing, began his poetic career in the twenties with tales of shipwrecks and whale hunts; he would later write *Brébeuf and His Brethren* and *Towards the Last Spike*, two epics of Canadian life. And Frederick Philip Grove, the most significant figure in Canadian fiction at that time, wrote of the Manitoba pioneer in such a way that his novels represented both the struggles of the pioneers in Canada and the struggles of the pioneering artists.

Shortly before this time the Group of Seven, painters who shared a commitment to a fresh rendering of the Canadian landscape, found a symbol of their country in the Precambrian shield. Their paintings depicted the rugged and uninhabited regions of Ontario. Seeking to "bring out everything in the landscape as a matter of design and also, of course, of colour," as one of the group's members, Arthur Lismer, stated, their art captured the immense grandeur and power of the land. And at the same time Emily Carr was locating her paintings in her native British Columbia where timber and totem poles dominate the terrain.

The individual Canadian finds his home in a specific region, and Canadian literature and art continue to find homes within particular areas of the country—the

British Columbia of Emily Carr's paintings or Ethel Wilson's fiction, the Manitoba world of Margaret Laurence, the Ontario of the Group of Seven or Robertson Davies's fiction, the various Monterals of Hugh MacLennan or Mordecai Richler or Gabrielle Roy, E. J. Pratt's Newfoundland.

For many years Northrop Frye has been a central figure in the Canadian literary scene. His Canadian studies have offered new ways of approaching his country's literature. In his essay for this book, "Haunted by Lack of Ghosts," he presents a reflective survey and history of Canadian poetry which reveal its variety and maturity. "Earlier Canadian poetry," he writes, "was full of solitude and loneliness, of the hostility or indifference of nature, of the fragility of human life and values in such an environment. Contemporary Canadian poetry seems to think rather of this outer leviathan as a kind of objective correlative of some Minotaur that we find in our own mental labyrinths." To complement this opening essay, Peter Buitenhuis turns to Canada's most significant poet, E. J. Pratt, and offers a detailed study of the nature and importance of his writings.

In "Possessing the Land," the third essay of this volume, George Woodcock explores the historical development of English Canadian fiction. As he questions the presence of realism in the novel, he uncovers "a genuine Canadian twentieth-century romanticism, which must use fantasy and dreams as paths to reality, which must accept myth as the structure that subsumes history, which in its ultimate degree of the fantastic must recognize and unite with its opposite, satire, the logically absurd extension of realism." The center of Margaret Atwood's study, "Canadian Monsters," is recent fiction in which there is a curious presence of supernatural elements. For Stephen Leacock in the early part of this century, Canada was "a land of hope and sunshine where little towns spread their square streets and their trim maple trees beside placid lakes almost within echo of the primeval forest." The locale of the books Margaret Atwood discusses is the primeval forest, as she concentrates on the unexplored and uncharted terrain of the supernatural and the magical.

In the fifth essay, "Stephen Leacock," Douglas Bush goes back to the turn of the century to consider the early days of Canada and its literature. A wry humorist who liked to point out the foibles of society and himself, Leacock becomes emblematic of early Canadian literature. With his unassuming amiability and self-deprecating sense of humor he lacks the kind of self-consciousness which has characterized more recent developments in the Canadian literary world.

Drama is the latest development in Canada's literary culture, and Brian Parker's essay explores Canadian drama which combines local subject matter with various experiments in spatial form expressed in the metropolitan Montreal of Michel Tremblay's plays, the rural Ontario of James Reaney's, and the West Coast Indian world of George Ryga's. "Is There a Canadian Drama?" is also a commentary on some similarities between English and French Canada as it focuses on the plays of both cultures. Although these similarities reveal an exciting sense of a single Canadian literature, it is, nevertheless, an indisputable fact that Canada has two native traditions, English and French, which in drama as elsewhere are ultimately distinct.

The seventh essay, "Quebec Literature in Its American Context," turns to the world of French Canada to trace the development and nature of its literature. Canada's first major period as a colony stretched from 1534 to 1760, from the landing of Jacques Cartier on the shore of the Gaspé Peninsula to the Articles of Capitulation whereby the French surrendered Canada, or New France, to English control. The Battle of the Plains of Abraham outside Quebec City in 1759, where both the English leader, Wolfe, and the French leader, Montcalm, fell, sealed the fate of New France and marked the establishment of English authority. By the Articles of Capitulation of 1760, the French transferred Canada to the English; the French fleur-de-lis, which had flown proudly over the outposts of the country, was replaced by the Union Jack.

The year 1760 marked the end of the struggle of two empires, France and England, and the creation of a new colony, British Canada. The era of New France gave way to the age of British North America, and the Articles of Capitulation foreshadowed the British North America Act of Confederation of 1867. By the Peace of Paris of 1763, when the population of Canada was sixty thousand, France officially ceded Canada to England. Despite their seeming defeat the French in Canada were made stronger by their new position in an English colony; they were forced to assert their own individuality against the domination of the English. With a strength and determination embedded in their Catholic religion, their own language and cultural traditions, and their lands along the Saint Lawrence, the French preserved their Canada and made it an active and defined world of literature and culture.

By the Quebec Act of 1774, passed in England where the government was wary of the growing unrest in the American colonies, French Canada received distinctive recognition and status within the colony; a policy of assimilation was rejected in favor of separate identities for the two founding peoples of Canada. By bestowing upon French Canadians certain specific rights and privileges, the act ensured that Quebec would retain its special position. Any future attempts to unite the two peoples would be almost impossible because of this act, which increased and assured the French feeling of separateness. The British North America Act reiterated the dual nature of Canada by establishing two official languages and the complete freedom and rights of two religions; confederation formed itself on the basis of continued cultural equality.

The need to preserve French Canadian traditions gave an urgency and a dignity to Quebec literature which never appeared with the same force in English Canada. Quebec literature flourished, not only because of Quebec's need to assert its identity through art, but also because of its ability to focus, as indeed it was forced to do from the time of the Articles of Capitulation, on its own immediate and defined region. Thus in 1888 G. Mercer Adam, an English Canadian writer and publisher, could look at French Canada with both understanding and jealousy:

> In the case of English-speaking Canada, there is, we think, little doubt that patriotism and national sentiment might be largely fostered by a literary spirit, particularly were it given that encouragement which the Canadian intellect should now extend to it. In this matter we might well take a lesson from the sister Province. French Canada, it is well known to those who look below the surface, makes large use of the literary spirit, not only in preserving national traditions, but in perpetuating racial ideas in religion, in politics, in her institutions, as well as in her language and literature. She not only honours her literary men, but maintains and nourishes her national life on what they bring forth.

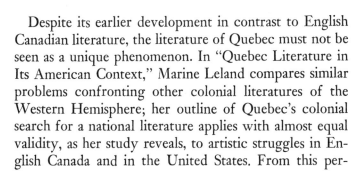

Despite its earlier development in contrast to English Canadian literature, the literature of Quebec must not be seen as a unique phenomenon. In "Quebec Literature in Its American Context," Marine Leland compares similar problems confronting other colonial literatures of the Western Hemisphere; her outline of Quebec's colonial search for a national literature applies with almost equal validity, as her study reveals, to artistic struggles in English Canada and in the United States. From this perspective of the evolution of American literatures she illuminates some distinguishing features of Quebec literature.

The final essay, "Canada: The Borderline Case," is Marshall McLuhan's first extended study of his homeland. For many years he has used Canada, "the land of rye and caution" as he once described it, as an ideal nineteenth-century perspective from which to probe the growing complexities of modern communications. Now he turns his attention to his own country in a provocative analysis of the frequently debated question of the Canadian identity. Finding many similarities between Canadians and their southern neighbors, he reveals some important features which ultimately separate the Canadian as North American from the citizen of the United States.

Throughout Canadian history the United States has played an important role in the slow growth of Canada as a nation. Although 1776 might not seem an important date in Canadian history, Canada's unwillingness to become part of the American Revolution is a most significant and far-reaching fact. Remaining loyal to England and eschewing the desire for assertive independence, Canada found itself in a peculiar position, situated beside a massive and developing independent country that had rejected the form of government and the ties with England which Canada itself was continuing to maintain. In a few years the Loyalists, the residents of the United States who rejected its revolution and preferred to remain loyal to the English crown, came to Canada; the northern colony became a haven for those Americans who wanted to live in an English colonial world.

In the War of 1812 between Britain and the United States Canada again rejected the republican democracy south of it. The American invasion of Canada failed not only because it was badly managed, which it was, but also because Canadians decisively denounced the American claims. Canada, not England, it can be argued, was the enemy that defeated the United States. The outcome made the colony see itself as more than a battleground; Canada was slowly becoming its own world, and the War of 1812 produced fresh pangs of self-consciousness. It is not a coincidence that about 1815 cries for patriotic rebellions, planned agitations, and Canadian freedom began to be heard.

The rebellions in Lower and Upper Canada in 1837 led to Lord Durham's *Report on the Affairs of British North America* (1839), a seminal document in the history of Canada's growth into nationhood and another refusal to follow the American form of democracy. In advocating responsible government for Canada, the *Report* showed preference for a government that embodied the principles of the British parliamentary system and rejected again revolution, American-style, motivated by the ideals of Jacksonian republican democracy.

The British North America Act of 1867 became the realization of Durham's *Report*. Its fundamental principles, responsible government and parliamentary sovereignty, guaranteed that Canadian federalism would be different from American federalism which, based on a written constitution, relied upon the separation of powers in the national government and upon the checks and balances inherent in the interpretation of the courts. The second major distinction of the Act which further separated Canadian government from the American system was the explicit preference for a strong central government over a commitment to states' rights; this adherence to British constitutional practice was also a reflection of the contemporary attitudes of Canadian statesmen, who saw that the issues of states' rights were being tried on the battlefields of the American Civil War.

Unlike the United States, Canada did not assert its nationhood. The American Declaration of Independence is a positive assertion of principles, a concrete embodiment of idealism in contrast to the pragmatism of the British North America Act. In declaring their independence from England, Americans found it necessary to define themselves and their way of life. Their expressed principles, focusing on the individual and his rights, stand in further contrast to the restrained social compromises which underlie the British North America Act. And while the United States had such spokesmen as Thomas Jefferson to enunciate its way of life, Canada did not have any writers or orators of a stature sufficient to assert the distinctive nature of the land and its inhabitants, nor did it feel the necessity of defining itself. The question of the Canadian identity, the kind of question which would be asked only of a colony, never occurred to the architects of confederation. Set adrift, in one sense, from England, their mother country, and fearful of possible annexation by a rapidly expanding United States, the four original provinces of Canada came together in 1867 in order to ensure their own continued existence.

Although the United States set for itself a series of goals and ideals, Canada formed itself in a pragmatic and not idealistic manner. The romance of the frontier pushed Americans westward, but when Canadians moved westward, they traveled only to link the British settlements on the West Coast to the original four provinces. Compromise, caution, and accommodation characterized the distinctly unaggressive development of Canada.

Many commentators on the Canadian scene lament Canada's lack of a defined and distinctive identity; others try desperately to offer various and ultimately inadequate definitions. In "Canada: The Borderline Case," Marshall McLuhan finds a major distinction between Canada and its southern neighbor in the absence of definite commitments and ideals in Canada. Having lived so long in a colonial world where a sense of identity is minimal, yet situated beside the powerful presence of the United States, Canadians are now the people best prepared, he argues, to respond to the growing complexities of the modern world.

For many years Canadians were reluctant to speak about their own culture; affairs of other countries occupied their attention. Recent decades have produced a dramatic change. The nineteenth-century Canadian boast "We keep our opinions to ourselves if we think people will disagree with them" seems the laughable plight of our colonial ancestors. The caution of the colonial has given way to the concern of the modern Canadian.

Caution makes a colony continually look to the future as the realm of its possible maturity. And Canada has always had a fixation on the future. Wilfrid Laurier's buoyant proclamation that "the twentieth century shall be filled by Canada" is only an exaggerated reiteration of Susanna Moodie's prophecies. So common is this future-orientation in much of Canada's literature that more than a decade ago Northrop Frye noted: "Adolescent dreams of glory haunt the Canadian consciousness (and unconsciousness), some naive and some sophisticated. In the naive areas are the predictions that the twentieth century belongs to Canada, that our cities will become much bigger than they ought to be, or like Edmonton and Vancouver, 'gateways' to somewhere else, reconstructed Northwest passages. The more sophisticated usually take the form of a Messianic complex about Canadian culture, for Canadian culture, no less than Alberta, has always been 'next year country.' "

For the pioneers in Canada's history and literature, Canada has always been "next year country." Yet their efforts hastened, indeed created, political and literary nationhood. The faith of Susanna Moodie and Thomas D'Arcy McGee led to the creation of a country which grew up in the twentieth century.

Since the time of Stephen Leacock Canada has acquired a political character which has received international recognition. Its distinctive literature and culture have become part of the consciousness of cultivated men and women beyond its borders. The end of the Second World War found Canada a nation in a modern world where there were two global powers, Russia and the United States, and Canada began to exert its own pressure in world politics; its actions were always patient, moderate, and conciliatory, three qualities which characterize the slow development of the country itself. Throughout the Korean War Canada urged restraint and compromise. The role of peacemaker seemed natural for a country that had maintained a quiet colonial reserve for so many years. In the fall of 1956 Canada denounced British and French imperialism in the Suez Canal crisis and sought to reconcile British and American differences created by the tension; in the following year Lester Pearson, formerly president of the United Nations General Assembly, helped to form the United Nations Emergency Force, which brought the Suez crisis under control. International recognition of the rectitude of the Canadian position led to the award of the 1957 Nobel Peace Prize to Pearson.

In the sixties Canada proclaimed to the world a new sense of pride in its own nationhood. In 1964 Lester Pearson, then prime minister, proposed the adoption of a national flag which did not contain the Union Jack; the proposal encountered strong opposition, some dissidents maintaining that the new maple-leaf flag was catering to Quebec opinion, others demanding retention of the Red Ensign (with the Union Jack prominent in its corner) as a symbol of Canadian tradition. On February 15, 1965, the maple-leaf flag was adopted only after closure was applied to stop a conservative opposition's filibuster. Such opposition, however, did force the prime minister into a typically Canadian conclusion; he sponsored a compromise whereby the resolution for the new flag included a proclamation that the Union Jack has official status as a sign of Canada's allegiance to the queen and a symbol of its membership in the commonwealth. The immediate and prominent display of the maple-leaf flag throughout the land after its official adoption showed that the country was prepared and eager to endorse the symbol of Canadian nationhood.

The high point of the celebration of Canada's centennial in 1967 was the international exposition Expo 67, in Montreal. Named "Man and His World," Expo had a significance far beyond the large number of countries which brought their exhibits to Canada. Pearson defined the importance of Expo: "The lasting impact of Expo 67 will be in the dramatic object lesson we see before our eyes today—that the genius of man knows no national boundaries, but is universal." But Expo had a special importance, as Pearson noted, for Canadians: "Anyone who says we aren't a spectacular people should see this. We are witness today to the fulfillment of one of the most daring acts of faith in Canadian enterprise and ability ever undertaken."

Canada's political growth in recent decades is paralleled by an equally impressive literary growth. The vitality of contemporary Canadian literature is testimony to the significance of the country's literary nationhood.

The Canadian Imagination reflects the variety of Canada's literary culture. In the vigor and complexity of modern Canadian poetry that Northrop Frye studies, in the many forms of Canadian fiction that George Woodcock and Margaret Atwood explore, in the recent developments of Canadian theater that Brian Parker analyzes, and in the Quiet Revolution where Marine Leland's account of Quebec literature culminates, Canada is exploring and expressing the challenge of its cultural nationhood. For the contemporary figures in Canada's history and literature, for the observed as well as the observers, Canada is a country of the present.

I

Haunted by Lack of Ghosts

Some Patterns in the
Imagery of Canadian Poetry

Northrop Frye

Very few historical and cultural statements can be made about Canada that do not have obvious counterparts in the United States. At the same time, social developments in a country which has amassed a huge population and has become a great imperial power may have a quite different imaginative resonance in a country with a sparse population and a minor world influence. For example, railways were built across the United States to the Pacific, and the romance of railway-building, along with the accompanying scandals and exploitations, have been factors of unquestionable importance in American culture. But in Canada the building of a single railway line was a matter of life and death to the infant nation, and the completion of it, against almost insuperable obstacles, was not one of many incidents of expansion but a central devouring obsession. Similarly, in the nineteenth century, an American boasting of the great size of America was helping to increase his own feeling of identity with it, whereas in Canada the background of immense rivers, lakes, and islands that very few Canadians had ever seen tended rather to weaken the sense of an identity that was already precarious.

In the United States, expansion into the West brought with it almost everywhere a sense of new opportunities for life in a new land. But while the Canadian expansion into the north looks vast enough on a map, the inference that there is unlimited room for people in Canada is an illusion. As the Canadian historian, W. L. Morton, says in *The Canadian Identity*, "The great staple trades have been extensive, in-gathering trades . . . most of Canada is simply a hinterland extensively exploited from the soil base of the St. Lawrence and Saskatchewan valleys, and from the delta of the Fraser." Increased immigration, in Canada no less than in Australia, means primarily an increase in the population of two or three cities which are already too big. The fact that the country grew up from two peoples speaking different languages meant that nobody could ever know what a "hundred percent Canadian" was, and hence the population became less homogeneous. An ethnic minority in any case is more conspicuous in a smaller population. And while we hear a good deal about separatism in Quebec, every part of Canada has strong separatist feelings: the Atlantic Provinces and western Canada also tend to feel that they are, vis-à-vis central Canada, in the same mercantile bind that the United States was in before 1776, and that they are forced to export at a lower price, and import at a higher price, than they would do if they had more autonomy.

Canada was first settled, like the United States, in the seventeenth century, but, in striking contrast to the United States, there was nothing culturally distinctive about Canada's eighteenth century, and the country went directly from seventeenth-century Baroque expansiveness to nineteenth-century Romantic expansiveness. There are some curious reversals of American historical movements in Canadian history. The Americans had first a revolutionary war against a European power, followed by a civil war within the country itself. Canada had a civil war first, which was a struggle of European powers on its soil, followed by a war of independence against the United States—at least, so far as the War of 1812 had any meaning at all for Canada, that was its meaning. A generation or two ago, girls in Quebec convent schools were taught that the British conquest was the will of God, saving them from the atheistic horrors of the French Revolution. It might have been added, with some justification, that the British conquest also preserved the French language and culture itself in Canada. The French lost the country primarily because they had very little interest in keeping it, and if they had held it they would doubtless have sold it, as they did Louisiana.

In any case Canada was founded on the Quebec Act of 1774, which recognized the *de facto* situation that while the British were technically the conquerors, the country could not survive as a British possession unless a settlement was made which guaranteed rights to the French. The Quebec Act was a conservative measure, conforming to Edmund Burke's principle of a synthesis containing opposed principles, in contrast to the revolutionary, and therefore more dialectical, attitude established by the victorious Whigs in the United States. Its revolutionary basis, along with the written constitution which was an integral part of that basis, makes for a deductive and continuous pattern in American life, as the constitution is reinterpreted or, in the last resort, amended. In Canada a discontinuous, *ad hoc*, illogical series of bargains and compromises succeeded the Quebec Act. Margaret Atwood's book on the spirit of Canadian literature, *Survival*, has become very influential partly through its inspired choice of a title: the word "survival" in itself implies a discontinuous series of crises, each to be met on its own terms, each having to face the imminent threat of not surviving.

For all its centrifugal expansion, the American consciousness revolves around one or two centripetal symbols of the nation as a whole, notably the President and the flag. In Canada the parliamentary system of election places much less emphasis on the party leader as a personality, and it is even more significant that Canada had no official flag of its own until the middle of the twentieth century. Francis Sparshott, in a poem called "Episode in Frederick, Md.," muses obliquely about this:

"Spare, if you must, this old grey head,
But shoot your country's flag!" she said.
"You got it wrong, you stupid bag.
You mean, '*Don't* shoot your country's flag.' "
"Yes, yes, young man, that's what I said:
Shoot if you must this old grey head."
"Pardon me, lady, that is not
What you first said you wanted shot."
Then down the street the General came,
His sword unsheathed, his eyes aflame.
"Sergeant! Don't contradict the lady.
Holes in the head she's got already;
Six more won't make no never mind.
Present! . . . Aim! . . . FIRE:"
                    Still down the wind
Streams the bright symbol of her honor,
But Mrs. Fritchie is a goner.
So now the Yanks have both a flag
And a distinctive national hag.

The author tells me that he was not aware, in writing the last line, that Canada also has had, in a sense, a distinctive national hag. No genuine portrait of English Canada's best-known heroine, Laura Secord, exists, and the deficiency is made up for by a grisly reproduction of a male elder statesman, with the beard removed and a shawl put over the head, purporting to represent her in old age. I mention this because it illustrates so clearly the perennial Canadian problems of publicizing the heroes of a country which has manifested a great deal of remarkable courage but has never responded with much warmth to charismatic leadership. Canadian heroes include such ambiguous figures as William Lyon Mackenzie, leader of the 1837 rebellion against the "Family Compact" (the Tory establishment in nineteenth-century Ontario),

whose role became very unheroic when the shooting
started, but who nonetheless still stands for the noncon-
formist conscience of Canada, an unwillingness to
knuckle under to any kind of foreign or domestic domination. Thus Dennis Lee, in a poem called "1838":

> The British want the country
> For the Empire and the view.
> The Yankees want the country for
> A yankee barbecue.
> The Compact want the country
> For their merrie green domain.
> They'll all play finders-keepers till
> Mackenzie comes again.
>
> Mackenzie was a crazy man,
> He wore his wig askew,
> He donned three bulky overcoats
> In case the bullets flew.
> Mackenzie talked of fighting
> While the fight went down the drain.
> But who will speak for Canada?
> Mackenzie, come again.

Seventeenth-century Europe brought three cultural
imports into the New World of North America. One
was the revolutionary monotheism of Christianity, with
its horror of "idolatry," that is, the sense of the numi-
nous in nature. For Christianity, the gods that had been
discovered in nature were all devils: man could raise his
consciousness toward the divine only through human institutions. It followed that a natural religion like that of
the Indians simply had to be extirpated if the Indians
were to realize their human potential. The second was
the Baroque sense of the power of mathematics, the results of which can still be seen in the grid patterns of our
cities, in the concession lines in the rural areas, and in the
great burden of geometry that North American life in
particular carries. The third was the Cartesian egocentric

consciousness, the feeling that man's essential humanity was in his power of reasoning, and that the nature outside human consciousness was pure extension: a turning away from nature so complete that it became a kind of idolatry in reverse.

A friend of mine, watching two Western farmers driving fence stakes and hearing one say to the other, "Put 'er in a coupla inches west," remarked that a consciousness as closely geared to the points of the compass as that was obviously in intimate touch with the land. I was inclined to disagree, feeling that it was a consciousness of nature as a territory but not as a home. It goes with the feeling that improved human communications means a straighter and therefore less interesting path through nature, until with the airplane the sense of traveling through nature itself disappears. I said in an earlier article on Canadian literature that the Canadian problem of identity seemed to me primarily connected with locale, less a matter of "Who am I?" than of "Where is here?" Another friend, commenting on this, told me a story about a doctor from the south (that is, from one of the Canadian cities) traveling on the Arctic tundra with an Eskimo guide. A blizzard blew up, and they had to bivouac for the night. What with the cold, the storm, and the loneliness, the doctor panicked and began shouting "We are lost!" The Eskimo looked at him thoughtfully and said, "We are not lost. We are here." A vast gulf between an indigenous and an immigrant mentality opened at that point; the possibility of eventually closing this gulf is the main theme of what follows.

Yeats speaks in one of his prose works of the Port Royal logicians, followers of Descartes, who cut up animals alive because everything outside man was a machine to them and they simply could not believe that anything without human consciousness could feel pain. The attitude of the Canadian fur trade, spreading traps over the north to catch animals, was not very different: for it, the mink, the beaver, and the silver fox were not living creatures but only potential fur coats. A growing sense of guilt about this attitude gives a peculiarly haunting resonance to the theme of the death of an animal in Canadian literature. (See, for example, Al Purdy's "The Death of Animals" in *Poems for All the Annettes* [1962], a poem too long to quote and too intricate to quote from.) Similarly, the destruction of the native culture, more particularly of its religion, leaves us with the feeling well described by the philosopher George Grant in *Technology and Empire* (1969):

> That conquering relation to place has left its mark within us. When we go into the Rockies we may have the sense that gods are there. But if so, they cannot manifest themselves to us as ours. They are the gods of another race, and we cannot know them because of what we are, and what we did. There can be nothing immemorial for us except the environment as object.

Much the same thing is said in poetry by Douglas LaPan, in a poem significantly called "A Country without a Mythology":

> No monuments or landmarks guide the stranger
> Going among this savage people . . .
>
> And not a sign, no emblem in the sky
> Or boughs to friend him as he goes; for who
> Will stop where, clumsily contrived, daubed
> With war-paint, teeters some lust-red manitou?

A parenthetical remark in Leonard Cohen's novel *Beautiful Losers* links a similar feeling of guilt to the colonial mentality of Canadians:

> Some part of the Canadian Catholic mind is not certain of the Church's victory over the Medicine Man. No wonder the forests of Quebec are mutilated and sold to America.

From my study of Canadian literature, in particular, I have found much evidence for the critical principle of the fallacy of imaginative projection, that is, the notion that a poet can confront some impressive object like Niagara Falls or Lake Louise and become "inspired" by it. An egocentric consciousness, Pascal's thinking reed, in the center of a country as huge and unresponsive as Canada finds the environment less impressive than oppressive. It is not only that nature is so big and the winters so cold, but also that there is a lurking feeling that if anything did speak to the poet from nature it would speak only to condemn. That is why I have adopted for my title the last line of Earle Birney's poem "Can. Lit.": "It's only by our lack of ghosts we're haunted." There are gods here, and we have offended them. They are not ghosts: we are the ghosts, Cartesian ghosts caught in the machine that we have assumed nature to be. Hence the characteristic Canadian feeling noted by the scholar and critic Robert McDougall:

> In our literature, heroic action remains possible, but becomes so deeply tinged with futility that withdrawal becomes a more characteristic response than commitment. The representative images are those of denial and defeat rather than fulfilment and victory.

One obvious corollary of this feeling is the sense that "civilized" man, with his economy of waste, his relentless plundering of a nature which he thinks is there only to be exploited by him, his infinite capacity to litter his surroundings with every conceivable variety of excrement is the essential principle of pollution in nature, a monstrous deformation or cancer that nature itself has produced by mistake. Thus Margaret Atwood, in a poem called "Backdrop Addresses Cowboy," where the cowboy is perhaps less a cowboy than a symbol of the more fatuous forms of mass culture:

I am also what surrounds you:
my brain
scattered with your
tincans, bones, empty shells,
the litter of your invasions.

James Reaney, studying "Winnipeg Seen as a Body of Time and Space," makes an explicit contrast with the native relation to nature:

Winnipeg, what once were you? You were,
Your hair was grass by the river ten feet tall,
Your arms were burr oaks and ash leaf maples,
Your backbone was a crooked silver muddy river,
Your thoughts were ravens in flocks, your bones were
    snow,
Your legs were trails and your blood was a people
  Who did what the stars did and the sun . . .

Then on top of you fell
A Boneyard wrecked auto gent, his hair
Made of rusted car door handles, his fingernails
Of red Snowflake Pastry signs, his belly
Of buildings downtown; his arms of sewers,
His nerves electric wires, his mouth a telephone,
His backbone—a cracked cement street. His heart
An orange pendulum bus crawling with the human fleas.
Of a so-so civilization—half gadget, half flesh—
  I don't know what I would have instead—
  And they did what they did more or less.

The phenomenon described is hardly peculiar to Canada, but again it has a distinctive resonance in a country where there is so much nature that ought to be unspoiled. The theme celebrated in science fiction, of nature's eventual revenge, seems to be less frequent in Canadian poetry, although E. J. Pratt, in a late poem called "The Good Earth," notices in passing that the death wish in man himself is partly a form of that revenge:

Hold that synthetic seed, for underneath
Deep down she'll answer to your horticulture:
She has a way of germinating teeth
And yielding crops of carrion for the vulture.

A curious schizophrenia can be seen in a good deal of nineteenth-century Canadian poetry, the sense of loneliness and alienation urgently demanding expression along with a good deal of prefabricated rhetoric about the challenge of a new land and the energetic optimism demanded to meet it. The latter mood often attempts to suppress or, failing that, to outshout the former one, but with little consistent success. Again, Margaret Atwood, who has inherited Pratt's instinct for what is imaginatively central in Canadian sensibility, studies this split consciousness in her *Journals of Susanna Moodie*. This book of poems follows the life of the redoubtable Susanna Strickland, who after her marriage came out to Ontario in the eighteen-thirties and wrote *Roughing It in the Bush*. Toward the end of the sequence, in a poem called "Thoughts from Underground," the poet describes the conflict in her heroine's mind between her very real hatred for the country that had caused her so much suffering and the rhetoric that she thought she ought to be producing about its material progress and cultural enlightenment:

> Then we were made successful
> and I felt I ought to love
> this country.
>   I said I loved it
> and my mind saw double.
>
> I began to forget myself
> in the middle
> of sentences. Events
> were split apart.

A similar rhetorical epilepsy may be observed in some of the semiofficial poets of the confederation period and

later, notably Charles G. D. Roberts and Bliss Carman.
Roberts begins a poem called "Canada" thus:

> O Child of Nations, giant-limbed,
>   Who stand'st among the nations now
> Unheeded, unadorned, unhymned,
>   With unanointed brow,—

This apostrophe is also an invocation, not a genuine
invocation, such as Homer would make to a Muse or
some shaping spirit of poetry asking it to take over
the poem, but one addressed to Roberts himself and
intended to help him work himself into the proper emotional state for a sublime ode. The rest of the poem illustrates the principle that invocations addressed to oneself
are seldom answered. Here is Bliss Carman, at the close
of a poem which has become perhaps less celebrated than
notorious in Canadian literature:

> Only make me over, April,
> When the sap begins to stir!
> Make me man or make me woman,
> Make me oaf or ape or human,
> Cup of flower or cone of fir;
> Make me anything but neuter
> When the sap begins to stir!

The critic E. K. Brown remarks on this passage that the
tone is "jaunty" and that the jaunty cannot also be
poetic. I think myself that Carman has fallen foul of
another well-known literary principle, the positive force
of the negative statement. One who says "the day was
not hot and stifling" has said something much hotter than
he means; and when Carman prays to be made "anything
but neuter" he is sowing a doubt in his reader's mind
whether, when the sap rises in spring, the poet will be
able to rise with it. Both poets, especially Carman, wrote
a good deal of verse dedicated to the power of positive
thinking, but the tone is almost invariably forced, and

invites Emily Dickinson's dry comment on Joaquin Miller, "Transport is not urged." Yet both Roberts and Carman could be haunting and eloquent poets as long as their tone was nostalgic, elegiac, or plangent: Carman's "Low Tide on Grand Pré" is a fine example. So the question naturally comes to mind: why were these poets so much better at whimpering than at banging?

The answer has already been implied: the nostalgic and elegiac are the inevitable emotional responses of an egocentric consciousness locked into a demythologized environment. Wherever reason is regarded as the distinctively human element in consciousness, the impulse to write poetry remains rhetorical (in the sense of oratorical), preoccupied with versifying prose statements and talking about emotional attitudes instead of presenting them. Eventually it becomes clear that the focus of such a response, in such conditions, is the moment of death. Death is the one point at which man and nature really become identified; it is also, in a sense, the only event in which the genuinely heroic aspect of human life emerges. A life in which energy is expended in subduing a tiny fraction of space has little room for the heroic, until death rounds off the total effort and gives it another dimension. Without death, the struggle would seem only unending and hopeless. John McCrae, the author of "In Flanders Fields," was a poet much possessed by death, and he has a poem called "The Unconquered Dead" in which one chilling phrase identifies the heroic with the ability to die:

> We might have yielded, even we, but death
> Came for our helper.

In such a setting the Indian appears as a noble savage in the sense that his life is so largely one of stoically enduring both the sufferings imposed by nature and those he inflicts on himself and others. In Duncan Campbell Scott's "The Forsaken," an Indian woman, trying to get

food for her baby in winter, baits a fishhook with her
own flesh. Later, as an old woman whom the tribe can
no longer afford to feed, she is abandoned and left to lie
down in the snow to die. Similarly, in Pratt's *Brébeuf
and His Brethren*, the martyrdom of the Jesuit missionaries is nothing that they are seeking for itself, but it is
the one real triumph of their service of Christ.

While some nineteenth- and early twentieth-century
Canadian poets were rhetoricians, others understood
better that the central poetic impulse is imaginative and
not rhetorical, and that its most direct product is mythology, which is essentially the humanizing of nature.
Charles Mair, author of *Tecumseh*, produced in 1901 a
rather maundering poem called "Summer," of this general texture:

> Or, if Fancy still would trace
> Forms ideal, forms of grace,
> Still would haunt, in dreamy trance,
> Kindred regions of Romance,
> Let her now recall the sweet
> Image of lorn Marguerite.

What is interesting about this poem is that it is a completely rewritten version of a poem written in 1868,
which was both explicitly mythological and very much
livelier:

> And let nymph-attended Pan
> Come in habit of a man,
> Singing songs of reeds and rushes,
> Elder brakes and hazel bushes.
> See him swing and jig about,
> Whilst the merry, rabble rout
> Chases round with joined hands,
> Twitching slily, when he stands,
> At his back, his garments tearing,
> All his swart, brute-buttocks baring.

Mair eventually came to realize that his 1868 muse was the authentic one, and her genteel 1901 sister a phony. In Isabella Crawford's extraordinary narrative poem *Malcolm's Katie* (1884), there is an explicitly mythical section beginning "The South Wind laid his moccasins aside," which contains the following passage:

> In this shrill moon the scouts of winter ran
> From the ice-belted north, and whistling shafts
> Struck maple and struck sumach—and a blaze
> Ran swift from leaf to leaf, from bough to bough;
> Till round the forest flash'd a belt of flame
> And inward lick'd its tongues of red and gold
> To the deep, tranced, inmost heart of all.
> Rous'd the still heart—but all too late, too late.
> Too late, the branches welded fast with leaves,
> Toss'd, loosen'd to the winds—too late the sun
> Pour'd his last vigor to the deep, dark cells
> Of the dim wood. The keen, two-bladed Moon
> Of Falling Leaves roll'd up on crested mists
> And where the lush, rank boughs had foil'd the sun
> In his red prime, her pale, sharp fingers crept
> After the wind and felt about the moss,
> And seem'd to pluck from shrinking twig and stem
> The burning leaves—while groan'd the shudd'ring wood.

There are several things to notice here. In the first place, the progression of seasons, with its great cycle of color that emerges in spring, bursts into flame in the fall, and dies out in the winter, is seen as a kind of battle of Titans. Nature here is not a Cartesian extension in space, but a field of conflicting energies which are seemingly just about to take on the forms of mythological beings. Second, for all the riot of color, the "inmost heart of all" does not quite come to life: something makes that "too late," and we are pulled around to death and winter again. The process is almost an allegory of the Canadian poetic imagination, making a tremendous effort to rouse itself and create a reborn mythology out of the abandoned Indian one, an effort still premature and collapsing before its fulfillment, but indicating that something new is on the way. The direct vision of nature in this passage is equally remarkable. Isabella Crawford has done in words much what the painter Tom Thomson was later to do in his art: evoking a dissonance of color that seems like an autonomous force of life itself bursting through the tree trunks, the sumac, and the sky.

Speaking of painting, the British painter and writer Wyndham Lewis, who spent some years in Canada during the Second World War, makes this comment about A. Y. Jackson, one of the twentieth-century Group of Seven landscape painters, perhaps with an underlying allusion to the Carman poem already cited:

> Jackson is no man to go gathering nuts in May. He has no wish to be seduced every spring when the sap rises —neither he nor nature are often shown in these compromising moods. There is something of Ahab in him; the long white contours of the Laurentian Mountains in mid-winter are his elusive leviathan.

The leviathan also recurs in Wilfred Watson's fine poem on another Canadian painter, the British Columbian Emily Carr:

> Like Jonah in the green belly of the whale
> Overwhelmed by Leviathan's lights and liver
> Imprisoned and appalled by the belly's wall
> Yet inscribing and scoring the uprush
> Sink vault and arch of that monstrous cathedral,
> Its living bone and its green pulsing flesh—
> Old woman, of your three days' anatomy
> Leviathan sickened and spewed you forth
> In a great vomit on coasts of eternity.

The image of being swallowed by the leviathan is an almost inevitable one for Canada: the whole process of coming to the country by ship from Europe, through the Strait of Belle Isle and the Gulf of Saint Lawrence and then up the great river, suggests it, again a marked contrast to the United States, with its relatively straight north-south coastline. In Pratt's narrative poem on the building of the Canadian Pacific Railway, *Towards the Last Spike*, the dragon image appears, the symbol of a nature so totally indifferent to man and his concerns that it is irrelevant to wonder whether it is dead or alive:

> On the North Shore a reptile lay asleep—
> A hybrid that the myths have conceived,
> But not delivered, as progenitor
> Of crawling, gliding things upon the earth . . .
> This folded reptile was asleep or dead:
> So motionless, she seemed stone dead—just seemed:
> She was too old for death, too old for life . . .
> Ice-ages had passed by and over her,
> But these, for all their motion, had but sheared
> Her spotty carboniferous hair or made
> Her ridges stand out like the spikes of molochs . . .
>
> Was this the thing Van Horne set out
> To conquer?

Van Horne was the builder of the Canadian Pacific Railway, and the stretch of Precambrian shield in northern Ontario was one of his most formidable obstacles.

In the Bible, of course, the leviathan swallows Jonah, a prototype not only of Emily Carr but of the Jesus who descended to the world of death and hell for three days. In the closely related myth of Saint George and the dragon, Saint George dies along with the dragon he kills, and has to be separately brought to life. What such myths appear to be telling us is that the leviathan is the monster of indefinite time and space surrounding us on all sides: we are all born inside his belly, and we never escape from it; he is the body of death from which we cannot be delivered. The Christian, Baroque, Cartesian attitude that the white invaders brought from Europe helped to ensure that in Canada the sense of being imprisoned in the belly of a mindless emptiness would be at its bleakest and most uncompromising. As we have seen, the ego's one moment of genuine dignity in such a situation is the moment either of death or of some equally final alienation. Among the poets of the generation of Roberts, Carman, and D. C. Scott, Archibald Lampman achieved the highest consistent level of poetry, partly because he was prudent enough to stick to elegiac moods. His poems are almost invariably those of a solitary watcher of the nature around him: the idiom is strongly Wordsworthian, but the greater sense of indifference in the landscape makes him more conscious of his solitude than Wordsworth:

> I sat in the midst of a plain on my snowshoes with
>   bended knee
> Where the thin wind stung my cheeks,
> And the hard snow ran in little ripples and peaks,
> Like the fretted floor of a white and petrified sea.
>
> And a strange peace gathered about my soul and shone,
> As I sat reflecting there,
> In a world so mystically fair,
> So deathly silent—I so utterly alone.

The poem, called "Winter-Solitude," expresses a kind of serenity that Lampman constantly sought. Margaret Avison presents us with a similar landscape but a different response to it:

> But on this sheet of beryl, this high sea,
> Scalded by the white unremembering glaze,
> No wisps disperse. This is the icy pole.
> The presence here is single, worse than soul,
> Pried loose forever out of nights and days
> And birth and death
> And all the covering wings.

I have quoted this passage elsewhere, but keep returning to it because, apart from its great eloquence, the poem from which it comes is called "Identity," and what it shows us is an identity driven into a last stand of such total isolation that it can define itself only by extinction, unless it can make some effort of rebirth.

I earlier quoted George Grant as saying that the gods of the Rockies are the gods of another race, and that we can make no contact with them because of what we are, and what we did. The statement sounds irrefutable, at least in prose, but it is not what the present generation of poets is saying. John Newlove, for example, in a poem called "The Pride," says,

> not this handful
> of fragments, as the indians
> are not composed of
> the romantic stories
> about them, or of the stories
> they tell only, but
> still ride the soil
> in us, dry bones a part
> of the dust in our eyes,
> needed and troubling
> in the glare, in
> our breath, in our
> ears, in our mouths,
> in our bodies entire, in our minds, until at
> last we become them
>
> in our desires, our desires,
> mirages, mirrors, that are theirs, hard-
> riding desires, and they
> become our true forebears, moulded
> by the same wind or rain,
> and in this land we
> are their people, come
> back to life.

In this poem the Indians symbolize a primitive mythological imagination which is being reborn in us: in other words, the white Canadians, in their imaginations, are no longer immigrants but are becoming indigenous, recreating the kind of attitudes appropriate to people who really belong here. We may remember that "primitive" poetry, which is created in a society where the poets are the custodians of culture and learning, is very direct in its impact, sometimes needing footnotes for those outside its orbit of allusions, but not at all inclined to talk around or avoid its subject. Thus a Haida song as translated, or adapted, by Hermia Fraser:

> I cannot stay, I cannot stay!
> The Raven has stolen the Child of the Chief,
> Of the Highest Chief in the Kingdom of Light.
>
> The Slave Wife born from the first clam shell
> Is in love with the boy who was stolen away,
> The lovers have taken the Raven's fire.
>
> The Slave who was born from the first clam shell
> Has made love to the wife who was born from the shell,
> This Slave man has stolen her treasures away.

The Haida lived on the Queen Charlotte Islands off the coast of British Columbia. Living there now is the extraordinary poet Susan Musgrave, who has produced four volumes of verse in the first twenty-five years of her life, and who shows throughout them strong imaginative links with a people whom she clearly thinks of as poetically her ancestors. In a poem called "Witchery Way" the sense of an indigenous creative power reforming in the present and immediate future seems indicated in the phrase about "the dark seed of their coming":

> Sometimes an old man
> crouches at the river—

sometimes he is someone
whose bones are not formed.

Sometimes an old woman
with fisher-skin quiver,
sometimes on the low bank
is hungry after blood . . .

Sometimes an old man
whispers down the smoke hole,
sometimes an old woman
furrows in the wind.
My skin is thick
with the dark seed
of their coming—
the blade of a fine axe
wedged between my eyes.

It should go without saying that I am not speaking of the
content or subject matter of such poems, but of the
imaginative attitude that produces their structures.

A poetic consciousness formed within the leviathan of
Canadian nature, feeling that it belongs there and can no
longer think of itself as a swallowed outsider, would
naturally be preoccupied with two themes in particular:
the theme of descent into the self and the theme of forming, within that self, an imaginative counterpart of what
is outside it. The sense of a responding imagination
which is part of its surroundings, and not a detached
consciousness rolling over it like so much tumbleweed,
already appears in Lampman and is in fact the reason
why so much of his work is focused on the theme of
serenity. Thus in a poem called "Storm":

O Wind, wild-voicèd brother, in your northern cave,
    My spirit also being so beset
With pride and pain, I heard you beat and rave,
    Grinding your chains with furious howl and fret,
Knowing full well that all earth's moving things inherit

The same chained might and madness of the spirit,
    That none may quite forget.

The same kind of microcosmic imagery continues in Irving Layton's "The Cold Green Element" and in A. M. Klein's very central poem, "Portrait of the Poet as Landscape," which concludes:

Therefore he seeds illusions. Look, he is
the nth Adam taking a green inventory
in the world but scarcely uttered, naming, praising . . .
For to praise

the world—he, solitary man—is breath
to him . . .

These are not mean ambitions. It is already something
merely to entertain them. Meanwhile, he
makes of his status as zero a rich garland,
a halo of his anonymity,
and lives alone, and in his secret shines
like phosphorus. At the bottom of the sea.

The closing lines echo Eliot on the poet as catalyst and Keats on the poet's lack of identity, but the final phrase comes out of the belly of the Canadian leviathan, for the leviathan, as no one knew better than Klein, is a sea monster.

Earlier Canadian poetry was full of solitude and loneliness, of the hostility or indifference of nature, of the fragility of human life and values in such an environment. Contemporary Canadian poetry seems to think rather of this outer leviathan as a kind of objective correlative of some Minotaur that we find in our own mental labyrinths. The mind has become a dark chamber, or *camera obscura*, and its pictures are reflections of what is at once physical and human nature. A poem of Gwendolyn MacEwen, "Dark Pines under Water," explicitly links the poetic consciousness with reflection and descent:

This land like a mirror turns you inward
And you become a forest in a furtive lake;
The dark pines of your mind reach downward . . .

There is something down there and you want it told.

Similar themes of descent are in Margaret Atwood's
work, especially *Procedures for Underground*, in Eli
Mandel's *Fuseli Poems*, and, very remarkably, in Jay
Macpherson's *Welcoming Disaster*, a sequence in which
the sections have such titles as "The Way Down" and
"The Dark Side." The imagery of this book, of a perilous descent into a world which is at once a world of
fear and of love, of horror and of creation, recurs in
Alden Nowlan's "Genealogy of Morals":

Take any child dreaming of pickled bones
shelved in a coal-dark cellar understairs
(we are all children when we dream) the stones
red-black with blood from severed jugulars.

Child Francis, Child Gilles went down those stairs,
returned sides, hands and ankles dripping blood,
Bluebeard and gentlest saint. The same nightmares
instruct the evil, as inform the good.

The conception of nature as a mechanism, which began to take its modern form in the seventeenth century,
meant, of course, that Western man was developing an
increasingly mechanistic civilization. Canada was opened
up by the technology of navigation and surveying and
held together by the technology of transportation,
which has left its mark in the great bridges and railways
and seaports and in the network of canals in southern
Ontario. Up to, say, the Second World War, the inar-
ticulate aspect of communication was the one that had
top priority. Pratt's fascination with the rumbling and
creaking of machinery, his constant awareness of the
throbbing engines at the heart of the ship, indicated that

poetry had with him become sufficiently aware of its surroundings to make poetic imagery out of technology. The development of technology makes for a growing introversion in life, with the high-rise apartments and office buildings, the superhighways, where falling asleep is one of the hazards, the tunnel-like streets, with pedestrians hustled out of the way of motor traffic as peasants used to be on the approach of nobility. Even in Pratt, society is held together only by the emergencies of "survival."

Culturally, this introversion reached its height with the blind man's medium of the radio and the deaf man's medium of the silent movie, the latter being a close relative of the puppet show. The television set is technically even more introverted, setting up a round-the-clock fantasy world that we can stay in without even making the effort of joining an audience. And yet the centering on both sound and vision sets limits to the introversion. Turn off the sound, and we are in the world of the puppet show again, totally uninvolved; turn off the screen and listen to the sound track, and a similar detachment occurs. But in the fully centered medium, for all the avoiding of reality, we are occasionally compelled to see glimpses of an actual and very human world. Whether cabinet ministers or Eskimos, people are ultimately compelled to look like people on television, instead of like abstractions of charisma or legend. The television set seems to me to provide an analogue, in the mass media, to the imagery of descent that I have been trying to trace in poetry, which ends not in introversion but in an intensely centered vision.

Besides television, the airplane is a technological development which has begun to make more human sense of the colossal space of Canada. Nature as seen from a plane forms patterns reminding us of the more abstract painters, Borduas and Pellan and Harold Town, who have succeeded the Group of Seven, but it figures less in the imagery of poetry, poets being, for the most part, children of the earth mother rather than the sky father. An analogy to the aerial perspective, which I think may be something more than an analogy, is the attitude to tradition in contemporary Canadian poetry. Tradition is usually thought of as linear, and as forming a series of conventions which continually go out of date, so that a poet has to be careful not to become associated with an obsolete fashion. In Canada tradition has become, in the last generation or so at least, a much more simultaneous and kaleidoscopic affair, reminding us perhaps of the welter of historical allusions in the costumes of young people. The echoes of Spenser in James Reaney's *A Suit of Nettles,* of descent themes from Ishtar to Boris Karloff movies in Macpherson's *Welcoming Disaster,* of prosodic devices from Old English to concrete poetry in Earle Birney, while they certainly assume a cultivated reader, are both unforced and unpedantic, and illustrate very clearly the advantage, for a Canadian poet, of being able to look down on tradition all at once, instead of being pushed ahead of it like the terminal moraine of a glacier. In the words of the critic Milton Wilson:

> But one of the advantages of a poetry less than a hundred years old is that all the things that couldn't happen when they should have happened keep happening all the time . . . Having begun a millennium too late, there is not much point being correctly fashionable.

Canadian literature has always been thought of as having its center of gravity in the future. Now that it has come into the present also, it may, by being where it is as well as what it is, help to make its own contribution to the future that we all hope for—not the apocalyptic futures of fantasy and nightmare, but a future in which Western man has come home from his exile in the land of unlikeness and has become something better than the ghost of an ego haunting himself.

II

E. J. Pratt

Peter Buitenhuis

It is generally agreed that Edwin John Pratt (1882–
1964) is, as yet, Canada's most significant poet. And yet
he is almost unknown in the United States, except, of
course, in those quarters where scholars make it their
business to study the culture of Canada.

There have been some significant exceptions to this
general darkness of neglect south of the border. William
Rose Benét wrote a fine introduction to the American
edition of Pratt's *Collected Poems* (1945); Robert Hill-
yer discerningly reviewed this work in *Saturday Review* in 1946, and Henry Wells published an article
on Pratt in *College English* in the same year. For the rest
there is silence.

This benign and limited acceptance was broken by
one notable blast against Pratt's work that appeared in
Poetry in September 1945 as a review of the *Collected
Poems*. This review suggests some of the reasons for the
neglect of Pratt's work, and must be dealt with in any
serious assessment of it. Winfield Townley Scott, after
some remarks about Canada's colonial status and the
slow emergence of its independence, asserted that Pratt's
work was "by our standards a hundred years out of

date." Pratt couldn't be blamed for this, Scott blandly went on, living where he did when he did. After all, his work was an advance on that of Bliss Carman, but he had to say, "without condescension as without dishonesty, that his verse is dull." In support of this condemnation, Scott went on to quote a linking narrative passage from *Brébeuf and His Brethren* and excerpts from two of the lesser poems. I suppose selective quotation could be used to consign to perdition the work of almost any poet not generally known to the reading public of another country. The more telling part of Scott's attack is made in his reference to Gertrude Stein's statement that, in the twentieth century, events are not interesting. Modern writing—and she cites her own *The Making of Americans*, Joyce's *Ulysses*, and Proust's *Remembrance of Things Past* in the passage—is about the *reverberations* of events.

In the thirty years since that review was written, what has come to be known as the postmodern movement in writing has emerged in the Western world. Miss Stein's statement no longer holds true. That intense concern with reverberations, as particularly seen in the work of Henry James, Virginia Woolf, Eliot, and Faulkner, to name only a few, has given way to a renewed interest in the event, the actual. In prose, the work of Bellow, Malamud, Mailer, and the so-called nonfiction novelists could be mentioned, whereas in poetry, Lowell, Olson, and others could be cited as instances. Given this context, Pratt's achievement can be seen more clearly for what it is.

I am not, of course, claiming Pratt for the postmodernists. He was in many ways rooted firmly in the nineteenth century and was particularly influenced by Browning, Tennyson, and Thomas Hardy. Stronger influences than these were his growing up in Newfoundland and his years of study, research, and teaching at the University of Toronto.

Pratt's father was a Yorkshire-born Methodist minister, his mother was the daughter of a Newfoundland sea captain, and he was born in a Newfoundland fishing village. Seldom has a man been more faithful to his heritage. His fascination with the sea is evident in the earliest and confirmed in the latest of his poems. He was also concerned throughout his career with the moral nature and the soul of man. For a long time, indeed, he was headed toward the ministry. After early education in outport schools, he attended St. John's Methodist College. Then, after a variety of odd jobs (including hawking his own brand of patent medicine around Newfoundland villages) and some preacher-probationer work, he went to Victoria College, Toronto, to study philosophy. He did an M.A., with a thesis on demonology, and a Ph.D. with a thesis on Pauline eschatology. In between he received a B.D. and was ordained into the Methodist ministry. But there is evidence that he could not remain content within the confines of the church. He studied psychology and became a demonstrator in the science; he read deeply in anthropology and in literature, and in 1920 he joined the Department of English of Victoria College. The appointment was made by Pelham Edgar, a celebrated teacher and one of the first critics of Henry James. It was a brave move, since Pratt had no literary training. Edgar modestly wrote later in his life that if he had a right to immortality, it was through that appointment. It was then, in his late thirties, that Pratt began seriously to write poetry, although he had published some juvenilia in the Victoria College undergraduate literary magazine *Acta Victoriana* between 1909 and 1918.

Something should be said of that intellectual milieu in which Pratt flourished until his retirement from the college thirty-two years later. Victoria College is the United Church college (Methodist-Presbyterian) in the federated University of Toronto. In some ways it was the quintessence of the Ontario mind, bourgeois, austere, dry, with a tradition both strongly theological and liberal. It nurtured many strong teachers, critics, and writers, including E. J. Robbins, Northrop Frye, and, in a later generation, Margaret Atwood and Dennis Lee. Nevertheless, for a beginning writer, Toronto in the twenties would hardly seem to have been the ideal place for development. After working on the Toronto *Star* Hemingway fled the place for the greener pastures of Paris, to be followed for a briefer sojourn by Morley Callaghan. But for Pratt it seems to have been ideal. The *Canadian Forum* was eager to publish and discuss his work, he had congenial colleagues whom he could tap for various kinds of information, and he had a wide circle of friends and, outside the college, cronies who became his loyal feasting and drinking companions.

It was at Victoria College, as a fledgling assistant professor of English, that I first met Ned Pratt. Although he had retired from the college some years before, as long as he could make it down from his Rosedale home he kept up the habit of lunching twice a week at the Senior Common Room. He had a great fund of anecdote and a precious gift of friendship, even for someone so much younger than himself. Along with the other lunchers at that austere but good table, I basked in the glow of his stories and the warmth of his benevolence. Later on, after I had read a good deal of his work, I was to recall Henry James's short story "The Private Life," which was based on his observations of Robert Browning. James frequently encountered the dining-out Browning, smooth, debonair, eminently social, and then turned to the poetry to find the image of a complex, difficult, even lonely individual. He could reconcile the two Brownings only by inventing an alter ego, a serious shade who sat upstairs at the writing table while the social mask went down to dinner. Something of this doppelgänger quality was to be found, I think, in Pratt. Many of the studies of the man stress his sociability, and they repeat, sometimes ad nauseam, the anecdotes, particularly those of his Newfoundland days, that attached themselves like limpets to the poet. The alter ego has consequently often suffered isolation, as the commentators have caroused with the smiling public man downstairs. The poet George Johnston was probably closer to the truth of the man when he wrote in an obituary notice, "For all his friendliness and good fellowship there was something awesome and aloof about him, so that for my part, although I always felt at home in his company, I could not imagine being intimate with him." He found the same to be true of Pratt's poetry: "It is grand, moving, serious; one feels at home with it but not intimate."

There is also in Pratt's intellectual tradition a high seriousness that is part of what seems to us the aloofness of the nineteenth-century man of letters. He was profoundly influenced early in his life by the evolutionary theory. Whereas the ideas of Darwin, Spencer, and Huxley had their strongest effect in Britain in the late nineteenth century, they were still current enough in Canada in the early twentieth to be issues of controversy, as they were in the southern parts of the United States. In the still-primitive conditions of the Canadian Far West and the Eastern seaboard, where Pratt grew up, the wilderness of plain, sea, and rock gave a meaningful setting to the clash of forces taking place within society. Pratt's work is filled with images of primitive nature and evolutionary history. It seemed natural to him to write of molluscs, of cetacean and cephalopod, of the Pliocene epoch, of Java and Piltdown man. The evolutionary process early became and always remained the central metaphor of his work. It gave him the themes of his best lyrics and provided him with the solid framework within which he could achieve an epic style. The evolutionary metaphor persisted in Pratt's work long after it had ceased to have much force for the twentieth-century poetic and philosophic mind.

The evolutionary theory came into conflict, of course, with the Christian belief in which Pratt had been brought up, and it probably had a good deal to do with his decision to leave the ministry. What he later came to believe has been the subject of continuing debate in Pratt criticism. Commentators have called him a Christian humanist, an agnostic, and an atheist. In a close examination of the question in *E. J. Pratt: The Evolutionary Vision* (1974), Sandra Djwa concluded that Pratt's synthesis of evolutionary thought brought him to a belief that was "both Christian and humanistic." On reflection, I have come to believe that Pratt, like many poets, could not commit himself finally to any dogma, but was interested in dramatizing the problem of belief in a variety of contexts. Such a dramatization is found in the poem "The Iron Door," written after the death of his mother. The door closes after the dead, but Pratt in a vision catches

> the sense
> Of life with high auroras and the flow
> Of wide majestic spaces;
> Of light abundant; and of keen impassioned faces,
> Transfigured underneath its vivid glow.

The vision fades, but not even the "blindness falling with terrestrial day" can "cancel half the meaning of that hour . . ." Pratt does not commit himself to either a denial or an affirmation of an afterlife, but he does show that belief itself is a reality that can transform life and give even the skeptical earthbound mind a vision of beauty and meaning.

The question of belief is central to Pratt's most successful poem, *Brébeuf and His Brethren* (1940). On the one hand, Vincent Sharman can claim that the poem is a kind of ironic put-down of the achievement of the seventeenth-century Jesuits in their attempt to convert the Indians to Catholicism. He believes the conclusion of the poem "The Martyrs' Shrine" to be a bitter indictment of twentieth-century Canadians. And on the other, I heard a paper presented at a 1976 conference on E. J. Pratt in Ottawa in which the writer claimed that the poem was a sustained and deliberate apologia for what the Jesuits did, full of high praise for their bravery and belief.

However, Pratt, as both a writer of epic and an historian, has an all-encompassing view of the events and can include both the irony and the achievement. He made a close reading of both the *Jesuit Relations* and Parkman's version of the events in *The Jesuits in North America in the Seventeenth Century*. Unlike Parkman, Pratt was able to escape quite successfully from his Protestant upbringing to write a remarkably sympathetic account of the mission. Yet he was too much aware of the larger forces at work on the continent to subscribe entirely to the orthodox church view. *Brébeuf* is about the whole French imperial effort in New France. That effort had a secular as well as a sacred mission. The duality of the theme is mirrored in the character of the warrior-priest, Brébeuf, himself. References to Richelieu, Mazarin, and the lilies of France demonstrate Pratt's concern with both forces and serve to show that, to some extent at least, the Jesuits were being used by the French ministers of the crown to further their dreams of empire. A converted native population would be a friendly one, and the importance of Indian alliances in the struggle among the French, Dutch, and British for control of North America can hardly be overstated. In the French and Indian wars of the eighteenth century, the combination of French soldiers and Iroquois warriors was to bring France as close to winning the continent as it ever came, before Wolfe put an end to those ambitions with the capture of Quebec in 1759.

Brébeuf and His Brethren abounds in ironies. The priests have the task of converting the natives to a sophisticated and quite abstract system of belief. But the Indians are seen as far down on the evolutionary scale. Behind the Frenchmen are centuries of culture and learning, the achievements of the French cathedral-builders, the traditions of chivalric warfare, the splendors of Renaissance cuisine and viniculture. This civilization is juxtaposed with the filthy primitivism of the Indians, with their smoke-filled lodges, revolting food, and savage warfare. Pratt's descriptions not only stress the enormous difficulty of the Jesuits' task, but also underline the virtual certainty of its failure.

The narrative demonstrates how closely a tribe's or a nation's religion is a product of a culture and its needs, and it establishes a real sympathy for the bewildered natives. Obviously, a religion that promises a heaven without hunting, war, feasts, and tobacco was about as useful to the Indians as a tomahawk without a head. Only the Jesuits' resort to the primitive symbolism of the Christian hell could make much impression on the imagination of the Indians. Again and again, the Jesuits are forced to oversimplify and substitute to convey even the crudest notions of their religion. What happens, in effect, is that they have to go backward many centuries along the path of evolution to make any contact with the savages. The ultimate meeting of minds of Jesuit and Indian comes not on the question of belief but on the common ground of physical endurance. One after another, the priests go to their excruciating deaths, torn and racked by tortures that surpass in refinement even those devised by the Medici. Some of the most effective parts of the poem deal with details of torture.

Pratt stresses that it was no mean achievement of Christian belief and culture to arm men more effectively against torment than could the most stoic capacity for endurance demanded by the Iroquois code. The final magnificent set piece of Brébeuf's torture—which Goya commemorated in a horrifying painting—shows how the priest reverts to his warrior heritage, becomes a lion at bay, and gives his foes "roar for roar" until he conquers this secular source of defiance to come to rely at last on the vision of that earlier crucifixion.

The design of the poem finely echoes its central conflict—the Old World against the New, Catholicism versus savagery. It is put together in mosaic form, usually under yearly dates, charting the triumphs and the heartbreaks of the missionaries. It is carefully built, piece by piece, so that an overwhelming sense of the myriad problems facing the Jesuits is conveyed. From the 1635 section on, the tension slowly mounts as the reader is made increasingly aware of the terrible and inevitable destruction facing the priests. The succession of captures, tortures, and murders works toward its climax in the martyrdom of Brébeuf. The priests scarcely emerge as individuals, as is fitting. Theirs is a joint venture, and the successes and sufferings are shared. At the same time, they become representatives of historical forces, as do the Indians, so that the conflict between the two groups is both elemental and unavoidable. Yet the poem is saved from impersonality by the innumerable details of ceremonials, meals, vegetation, lodge construction, language, and gesture. It is moved forward by a tremendous narrative energy that Pratt, almost alone among twentieth-century poets, possesses. The blank verse is heavily alliterative, but not oppressively so. The rhythms are varied by many run-on lines, and the harmony is established by a sure control of assonance and contrast. Close analysis will reveal the skill with which Pratt adapted the rich variety of syntactical patterns inherent in English to the demands of his metrics.

In *Brébeuf, contra* Winfield Townley Scott, there are innumerable gems of phrasing, such as "the subtle savagery of art," "the rosary against the amulet," "hermit thrushes rivalled the rapture of the nightingales," "gardens and pastures rolling like a sea / From Lisieux to Le Havre." In each of these phrases, the broad themes and conflicts of the poem are suggested, just as in the least metaphor or image, reverberations are sounded that echo through the poem, enrich its texture, and strengthen its form. Verbal sketches abound:

                                    At the equinoxes
Under the gold and green of the auroras
Wild geese drove wedges through the zodiac.

                                    They suffered smoke
That billowed from the back-draughts at the roof,
Smothered the cabin, seared the eyes; the fire
That broiled the face, while frost congealed the spine.

Themes, metaphor, and vision come to a climax in the
death of Brébeuf, as the Indians search for the source of
that enormous vitality and endurance:

                                    Was it the blood?
They would draw it fresh from its fountain. Was it the
     heart?
They dug for it, fought for the scraps in the way of the
     wolves.
But not in these was the valour of stamina lodged;
Nor in the symbol of Richelieu's robes or the seals
Of Mazarin's charters, nor in the stir of the *lilies*
Upon the Imperial folds; nor yet in the words
Loyola wrote on a table of lava-stone
In the cave of Manresa—not in these the source—
But in the sound of invisible trumpets blowing
Around two slabs of board, right-angled, hammered
By Roman nails and hung on a Jewish hill.

Most of Pratt's other notable epic pieces are set on or
by the sea, which remained throughout his career the
source of his most deeply felt emotions and his most
effective imagery. His earliest published essay in the epic
form was *The Witches' Brew* (1925), an octosyllabic
mock-epic in which a drunken tomcat leads an attack on
behalf of the fishes on the warm-blooded creatures of
the earth. The humor seems now heavy-handed and the
satire too drawn out, but the poem was for Pratt a useful
experiment in the form of the long poem and in the
possibilities of great power struggles—an essential element in his epic vision from then on.

It was a short step from there to *The Cachalot* (1926), an account of a sperm whale's attack first on a kraken and then on a whaling ship. Comic elements are still there, as in the description of the whale's anatomy:

> And so large
> The lymph-flow of his active liver,
> One might believe a fair-sized barge
> Could navigate along the river.

In *The Cachalot*, however, Pratt, like Melville, marries a comic to a serious theme and gives an exciting picture of epic conflicts under and on the sea. Pratt had undoubtedly read *Moby-Dick*, but brought to the conflict his own sense of pace and drama. Both men loved the sea, and both were fascinated by the forces of the universe and found an appropriate symbol for that force in the sperm whale. The major difference between the narratives of *Moby-Dick* and *The Cachalot*—aside from length—is that Melville's whale survives the encounter with the whaling ship. Pratt's whale is merely that; unlike Moby-Dick he does not carry the weight of symbolic ambiguity, the profound mystery at the heart of things, an enormous and perhaps inextinguishable life-energy. Pratt's cachalot can be weighed and measured. He is tremendously powerful but finite; a creature of the sea, but warm-blooded. Caught, sleeping and unaware, by the whaling ship, he gives epic battle to the combined forces of man and technology ranged against him. It is a battle to the death, sustained with courage on both sides, and completed by a magnificent charge:

> All the tonnage, all the speed,
> All the courage of his breed,
> The pride and anger of his breath,
> The battling legions of his blood
> Met in that unresisted thud,
> Smote in that double stroke of death.

Epically, Pratt progressed from this titan to *The Titanic* (1935). The sinking of the great ship was a subject exactly fitted to Pratt's talents, requiring technical and historical knowledge, a sense of epic dimension, and, above all, an awareness of the ways of the sea and sailors. Sailors are notoriously superstitious. Centuries of experience have shown that when things can go wrong, through carelessness, indifference, or chance, they invariably do. It is a wise sailor who reads the signs of the skies or the pattern of events which may point to disaster. To heed them hurts nothing; to disregard them invites the fates. The omens on the maiden trip of the *Titanic* down the Solent are ignored as part of the pattern of pride which causes the captain to proceed at full speed through the ice field, when every other ship has slowed to a crawl.

Underlining and appearing to justify the captain's pride is the apparently foolproof construction of the ship, so brilliantly described by Pratt. The *Titanic* appears to be far more than a ship—it is a luxury hotel whose appearance and services seem to deny the limitations of any sea-borne vessel. The ship's luxury helps create the illusion of complete security which cocoons the first-class passengers. Only the gambling scene, rich in irony, indicates the peril toward which the ship is proceeding.

Meanwhile the iceberg, reduced from its cathedral-like shape to what Pratt calls the "brute / And palaeolithic outline of a face," drifts toward its rendezvous, its long claw stretched out underwater at precisely the depth at which it can rip through the double hull of the ship. The *Titanic* moves at top speed toward its destiny, ignoring the many radio signals from all around warning of the danger. The collision itself is barely felt by those on board, another irony underscoring the still apparent security of a ship doomed to rapid destruction.

The only thing which redeems the occasion is the heroism of a few men and women—the stokers and engineers who stay at the job down below, the officers, crew members, and passengers who stay calm, the wife and the small boy who give up their places in the lifeboats,

> In those high moments when the gambler tossed
> Upon the chance and uncomplaining lost.

All that power and luxury slide beneath the waves and leave behind them the iceberg, "the master of the longitudes." As Pratt wrote in his notes to the poem, "There was never an event outside the realm of technical drama where so many factors combined to close all the gates of escape, as if some power with intelligence and resource had organized and directed a conspiracy." The brilliant structure of the poem, with its matched opposites, all the way from the great ship and enormous iceberg down to rhymed decasyllabic couplet, emphasizes the form of this august event. Destruction is virtually certain to come to anyone who neglects the iron rules of the sea.

A maritime disaster is also the theme of another epic poem, *The Roosevelt and the Antinoe* (1930), which recounts how the captain and crew of the American liner *Roosevelt* rescue many of the crew of the sinking British freighter *Antinoe*. Even when things are done in the proper seamanlike manner, as they were in this incident, there is no guarantee of safety, as men are lost in spite of efficiency and heroism. In this poem, as in earlier work, the sea seems to be the ally of prehistoric forces. As a lifeboat is lowered into the water from the davits of the *Roosevelt*,

> Below, like creatures of a fabled past,
> From their deep hidings in unlighted caves,
> The long processions of great-bellied waves
> Cast forth their monstrous births which with grey fang
> Appeared upon the leeward side, ran fast
> Along the broken crests, then coiled and sprang
> For the boat impatient of its slow descent
> Into their own inviolate element.

Later in Pratt's career, when he came to write epics in celebration of the battle against Nazi tyranny, the image of the sea changed. For the sailors coming to the aid of the trapped soldiers in Pratt's poem *Dunkirk* (1941),

> Their souls had come to birth out of their racial myths.
> The sea was their school; the storm their friend.

Pratt's patriotism carried him at times into strident propaganda in *Dunkirk*, but in *Behind the Log*, written after the war in 1947, the language is freed from this flatulence and renders, in strikingly idiomatic blank verse, the reality lying behind the traditional laconic form of the logbook

> That rams the grammar down a layman's throat,
> Where words unreel in paragraphs, and lines
> In chapters. Volumes lie in graphs and codes,
> Recording with an algebraic care
> The idiom of storms, their lairs and paths;
> Or, in the self-same bloodless manner, sorting
> The mongrel litters of a battle signal
> In victories or defeats or bare survivals.

Here it is the centuries of tradition and duty as well as the boring, tiring, demanding, and occasionally heroic facts of convoy duty concealed in the log which Pratt seeks to transmute into poetry.

Ranged against the miscellaneous collection of freighters and the four escort vessels which constitute the convoy is the sea power of Naziism, the U-boat. In *Behind the Log* submarines are personified into

> Grey predatory fish [that] had pedigreed
> With tiger sharks and brought a speed and power
> The sharks had never known, for they had been
> Committed to the sea under a charter
> Born of a mania of mind and will
> And nurtured by a Messianic slogan.

The slogan is, I suppose, "Heil Hitler," and it represents for Pratt that abstract rhetoric and demonic lust for power and destruction which for him typified fascism. Against the rhetorical demonism is ranged the laconic language of the log: the complex web of signals, technologies, duties, observations, and rituals that make up the discipline of convoy duty.

Here again, as in *Dunkirk*, the sea becomes an ally. To exploit the alliance of the sea, the convoy turns north, to leave the beaten sea lanes

> And in the ambiguity of the wastes
> To seek the harsh alliance of the ice
> And fog, where Arctic currents were more friendly,
> And long nights blanketed the periscopes.

This alliance partly breaks down in clear weather and moonlight, and the U-boat wolf pack does get through to wreak a terrible havoc among the freighters. Men drown, are fried by burning oil, or blown to pieces in explosions. The escorts strike back. Hunting by sonar, they seek out their prey and destroy them by depth charges.

Suffering terrible losses, the convoy struggles on. In the end it is the work of disciplined men, their knowledge of the sea and navigation, their skill in handling ships and weapons, and the alliance with the waters that brings the convoy through. Pratt makes the point, perhaps the central point of modern war, that the ultimate victory is achieved not by the Nelson touch but by the combined, unrelenting tasks of many men. And he skillfully draws together the themes of *Behind the Log* in a complex web of imagery of writing, type, blood, body, and machinery. The whole is given a sacramental power by the pun on the word "mass" at the beginning of this excerpt:

> No one would mould the linotype for such
> A mass that might survive or not survive

Their tedium of watches in the holds—
The men with surnames blotted by their jobs
Into a scrawl of anonymity.
A body blow at the boilers would untype
All differentiations in the blood
Of pumpmen, wipers, messmen, galley boys
Who had become incorporate with the cogs
On ships that carried pulp and scrap to Europe.

The sacramental vision is given a further intensity by a later passage describing the blowing up of the tanker *Stargard:*

Where find the straws to grasp at in this sea?
Where was the cause which once had made a man
Disclaim the sting of death? What ecstasy
Could neutralize this salt and quench this heat
Or open up in victory this grave?
But oil and blood were prices paid for blood
And oil. However variable the time,
The commerce ever was in barter. Oil
Propelled the ships. It blew them up. The men
Died oil-anointed as it choked the *"Christ!"*
That stuttered on their lips before the sea
Paraded them as crisps upon her salver.

The insistent biblical imagery of baptism, anointing, communion, crucifixion, and resurrection transform the anonymity of the men behind the log into an identity with the individual who made the supreme sacrifice by dying on the cross. The point is subtly made that the deaths of these almost anonymous individuals cumulatively had an effect similar to the sacrifice of the Lord in bringing ultimate victory over the powers of evil.

In his last epic, Pratt forsook the sea to record the conquest of the land by the builders of the continental railroad. In *Towards the Last Spike* (1952) it is the perilous "sea of mountains" that the railroad men have to cross rather than the ocean seas, and it is a task requiring as much nerve and sinew as the other journeys. As in

Brébeuf and His Brethren, Pratt employs a mosaic technique to organize his disparate materials, but since *Towards the Last Spike* contains a good deal of political material, it is looser in form than his other epics. The gigantic nature of the theme tends to give an air of impersonality to the poem, and Pratt often resorts to personification in efforts to overcome this. He makes a monster out of the Laurentian shield and a lady out of British Columbia, just as Frank Norris personified the wheat and the railroad in *his* rail epic, *The Octopus.* Fortunately for Pratt, the giganticism of his geographical forces is almost matched by the human heroes, William Van Horne, the American railroad builder, and Sir John A. Macdonald, prime minister of Canada. The two men are complementary in the poem: Sir John, the rhetorician and skilled parliamentarian, supplies the dream of continental union; Van Horne, engineer and administrator, supplies the force and skill that make the dream come true. *Towards the Last Spike* is not narrative history—Ned Pratt was ironically asked by one of his critics where his coolies were—but it is the stuff of myth, a vigorous, trenchant, swiftly moving narrative in which a nation's ideals and aspirations are given expression and form. Pierre Berton's history of the building of the railroad, *The National Dream,* gives the full story, but does not have the mythical dimension of *Towards the Last Spike.*

A. J. M. Smith has called Pratt "the only Canadian poet who has mastered the long poem." My agreement with this dictum is one reason why I have not left myself much space in which to discuss his shorter poems. Some of them are fine achievements of precision and perception, but it is significant that the most fruitful source of lyric poetry—love—seemed closed to him. One of the few love poems in his canon, "Like Mother, Like Daughter" (1937), clearly shows Pratt's ambivalence about the ruling passion:

You caught the *male* for good or ill,
And locked him in a golden cage.

There are references to Keats's forlorn knight-at-arms in
the first stanza, while the catalog of women heroines in
the poem, "Helen, Deirdre, Héloïse/ Laura, Cleopatra,
Eve!" seems more catastrophic than celebratory. For
Pratt the domain of women seemed to represent tempta-
tion and imprisonment, while that of men represented
adventure, liberation, and the possibility of heroic
action. In "The Deed," for example, Pratt wonders what
has happened to the beauty which inspired lovers to sing
serenades, minstrels to praise cavalcades, and the poets to
write of fruits, flowers, and birds. His own answer is
that beauty for him lies not in these things, but in the act
of heroism—the almost hopeless dive for the boy's body
by an unnamed swimmer:

This was an arch beyond the salmon's lunge,
There was a rainbow in the rising mists:
Sea-lapidaries started at the plunge
To cut the facets of their amethysts.

So it can be claimed that Pratt's lyric impulse expressed itself not in the conventional themes, but in ver-
sions of the heroic. These can be tragic in tone, as in
"The Deed," or comic, as in "Carlo," a poem about a
Newfoundland dog who rescues more than ninety
people from a wreck. At the end of the poem Pratt
promises to intercede with St. Peter at the heavenly gates
in the attempt to get the dog into heaven where he belongs. Pratt wrote several comic poems about animals,
but one of them, "The Prize Cat," ends in savagery
when the cat goes after a bird:

Behind the leap so furtive-wild
Was such ignition in the gleam,
I thought an Abyssinian child
Had cried out in the whitethroat's scream.

The tension between high breeding on the one hand and savagery on the other in fact supplies the subject for many of the shorter poems. Pratt was always concerned with the evolutionary process, but insisted, too, that the distance between caveman and civilized man is often as short in spirit as it is long in time. Ironically, some of man's greatest technological achievements tend to shorten the distance, as is shown in Pratt's most successful, and most typical, lyric, "From Stone to Steel":

> From stone to bronze, from bronze to steel
> Along the road-dust of the sun,
> Two revolutions of the wheel
> From Java to Geneva run.
>
> The snarl Neanderthal is worn
> Close to the smiling Aryan lips,
> The civil polish of the horn
> Gleams from our praying finger tips.
>
> The evolution of desire
> Has but matured a toxic wine,
> Drunk long before its heady fire
> Reddened Euphrates or the Rhine.
>
> Between the temple and the cave
> The boundary lies tissue-thin:
> The yearlings still the altars crave
> As satisfaction for a sin.
>
> The road goes up, the road goes down—
> Let Java or Geneva be—
> But whether to the cross or crown,
> The path lies through Gethsemane.

Here the journey of man is more like a circle than a straight line, but in a good many other poems the journey is terminated by death—usually death by water. Here again thematic concerns are similar to those in the epics. In the ironic little poem "The Drag-Irons," the dead captain comes up from Davy Jones's locker "with livid silence and with glassy look," a parody of his long years of command. Another poem on the same subject, but with a completely different tone, is "Come Not the Seasons Here," one of Pratt's quietest and most effective works. Probably the poem's model is Shakespeare's song "Come Away Death," although the imagery does not concern itself with death directly, but with the seasons. However, the traditional sense of growth associated with spring, summer, and autumn is undercut by the imagery: cuckoo, poppy, shed bloom, sere leaf, brown pasture. The kingdom of death takes over imperiously in the last stanza, in frozen air and glacial stone. This Canadian pastoral is, I take it, about the power of sorrow to destroy the perception of vitality in nature.

The Canadian environment presses in relentlessly on the subject matter of the short poems, as the titles themselves reveal: "The Toll of the Bells," "The Ground Swell," "The Fog," "The Shark," "A Dirge," "The Ice-Floes,"—all in Pratt's first collection, *Newfoundland Verse* (1923). "The Way of Cape Race," "A Prairie Sunset," "Putting Winter to Bed," "Frost," and "The Lee-Shore" appear in the second collection, *Many Moods* (1932). "The Unromantic Moon," "A November Landscape," "Myth and Fact," and "Newfoundland Seamen" are among his later poems. Canada does not offer a climate or a culture hospitable to the tender and lyrical impulses of man.

Canadian life has, on the other hand, been conducive to the development of man's ingenuity, toughness, and resistance. Margaret Atwood has made this the theme of her book about Canadian literature, *Survival*. There is a good deal of the survivor instinct in Pratt's work, but it is not often the grim and desperate affair that Atwood makes it out to be. In one of Pratt's most typical poems, "The Truant," survival becomes a joyful as well as a defiant necessity. The poem's purpose is to show the undying spirit of man when confronted by the ultimate tyrant, the Panjandrum, who represents himself as God, but is merely, as Northrop Frye has noted, "the mechanical power of the universe." Man refuses the Panjandrum's order to join the cosmic ballet and so is condemned by the god to endure palsy, deafness, blindness, old age, and other humiliations. Man merely laughs in the god's face, asserts that he himself created the god, discovered the organization of his universe, and

> Lassoed your comets when they ran astray,
> Yoked Leo, Taurus, and your team of Bears
> To pull our kiddy cars of inverse squares.

Condemned to death, he rings out his defiance, basing his case on the long history of man's resistance to force and tyranny. He ends, "No! by the Rood, we will not join your ballet." It is in this poem that Pratt's poetic personality of wit, humor, toughness, pride, and technical skill most clearly emerge.

Frye has concisely captured the particular quality of Pratt's individualism in his introduction to the second edition of *The Collected Poems* (1958):

> When everybody was writing subtle and complex lyrics, Pratt developed a technique of straightforward narrative; when everybody was experimenting with free verse, Pratt was finding new possibilities in blank verse and octosyllabic couplets. He had the typical mark of originality: the power to make something poetic out of what everybody had just decided could no longer be poetic material. He worked unperturbed while the bright young men of the twenties, the scolding young men of the thirties, the funky young men of the forties, and the angry young men of the fifties were, like Leacock's famous hero, riding off rapidly in all directions.

Twentieth-century poets in general either have tended to be ahistorical or have used history as a kind of rubbish dump from which to pluck bits and pieces to titillate their imaginations. Winfield Townley Scott reflects the antihistorical attitude in his condemnation of Pratt's use of events. But artists, even poets, cannot continue to evade or to play with history with impunity. Pratt's intellectual training and inclination enabled him to regard history as a great unfolding process from which he could select at will stories and incidents that could serve his large poetic purposes. He could consequently write epics of the Canadian experience, such as *Brébeuf* and *Towards the Last Spike*, that no other contemporary poet could have tackled. Most poets seem to have felt that there was nothing much worth saying about the Canadian past. Earle Birney's "Can. Lit." is an example:

> we French&English never lost
> our civil war
> endure it still
> a bloody civil bore
>
> the wounded sirened off
> no Whitman wanted
> it's only by our lack of ghosts
> we're haunted

Pratt suffered from no lack of ghosts, and he was able over the years to create a usable past for the contemporary Canadian imagination.

Pratt's roots in older poetic traditions also enabled him to write descriptively and lyrically about the Canadian landscape. In this endeavor he was, of course, preceded by many poets such as Marjorie Pickthall, Bliss Carman, and Archibald Lampman, but Pratt's scientific bent brought a new precision to his depiction of the Canadian scene, particularly in its severity and grandeur, that previously only the painters of the Group of Seven had adequately captured. Although Pratt remained preeminently a poet of the sea, and particularly of the rockbound, storm-lashed, Newfoundland coast that provided

him with his earliest images, he emerged from regionalism to discover the inland plains and mountains and to
record them with love and fidelity.

Canada did not find an adequate myth- and image-
maker in poetry until E. J. Pratt appeared. It was fortunate that the individualistic and slightly anachronistic
form of his imagination enable him to fulfill this role so
late in the national day, in an age when mythmakers had
all but disappeared.

III

Possessing the Land

Notes on Canadian Fiction

George Woodcock

In his conclusion to the new edition of the collectively written *Literary History of Canada* (1976), which brings the record up to 1972, Northrop Frye remarks on "the colossal verbal explosion that has taken place in Canada since 1960." And indeed, quantitatively there has been an extraordinary upswing in literary production, fostered by many circumstances, including cheaper printing processes, public subsidies to publishing, and a kind of creative surge, in some way connected with the rising up of national pride, without which these mechanical forms of assistance would have been useless. In most areas of writing the growth has been both qualitative and quantitative. A fresh sureness of voice and touch has appeared in poetry, where a surprisingly high proportion of the hundreds of new books—often by new poets—that have appeared each year have been distinctive in both tone and accomplishment. With a new sense of the past as myth as well as fact, the historians and biographers during the past decade and a half have been mapping out all the neglected reaches of the record of Canada as a cluster of regions and peoples rather than as a nation in the older European sense. Drama has moved out of the restricting field of radio, and plays that are both actable on stage and publishable as books have appeared with astonishing frequency over the past decade. Finally, criticism has achieved the kind of maturity and subtlety which is one of the signs of a literature's coming of age. When I founded the quarterly review *Canadian Literature* in 1959, good critics were not easy to find; now they are numerous and creative.

In fiction alone has the situation been different. There are not more books, but those that are published are astonishingly better in quality than all except a few novels of past decades, and their variety of approach has increased phenomenally. One of the most striking facts I encountered as I looked back over the decades in preparing this essay was that the average number of novels published yearly by Canadians has not changed in any marked way over the past forty years, in spite of the steady growth in population. According to Gordon Roper, writing in the first (1965) edition of the *Literary History of Canada*, some fourteen hundred volumes of fiction were published by Canadians between 1880 and 1920, an average of thirty-five a year. Between 1920 and 1940, according to Desmond Pacey, writing in the same *History*, the annual average number of Canadian works of fiction remained almost exactly the same, with seven hundred books appearing over twenty years. Between 1940 and 1960, according to figures presented by Hugo McPherson, there appears to have been an actual drop in publication figures, since he counts up only 570 works of fiction appearing over two decades, but I believe he did not count books published by Canadians abroad, so that the final figure can probably be taken as very near to the thirty-five that had prevailed so consistently between 1880 and 1940. I have not made a count for all the years between 1960 and 1976, but spot checks of two years during this period revealed figures of thirty-five and forty respectively, bringing us curiously close to that average of thirty-five volumes per year which prevailed between 1880 and 1940.

Yet despite the fact that no greater numbers of novels are being published by Canadians now than in 1890 or 1930 or 1950, and although far smaller areas on bookstore shelves are now occupied by works of fiction, there is no evidence that in Canada the novel is a dying or even a sickly genre; on the contrary, the novel and the short story both occupy positions of prestige in the 1970s, among both critics and scholars, which no kind of Canadian fiction occupied in earlier decades.

This apparently paradoxical situation exists mainly because popular fiction has been so largely superseded by television as a means of mental and emotional escape that it is no longer one of the mainstays of the literary industry. The great circulating libraries which once provided the basis of a living for hack fiction writers, including the monstrous regiment of "lady novelists," have almost vanished for lack of support, and both public libraries and personal collections of books devote far less space proportionately to fiction than they did up to twenty years ago. But it is far from the case that the novel, as a form of literary art, has lost prestige or significance in Canada.

The great change which has happened, while the number of books of fiction published in Canada remains so astonishingly constant over almost a century, is that the quality of craftsmanship has improved and the degree of original creation has increased steadily, decade by decade, since the 1920s. As Northrop Frye remarked of the period between 1880 and 1920, "not all the fiction is romance, but nearly all of it is formula-writing." Of Canadian fiction in the 1970s, it can be said that, while romance in a somewhat different form does indeed exist, only a small proportion of the books that are published can be regarded as formula writing, which survives mainly in the curious subculture represented by nurse romances, inferior crime novels, and soft porn, very little of which is actually written in Canada, owing to the control of the low-grade paperback distribution industry by companies which import mainly the products of American mass book production.

When I was invited to write this essay, it was tentatively suggested that I consider the relevance of realism to the Canadian literary tradition. I replied that any essay I might write would have a rather different approach, since realism as ordinarily defined (in terms of either Godwin's "things as they are" or Zola's naturalism or the Marxists' "social realism") had not played a very significant role in Canadian fiction. Where an important novelist—such as Frederick Philip Grove or Morley Callaghan or Hugh MacLennan or Mordecai Richler—has used techniques generally regarded as "realist," the realism has almost always turned out to be one of the secondary elements in what is primarily a moral drama (Grove), a homiletic parable (Callaghan), an imaginative gloss on history (MacLennan), or a satire (Richler) which uses fantasy as much as realism to gain its ends.

A few Canadian writers could indeed be called realists in the same way as we apply that label to American novelists like Frank Norris and Theodore Dreiser. Robert Stead, the early twentieth-century novelist of the prairies and author of *The Homesteaders* (1916) and *Grain* (1926), was perhaps the most important early representative of the tradition. A genuine realist of a later generation, Hugh Garner, retains some standing even today in the Canadian literary world and is respected for his short stories and novels of Toronto working-class life, such as *Cabbagetown* (1950). During the 1930s a few isolated novels of some merit might have been classed as vaguely "social realist," such as Irene Baird's still impressive chronicle of class struggle *Waste Heritage* (1939), perhaps the best of its kind to be written in Canada.

But the main development in Canadian fiction in fact bypasses the matter of realism, European or North

American, largely because Canadians, faced with the wilderness on one side and a dangerously powerful neighbor on the other, had little doubt as to the actual nature of their predicament; what they needed was the combination of mythology and ideology that would enable them to emerge from mere escapism and present a countervision more real than actuality. Hence the weakness of realism as a tradition in literature or, for that matter, in the visual arts, where a national consciousness was first expressed through the highly colored and emphatically outlined formalism of the paintings of the Group of Seven and Emily Carr.

What one does see, observing the transition that began in the later 1920s, is the change in the novel from formulaic and commercially motivated romance to a genuine Canadian twentieth-century romanticism, which must use fantasy and dreams as paths to reality, which must accept myth as the structure that subsumes history, which in its ultimate degree of the fantastic must recognize and unite with its opposite, satire, the logically absurd extension of realism.

Little Canadian fiction that was published before 1900 now seems worth rereading either for pleasure or for the kind of subliminally directed information that, at its most sensitive, literature can project over the centuries. The basic purpose of the early literature of any colonial culture, like the basic purpose of transplanted peasant folk arts, is not to define the future but to consecrate the past. Faced by the wilderness, man seeks to assert the familiar, not to evoke the unknown, and so colonial literature generally attempts to reenact against the backdrop of a new land the achievements of an abandoned way of life. Nothing could be more devastating as a symbol of this attitude than the fact that the English Oliver Goldsmith, who wrote "The Deserted Village," should be followed by a Canadian Oliver Goldsmith, seeking to repair the damage to the good life with that immeasurably more banal poem *The Rising Village* (1845).

Eighteenth-century Frances Brooke, writing the first of all novels of Canada, *Emily Montague* (1769), established in her account of a garrison-limited society a pattern of defensive writing that continued for more than a century, until in the confederation years the American threat grew less urgent and the northern wilderness more penetrable. And since the novel is perhaps the genre that most requires a sense of empathy with the actual, the touch of verisimilitude necessary to authenticate the transfiguration of fantasy, the nineteenth century in Canadian literature was not unjustly defined by the early critic John Bourinot, who in 1893 remarked favorably on the achievements of Canadians in history, poetry, and the essay, but added that "there is one respect in which Canadians have never won any marked success, and that is the novel or romance."

The most vigorous early Canadian fiction was in fact written by satirists in the Maritime Provinces who had no thought of writing novels, such as Thomas McCulloch in *Letters of Mephibosheth Stepsure* (1862) and Thomas Haliburton in *The Clockmaker* (1836). Both McCulloch and Haliburton wrote episodically, each delivering his own series of sermons in fiction, and their purpose of presenting the ills of society rather than developing the inner and individual worlds of that society's inhabitants prevented them from ever creating the kind of self-consistent world of the imagination which is the true fictional achievement.

McCulloch and Haliburton established a long Canadian lineage of ironists and satirists, and they encouraged among Canadians a fatal illusion that they are a humorous people, but in terms of the novel it was an impasse into which they led. Even the much revered Stephen Leacock, perhaps the best-known Canadian writer in the early decades of the present century, endowed with an extraordinary ironic sensibility and a great fund of sharp and true wisdom, failed in the essential fictional task because all his aims were, in the end, didactic rather than

creative. He wrote admirable and not always gentle
comments in fictional form on the world of actuality,
which so often distressed him with its crassness and
hypocrisy, but he never united those comments into the
kind of alternative world of the imagination which the
true novelist erects to confront—or to evade—the world
of actuality.

For most of the early Canadian novelists, writing was
a way of earning or supplementing a living, with—as a
special bonus—the hope of entertaining or edifying one's
readers added on to it. An astonishing proportion of
early Canadian fiction writers were clergymen of evangelical bent, only one of whom had the kind of talent
that transfigured the Reverend Charles William Gordon
into the novelist Ralph Connor and in the process developed one of the three or four fictional voices that still
speak out of the Canadian nineteenth century with a
degree of conviction. Connor was in no authentic sense a
realist, since his concerns were overwhelmingly didactic;
he wished to portray the essential drama—which under
his hand often turned into melodrama—of the spiritual
life, and he wished to show how that life could be rendered in the unpromising circumstances of Upper Canadian settlements of Highland immigrants like Glengarry
and in the vast spaces and the rough elemental society of
the new West that developed in the wake of the fur
traders. It would be hard to find anywhere in the literature of the British Empire a more vigorous exposition of
the doctrine of muscular Christianity than in such novels
by Ralph Connor as *Black Rock: A Tale of the Selkirks*
(1898), *The Sky Pilot: A Tale of the Foothills* (1899),
and *The Man from Glengarry* (1901). Yet Connor used
some of the devices of realism skillfully in developing his
heroic religious fantasies, and in some degree his books
do portray what life was like in both the pioneer East
and the pioneer West of Canada during the latter half of
the nineteenth century.

In his own way, Connor was in fact a fairly effective

exponent of the pseudorealistic North American local-color movement, with its aim of giving authenticity, through a vivid and detailed depiction of the setting and the characteristic local way of life, to a sentimental plot and a group of conventionally typed characters. Occasionally a book of this kind was so well done that it survived its time by the sheer appeal of the idyllic atmosphere it created; an example is Lucy Maud Montgomery's *Anne of Green Gables* (1908), with its haunting evocation of rustic Prince Edward Island, or, in a later decade, Mazo de la Roche's *Jalna* cycle of sixteen novels in which the improbable epic of an Upper Canadian squirearchical family is presented in a setting so plausibly circumstantial that for many years it was regarded, if not in Canada, certainly in Britain and even more in France, as an authentic portrayal of Canadian life.

Books like *Anne of Green Gables* and the *Jalna* cycle show how far the manipulation of authentic detail to give local color to a formulaic kind of romance might be stretched in a direction opposite that of true realism, and even in the very few remaining Canadian novels written before 1914 that stand out with some distinction, one sees the devices of verisimilitude being used for purposes that are essentially nonrealistic in their intent. In my own estimation two such books stand out with especial vividness as exceptions to the general mediocrity of Canadian fiction in that early age.

One is the solitary masterpiece of James De Mille, an academic who for the most part wasted a genuine talent on writing humorous potboilers and boys' adventure stories for the American market. *A Strange Manuscript Found in a Copper Cylinder* is the only book by De Mille that continues to be read; it never found a publisher during his life and was not brought out until 1888, eight years after his death. *A Strange Manuscript* has some distinction as the first utopian romance written by a Canadian, and almost the last. It is a vivid and haunting tale of bizarre adventures that take the narrator into a strange world within the earth, entered by a vortex near the South Pole—a world through which De Mille, by some skillful inversions of habits and customs, presents an effective satire on the hypocritical Victorian world in which he was forced to live and work. *A Strange Manuscript* has some distinct similarities to Samuel Butler's *Erewhon*, to Bulwer Lytton's *The Coming Race*, and to some of the romances of Jules Verne, and Canadian scholars—myself among them—have argued at length on what De Mille borrowed from whom or whether he borrowed at all. But even if it is partly derivative, *A Strange Manuscript* is a well-written and boldly speculative book, in quite another category from most of the banal adventure narratives which Canadian writers were publishing copiously at the time.

An even sharper mind than De Mille's is evident in Sara Jeannette Duncan's best book, *The Imperialist* (1904). Sara Jeannette Duncan was one of the many Canadians, like Richler, Norman Levine, and Margaret Laurence in our own age, who matured their talents in long years abroad, in Duncan's case in England and especially in India, which became the setting for many of her novels. Like Henry James, who much influenced her, she was greatly concerned with the accentuation of both virtues and failings that takes place when people transplant themselves into alien settings, like Canadians in Britain and the British in India, yet her qualities as a writer are most admirably shown in the only one of her novels that is set in Canada. *The Imperialist* is a many-leveled novel of sophistication and wit such as no other Canadian wrote before 1914 and few have written since, a study of political motivations but also of small-town Canadian manners, observed with an eye for the comedy as well as the pathos of ambition and written with great skill in, as Northrop Frye has remarked in his conclusion to the first edition of the *Literary History of Canada* (1965), "a voice of genuine detachment, sympathetic but not defensive either of the group or of herself, concerned primarily to understand and to make the reader see."

A similar, though less successful, effort to "understand and to make the reader see" is to be found in the work of the early twentieth-century writer Frederick Niven, Chilean-born and oriented in his writing toward western Canada as well as toward the Scotland of his childhood. Niven, again, was a writer who used some of the techniques of realism for other purposes, since basically he was a fictional historian—rather than an historical novelist—dedicated to presenting history as adventure. The romance of Western settlement activated Niven's imagination, but he continued to write historical fiction long after it had gone out of vogue, and his most ambitious novels—the trilogy concerning developments on the prairies and in the Rockies from the early to the late nineteenth century, *The Flying Years* (1935), *Mine Inheritance* (1940), and *The Transplanted* (1944)—never received the attention that was due their extraordinarily authentic recreation of time and place. Niven was weak in developing those conventional elements of the novel —character and plot; he tended to produce episodic pageants rather than sustained narratives. But he does anticipate in interesting ways the neoromantic concern for the magical continuum of the land and of the history it projects that has been so evident in the work of emerging Canadian poets and novelists in recent years.

It is a long step from the urban and urbane concerns of Sara Jeannette Duncan, but not so far from the action-in-a-landscape approach of Niven to the handful of turn-of-the-century writers who produced for the first time a characteristic Canadian group expression in prose that can be compared with the more solid and celebrated achievement of the much more personally knit Group of Seven in painting. These are the nature writers, the outdoorsmen, who emerge with Ernest Thompson Seton and Charles G. D. Roberts during the last years of the nineteenth century. The outdoors story and the animal story became very popular around 1900, and this was the first period in which Canadian writers began to draw the attention of the whole English-reading world. For a considerable period, such fiction was one of the main streams in Canadian writing, and, although the vogue tended to die away about the time of the Great War, a steady interest in outdoors writing has sustained later exponents, such as the ambiguous Archie Belaney who gained celebrity as Grey Owl and the British Columbian fisherman, naturalist, and novelist, Roderick Haig-Brown, who died as recently as 1976.

Of the two leading exponents of the animal story, Seton was the better naturalist and tended to be the more didactic, striving—with many lapses into pathos—to portray the actual lives of animals as nearly as possible and in this sense he was a realist. Roberts was the more philosophic and also the more melodramatic writer, tending to portray his animal heroes in extreme situations where they could be displayed as the tragic victims of destiny in an indifferent universe. His views are impregnated with the fashionable evolutionism of his time, but it is Huxley's pessimistic interpretation of Darwinism rather than Kropotkin's optimistic one that shadows his stories.

In seeking the common themes of Canadian writing and the myths that underlie them, contemporary Canadian critics have been inclined to make much of these turn-of-the-century creators of animal stories, and from their special viewpoint of cultural nationalism they are right, since here for the first time are writers working in Canada whom it is difficult to relegate to the fringes of more dominant literary traditions such as the English and the American. One may perhaps consider Duncan a lesser Edith Wharton, dismiss Niven as a minor Robert Louis Stevenson, but the Canadian animal writers were doing something quite different from either their British or their American counterparts. British animal stories have almost always been thinly disguised fables, acted out by men in animal skins to illuminate essentially human problems. (George Orwell's *Animal Farm* is an outstanding example, but even less obviously didactic works like *The Wind in the Willows* are just as essentially anthropomorphic.) American animal stories, like Faulkner's "The Bear" or Hemingway's *The Old Man and the Sea*, are almost invariably stories of antagonism and confrontation, man pitting himself against the animal who becomes the symbol of all that is hostile in nature. But Canadian animal stories are really about animals, and they are about animals with whom we are invited to empathize. We are invited to empathize with them—critics such as Margaret Atwood are likely to claim—because they are invariably portrayed as victims, and we, a multiply colonialized people, are victims, too.

It does not, however, require any such deference to literary theory to recognize that in such fiction the Canadian writer is at last beginning to respond to and utilize his environment directly and without fear; it is no longer necessary to interpose the screen of European forms and values between him and the world in which he is destined to live. It is Canada's own myths that Canadians must recognize, mediated through the images which at last can begin to be recognized in their true shapes. But even the animal writers of the turn of the century present us with the reality of the specific Canadian existence at one remove. For all his skill in evoking the lives of wild animals, Roberts failed when, in *The Heart of the Ancient Wood* (1902), he attempted to establish a meaningful relationship between human beings and the wilderness. Roberts failed because he created a sentimental identification of man with untamed nature rather than an organic link.

A much more successful exercise in bringing man into a fictionally viable relationship with the wilderness is Martin Allerdale Grainger's single novel, *Woodsmen of the West* (1908), a fine small novel which marks an almost unrecognized transition point in Canadian writing. It concerns the loggers of the British Columbian rain forests, and even now it is probably the best work of fiction that their way of life has ever inspired. Grainger, a man of extensive outdoors experience who later rose to a high executive position in the West Coast logging industry, approached his subject not out of a sentimental attachment to a mythical natural life or a principled desire to retreat from civilization, but from the standpoint of a man who goes into the forest to wrest a living—and, with luck, a fortune—from it. Grainger knows from experience all the mundane as well as the curious details of the logger's working life; he knows the psychological frustrations and the human conflicts that woodsmen endure, but he also knows the sense of freedom that counterbalances the memories of even the most uncomfortable of logging camps and leads the men back to what most people regard as a hard existence. If one seeks a work of true realism in Canadian fiction, *Woodsmen of the West* is probably as near to a perfect example as one is likely to come by. Yet, as is the case in all the classic examples of successful realism, the vision the novel creates survives when the world it portrays has vanished, so that Grainger's camps, belonging historically to what is now a very distant past, continue in our mind a detached existence in rather the same way that the birch woods of a lost Russia survive in all their rainy glitter in the pages of Turgenev's *A Sportsman's Sketches*, which is another way of saying that the pursuit of realism is self-defeating, since its achievements survive in exactly the same way as those of successful fantasy in the timeless world of the imagination.

Woodsmen of the West was a striking example of a phenomenon very common in Canada—the novelist who writes only one book, or only one good book, either because he is writing out of a vividly remembered but limited body of direct experience, as Grainger did, or because he has an intense but equally limited imaginative vision which can be encompassed within a single book.

The novels derived from direct experience are really by-products of the oddities of life in a pioneer society, and often, when they are rendered with natural artistry, as in *Woodsmen of the West*, they project a purer sense of locality than the writings of more professional novelists. Another especially pleasing example of this kind of book is that haunting fictional account, derived from family traditions, of the nineteenth-century Irish immigration to Canada *The Yellow Briar* (1933), by "Patrick Slater" (John Mitchell).

The books that stem from a sharp but unrepeatable personal vision are very often written in Canada by poets troubled by some theme they cannot find expression for in verse. An especially striking example is Leonard Cohen's *Beautiful Losers* (1966), a work of remarkable decadent fantasy which followed on the failure of Cohen's much more realistic and autobiographical first novel, *The Favourite Game* (1963). Earle Birney also wrote one very good novel of comic fantasy, *Turvey* (1949), a highly stylized Schweikian vision of the absurdities of war and the military mind, but followed it by an unsuccessful stab at social realism in his novel of Senator McCarthy's America, *Down the Long Table* (1955). And P. K. Page wrote a single and rather fine romantic novel, *The Sun and the Moon* (1944), under the nom de plume of Judith Cape.

Most of these solitary masterpieces, although they cannot be ignored by anyone who wishes to appreciate the variety of modern Canadian fiction, take their places on the verge of the genre. When poets have written novels they are usually individual feats of virtuosity that somehow emerge out of their poetry writing—the kind of things that in an age more tolerant to the long poem might have been rendered in satiric or romantic verse (such as Byron wrote in his time) and which have little relation to the general trends of contemporary fiction. It is certain that none of the books I have just mentioned—not even *Beautiful Losers* for all its dazzlement of the academic critics—has had much effect on the kind of books professional novelists write. Nevertheless, one solitary novel exemplifying a highly personal vision, Sheila Watson's *The Double Hook* (1959), did have a great influence on younger fiction writers, and to that I shall later be returning.

As the twentieth century continues, leaving behind it the troubled complacencies of the Edwardian age, characteristic Canadian ways of writing become more evident, especially in poetry and in fiction, although probably a majority of the novels being written in Canada in the thirties and even in the forties were in general character, if not in setting, hardly distinguishable from the romances or adventure stories being written elsewhere in the English-reading world, and even the novelists of that time whom we consider now to be the pioneers of present day Canadian fiction often carry with them the vestiges of alien influence. We all know those passages of Morley Callaghan which, taken out of context, might very easily be mistaken for Hemingway, and even before readers were aware of Grove's hidden career as a novelist in Germany, the affinities between him and European writers like Zola and Knut Hamsun were abundantly evident. Yet the stylistic influences which reached Canada as ripples of literary revolutions in Europe and America were not very important in their ultimate effects, for it was characteristic of Canadian fiction when it began to emerge as something special and distinguishable that its practitioners tended to be formally unadventurous and even conservative and to concentrate to a degree long abandoned by novelists in culturally more settled countries on the content of their books—on *what* they had to say rather than on *how* they said it. I remember very clearly my astonishment, on coming from Europe in 1949, at the importance Canadian critics attached to writers so formally conservative—even retrogressive—as E. J. Pratt and Hugh MacLennan; it took me a long time to accept that at certain stages in literatures, when they emerge from a kind of colonialism to take on their own identity, an emphasis on content rather than on form may be necessary and is to be encouraged. To this extent the recent Canadian school of thematic critics has been justified; a criticism of pre-1950s Canadian fiction based on the analysis of form would have been a task of supererogation, although the same attitude would not apply to the fiction of the past twenty years.

In the decades after 1918 there were still only a few Canadian novelists to whom we need pay attention. During the period between the wars the most popular Canadian novelist was probably Mazo de la Roche (she was certainly the most popular abroad, largely because she was writing a kind of international ladynovelism in which the setting was Canadian in a peculiar and distorted way), although if we consider fiction in a wider sense she had a rival in Stephen Leacock, who struck the chord of Canadian ironic self-deprecation so accurately that he still enjoys a repute considerably above his true merits. But if we are concerned with something more than popularity, if we seek the writers who in retrospect appear to have given in that generation the most authentic fictional expression of Canada and the Canadian consciousness, two men stand far above their contemporaries. They are the German novelist Frederick Philip Grove, who transformed himself into one of the two most memorable fictional chroniclers of Canadian prairie life, and Morley Callaghan, the Torontonian who chronicled the travails of people attempting to live with some meaning in the developing metropoles of eastern Canada.

With Robert Stead and Martha Ostenso (whose memorable *Wild Geese* appeared in 1925), Grove represents the beginnings of what eventually became a notable movement of prairie fiction that penetrated far more deeply into the actualities of Western life than Ralph Connor had ever succeeded in doing. To a considerable degree the members of this movement acted as the realistic chroniclers of the region. A succession of later writers, such as Sinclair Ross, W. O. Mitchell, Rudy Wiebe, and Robert Kroetsch have kept the prairies in the center of Canadian fiction, and this is appropriate, for the Great Plains have served as a uniting membrane to sustain whatever collective consciousness English-speaking Canada may in fact have. More than anywhere else, more even than in the North, man grapples on the prairies with that immensity of the environment which still haunts Canadians with the vestiges of wilderness terror, and therefore it is more on the prairies than anywhere else that Canadians can symbolically face and come to terms with whatever destiny unites them. When Canada was established, the first necessary act to ensure the survival of confederation was the acquisition and settlement of the prairies, and one of the basic differences between francophone and anglophone Canada—one of the sources of the present conflict—is that the people of Quebec took virtually no part in the great Canadian sweep westward that built up after 1870. The prairies were the place where the English and the immigrant peoples of continental Europe struggled to establish their roots in earth and achieved the one Canadian compromise that shows some appearance of lasting.

It is their consciousness of this background that gives prairie fiction a special interest to Canadian readers and gives to the novelists who write it a sense that in a special way not open to novelists in Ontario or the Maritimes or British Columbia they are giving form to the great symbols that express the relationship between man and the Canadian land. Everything in the prairies tends toward extremity—the climate, the winter isolation, the distances—and in response every human reaction tends toward intensity—of boredom, of faith, of despair, of prejudice, of hatred; it is no accident that the most bitter of all Canadian battles since the Conquest of 1760 was that fought at Batoche in a few tragic days of 1885.

Novelists tend to respond to this harsh environment

and its immoderate emotions with a combination of realistic method and symbolist intent, moving on with later
writers like Robert Kroetsch into a kind of superrealistic
fantasy. And it is this combination of approaches that has
almost certainly made Frederick Philip Grove, despite
his extraordinarily clumsy constructions and his ponder-
ousness in thought and language, the most significant to
contemporary readers of the prairie novelists who wrote
between the wars.

Grove arrived bearing with him, as part of his carefully concealed mental baggage, the heritages of the two
significant European movements of his time—naturalism
and symbolism. *The Master Mason's House*, which he
published in Germany as Felix Paul Greve in 1906 (it
has had to wait until 1976 for Canadian publication in an
English translation), is a late naturalist novel with ex-
pressionist overtones. But, as the translator of Wilde and
the acquaintance of André Gide and Stefan George,
Grove was also linked with the late days of symbolism,
and his prairie novels show the influence of both movements. They can be read as attempts at a realistic chroni-
cling of the hard life of early homesteaders. But if, as
Desmond Pacey, Grove's first biographer, argued in the
Literary History of Canada, Grove's *Settlers of the
Marsh* was "the first novel to introduce into Canada the
naturalism which, finding its chief source in Emile Zola,
spread over the whole Western world in the late decades
of the nineteenth century and the early decades of the
twentieth," then Grove's belated tribute to Zola (for
Settlers of the Marsh was not published until 1925) was
distorted by a melodramatic degree of pessimism which
makes one wonder how far Grove did in fact consider
that he was writing "naturalistically" or "realistically."
Certainly, insofar as we remember Grove, it is because
he made men and landscapes alike into symbols of a general human destiny, into emblems of collectively gener-
ated ideas, and so it is his least realistic book, *The Master
of the Mill* (1944), that we value most. What he has

constructed for us in this book is not merely the great symbol of the mill with its possessing family, but, bodied forth in human conflicts and misfortunes, the whole Heartbreak House of conflicting ideologies and interests in a Canada which he saw before his death moving into the crucial period of change from a colony to a nation, from a rural to an urban society, and—symbolized in the shift of venue from the prairie farm to the eventually mechanized mill—from pioneer innocence to technological experience with all its perils.

Few pairs of Canadian writers are more easy to contrast than Grove and Callaghan, the one seeking his huge symbols in a vast rural setting of high skies and fields a quarter-section large, the other working out his moral problems in the constricted setting of the city; one large and uncouth in the texture of his writing, the other lapidary to the point that any release from simplicity of form results in a complete breakdown of his writing (as has happened in Callaghan's three most recent novels, *The Many Colored Coat* [1960], *A Passion in Rome* [1961], and *A Fine and Private Place* [1975]).

Although he has continued to write into the century's and his own seventies, Morley Callaghan is in terms of effective achievement a writer of the late twenties and the thirties. It was during these decades that almost all his marvellously laconic short stories (collected in *Morley Callaghan's Stories* [1959]) were written, and it was during the latter decade that his three best novels appeared: *Such Is My Beloved* (1934), *They Shall Inherit the Earth* (1935), and *More Joy in Heaven* (1937). These novels reflect their times in ways often reminiscent of more deliberately political writers: Callaghan portrays mordantly the social tragedies and injustices of the depression years, the hypocrisies of the church, the presumptions of the state. But Callaghan is not drawn into the facile political solutions of the age, and always he returns to seeing the social situation in terms of individual lives. Within these lives, moreover, the essential factor is not adverse external circumstances; it is inner moral strength. Although his felicity in the use of descriptive detail may lead the superficial reader to dismiss him as a kind of realist devoted to simplicity of language, Callaghan is in fact a moralist, and his books take on their full significance only when we see them as sparely constructed parables on the human condition, their very conciseness and flatness of tone a moral matter.

To move into the 1940s is still to find the Canadian fictional landscape populated sparsely with novelists of power and vigor and originality, yet it is in this decade that three Canadian fiction writers obviously destined for lasting importance appear: Sinclair Ross with *As for Me and My House* in 1941; Hugh MacLennan with *Barometer Rising* in the same year, followed by *Two Solitudes* in 1945; and Ethel Wilson with *Hetty Dorval* in 1947, followed by *The Innocent Traveller* in 1949.

Ordered in this way, the trio brings us to one of the peculiar problems of the critic who is also a literary historian, when he is dealing with a nation and a literature that are in the process of emerging more or less simultaneously into self-consciousness. In such cases it is entirely possible that the writer who is the lesser artist may be the more important in a social and historical sense because his concern for things outside his art allows him to interpret more boldly and fully than the scrupulous artist the preoccupations of his community at a crucial point in its history. And when one is faced with the need to relate Sinclair Ross, Hugh MacLennan, and Ethel Wilson, it is obvious to anyone with an even modestly developed literary sensibility that Ross, at least in *As for Me and My House*, and Ethel Wilson in everything she wrote are vastly more subtle and complete in their fictional artistry than MacLennan.

Yet anyone with an ear for history—literary or other —must acknowledge the overhelming importance of MacLennan in Canadian writing during the forties, and the fifties as well. More than any other novelist he isolated and gave memorable expression to the significant political and moral issues of Canada in his time; more than any other writer he elucidated the collective problems that each man finds impinging on his personal existence in a country still in the process of self-creation. A consciousness of emergence into nationhood is the theme of *Barometer Rising*, the two nations within a single federation that of *Two Solitudes*, the perils of American dominance that of *The Precipice* (1948), and the constricting nature of the Calvinist heritage that of *Each Man's Son* (1951), while in the more complex structures of his last two novels, *The Watch That Ends the Night* (1959) and *Return of the Sphinx* (1967), many of these earlier themes are brought together in an approach that seeks to demonstrate how history lays its claims on our lives and may destroy them if we have not listened to the lessons of the past.

There is no writer other than MacLennan whom one could plausibly consider the Canadian Balzac, seeking to construct his country's special *Comédie Humaine* and trusting that if the themes are honest the forms will take care of themselves. At times he is splendid in every respect; *Each Man's Son*, which many critics ignore, is one of the best Canadian novels, precisely because the thematic impulse is subordinated to the Odyssean structure that delineates MacLennan's personal mythology. But all too often in MacLennan's books the themes take impetuous control, and we have such extraordinary failures of fictional proportion as the endings of his two first novels, *Barometer Rising* and *Two Solitudes*, both ruined to make a didactic point better reserved for an essay, or the whole structure of *The Precipice*, misbuilt in the effort to work out moral and social problems in logical terms. What makes one remember with a special warmth MacLennan's two latest novels is that neither *The Watch* nor *Return of the Sphinx* offers a facilely rational solution to the universal alienation each presents as the human predicament. In these last novels MacLennan has learned that fiction, like all the arts, may offer questions but can rarely give answers. If the sphinx does return, it is merely to present more enigmas.

MacLennan, it seems, had to go through two decades of creative travail to acquire a knowledge Ross and Wilson possessed from the beginning. Sinclair Ross, in spite of a long literary career during which what one always assumed to be terminal silences have been broken by long-maturing new works, is essentially a one-book man. Nothing he has written since *As for Me and My House* appeared in 1941 has attracted more than fleeting attention, and critical attempts to inflate his lesser works and make him appear in quantitative terms a major Canadian writer have always flagged before the embarrassing realization that it is *As for Me and My House* alone among his works that rends one's heart with a sense of pathetic frustration that few other Canadian novels have projected. The book is isolated even among Ross's works, no doubt because it is one of the few novels whose basic theme derives from an honest perception of the perpetual nightmare of all Canadian artists at the time *As for Me and My House* was being written—the failure of imagination and of creativity. In the Canada of that distant time these gifts lacked any meaningful focus, for in 1941 where could the artist in Canada look for validation?

And that is where Canadians writers have to be perpetually grateful to Hugh MacLennan, for in his time he understood that the literary imagination had to be given a focus, and in his own honest way he gave it by daring to express in fictional form what many people of that day feared to discuss in any more direct way. Through his flawed but vigorous novels he helped to liberate writers thematically and to turn their attention back to problems of form and sensibility rather than to problems of national destiny, although these have never been allowed to fall entirely out of sight since this has been, after all, as nationalist a generation as that of Yeats and Synge in Ireland. In the novels of Dave Godfrey and Marian Engel, in the verse of Al Purdy and Milton Acorn and many of the younger poets, in the historical writings of Donald Creighton, and in works of thematic criticism such as Margaret Atwood's *Survival*, the sense that Canadians are fighting as crucial a battle for their cultural independence as they fought for their political independence in 1812 is strongly manifest. The inclination that MacLennan once represented almost in solitude has found expression not only in the work of individual writers but also in the publishing houses set up in the 1960s to counter the tendency for foreign firms to take over native houses and in the strong inclination of Canadian periodicals of all kinds to take the stance that cultural colonization, particularly from the United States, remains a threat to be countered. Much of the sense of urgency that characterizes recent Canadian writing is linked to this resurgence of national feeling with its curious mingling of apprehension and pride.

Ethel Wilson always seemed much nearer to the younger writers who appeared during the 1950s than Callaghan or MacLennan ever did, although she was the oldest of these three writers. But she began to write far later in life, and although eventually she became one of my most valued friends, I never quite understood the process by which this handsome, charming Vancouver *bourgeoise* emerged in her closing fifties as a writer of extraordinary subtlety and sophistication. Had there been a long period of secret practice, of ruthless self-critical rejection, or had she been the fortunate subject of some sudden pentecost that turned her overnight into the consummate stylist and literary psychologist whom readers encountered with such astonishment when *Hetty Dorval* was published? It was never revealed, but her readers admired, and continued to admire for the brief period of her creative life (much less than two decades in all), the combination of assurance and adventurousness, the strange equilibrium between illusion and reality, the oracular sense of the power and irrationality of love that appeared in such novels as *Swamp Angel* (1954) and *Love and Salt Water* (1956) or in the sparkling dry and ironic stories collected in her last book, *Mrs. Golightly and Other Stories* (1961).

There was something of the catalytic imagination about Ethel Wilson, emerging for so few years, so late in life, to project an original, urbane vision across the landscape of an emergent literature, and there is no doubt that her influence on younger writers such as Margaret Laurence and Margaret Atwood came from more than mere friendship. The mention of Laurence and Atwood leads us, of course, into the highly active present of Canadian fiction in which, as I have suggested, few more novels are being published each year by Canadian writers than appeared in 1890 or 1930, but those which do appear are likely to be of far higher craftsmanship and far more original vision, partly at least for the simple reason that Canada offers no market for the kind of formula novels that provided the uninspired hacks of the past with the basis of a living.

How can one begin to discuss the many interesting novelists who have been active over the past twenty or twenty-five years in Canada? Should one start, for example, with the brilliant immigrants who came for a while, wrote remarkable books here which told us new things about ourselves and our world, such as Brian Moore's *The Luck of Ginger Coffey* (1960) and Malcolm Lowry's *October Ferry to Gabriola* (1970), influenced native writers (particularly in the case of Lowry) to the point of obsession, and then departed? What can one say of such figures in the context of the present essay except that they seemed to accentuate an obsession with human solitude already dominant in the Canadian literary consciousness and to encourage younger writers to explore it to the bizarre limits of fantasy, which became in the later 1950s an inescapable element in Canadian fiction? Or should one start in the complementary direction and consider how many Canadian writers have developed themselves as expatriates, and out of a combination of physical experience and cultural absorption have contrived to enrich their own writing and the Canadian fictional tradition as well, edging it further, by the introduction of exotica, in the direction of fantasy? There is Mavis Gallant, for example, who went to Paris and never came back; there is Mordecai Richler, who went to London and did come back, although what he will write as a returned expatriate still remains to be demonstrated. But other writers also went away and returned enriched to write their best work in Canada: Audrey Thomas and Dave Godfrey and, above all, Margaret Laurence, all of whom spent immensely impressionable periods in Africa and wrote such novels about their experiences as Thomas's *Mrs. Blood* (1970), Godfrey's *The New Ancestors* (1970), and Laurence's *This Side Jordan* (1960). In the case of Laurence, Africa provided the insights which unlocked her ability to perceive and to write about her own heritage, her own country, and there emerged that splendid series of time-obsessed myths of the Canadian prairie town from *The Stone Angel* (1964) down to *The Diviners* (1974), which Margaret Laurence has told us—in what one hopes will be an unfulfilled warning—may be her last novel.

Perhaps the most striking phenomenon of recent years in Canadian writing has been the tendency to loosen verisimilitude in the direction of fantasy and to abandon the chronological pattern of ordered sequence with effect following cause and consequence following action which characterized most of the novels written before the later 1950s, especially the novels on which writers like Callaghan and MacLennan based their careers. Here one of the most important books for itself and in terms of influence is Sheila Watson's single novel *The Double Hook* (1959), in which the rural tale of a decaying society is mingled with the native mythology of the vanished Indians to create a strange and superb fantasy of moral strife and spiritual terror. Mordecai Richler, whose *Apprenticeship of Duddy Kravitz* (1959) was a picaresque novel in the classic manner, moving on the inspired edges of credibility but essentially conventional in its sequential form, went on in books such as *The Incomparable Atuk* (1963) and *Cocksure* (1968) into the use of grotesque fantasy for the purposes of satire, although he has never in these later works repeated the triumph of *Duddy Kravitz* and is certainly perceived by now to be of much less central importance as a Canadian novelist than he seemed to be to many critics a decade ago.

In moving away from conventional structures and from the lingering demands of naturalistic theory, Canadian writers have also tended to abandon the didactic preoccupations of the generation of Callaghan and Mac-Lennan. They no longer feel the need to state political or moral positions, which now tend to find expression in other literary genres.

I do not suggest that there has been a diminution in the patriotic (as distinct from the stridently nationalist) frame of mind. But it is clear that, like the poets, the novelists have become concerned less with making thinly disguised policy statements than with the more basic functions of returning over time, of examining the foundations of history, of exorcising ancient guilts and celebrating ancient heroisms, of giving spirit to the land. Novels such as Rudy Wiebe's *The Temptations of Big Bear* (1975), Matt Cohen's *The Disinherited* (1974), and Robert Kroetsch's *The Studhorse Man* (1969) do not merely confirm for us the quality of writers whose first and promising novels had appeared in the later 1960s; they introduce a new sense of history merging into myth, of theme coming out of a perception of the land, of geography as a source of art. In the process they break time down into the nonlinear patterns of authentic memory at the same time as they break down actuality and recreate it in terms of the kind of nonliteral rationality that belongs to dreams.

These novels embody the difference between realism and a reality that is not merely material, between literal credibility and imaginative authenticity. There is, for example, a great deal of credibility about Hugh MacLennan's characters and their behavior; when they are not represented in sexual relationships (a notorious MacLennan weak point) they sound very much like the people one meets ordinarily in real life. But it seems extremely improbable that in real life people would literally do what they are represented as doing in, say, Margaret Atwood's *Surfacing* or Marian Engel's *Bear*, although both of these books strike one as entirely authentic once one has taken the initial step of suspending disbelief in the author's particular world of the imagination.

There are not indeed as many new novelists in Canada during the 1970s as there are new poets. To write a publishable novel, after all, still demands more industry and discipline than to write a publishable piece of verse. But the situation has changed to the extent that it is no longer possible to take one or two central figures and say that essentially this is their decade, as past decades seemed those of Grove and Callaghan, or of MacLennan and Ross. Today amazingly many good fiction writers are working in Canada (including many short-story writers whom the scope of this essay has not allowed me to discuss), and the variety of approaches and talents is more impressive than any dimly perceptible common attitude.

As I have hinted already, the indications are many that during the past twenty years the literature of Canada has gone through a process of maturing into a self-consistent entity, analogous to that which literature in the United States went through earlier in the century. That writers are liberated to follow highly individual courses, no longer dominated by the thematic demands which critics were detecting even early in the present decade, is one of the signs and also one of the effects of that maturity.

IV

Canadian Monsters

*Some Aspects of the
Supernatural in Canadian Fiction*

Margaret Atwood

I first became interested in Canadian monsters, not, as you might suspect, through politics, but through my own attempts to write ghost stories and through some research I happened to be doing on Sasquatches for the CBC program "Poem for Voices."[1] My collection of other people's monsters has not been systematically acquired, and there are probably glaring omissions in it. No sooner will this essay appear in print than some indignant student of the occult will, no doubt, chastise me for not having known that the central character in *I Was a Teenage Werewolf* was, like Walt Disney, a Canadian, or for some error of similar magnitude. I hasten to cover my tracks by declaring that, unlike my compatriots here assembled, I am not a professional academic, and my collecting and categorizing of monsters must be ascribed to an amateur, perverse, and private eccentricity, like that of, say, a Victorian collector of ferns. (Like many Canadian writers of my generation I started to read Canadian literature in self-defense; we got

1. "Oratorio for Sasquatch, Man and Two Androids," in *Poem for Voices* (Toronto: Canadian Broadcasting Corporation, 1970). The first eleven lines are not mine.

tired of people telling us there wasn't any and that we should therefore not exist, or go to New York.)

But criticism, even the proliferating Canlitcrit of the last decade, hasn't had much to say about this subject, probably because magic and monsters aren't usually associated with Canadian literature. In fact, the very term "Canadian literature" would seem to exclude them, in the popular mind at least, and the popular mind is not always wrong. Supernaturalism is not typical of Canadian prose fiction; the mainstream (with those useful qualifications, "by and large" and "so far") has been solidly social-realistic. When people in Canadian fiction die, which they do fairly often, they usually stay buried; mention of supernatural beings is as a rule confined to prayers and curses; God and the Devil appear in the third person but rarely in the first and are not often seen onstage. The divine and demonic levels of human existence may appear through analogy or symbol, but there aren't very many apotheoses or descents to the underworld, or even white whales, scarlet letters in the sky, or *Blithedale Romance* mesmerists. Canadian fiction on the whole confines itself to ordinary life on middle earth.[2] Recently, experimentalist Lawrence Garber began a story, "Susceptible to illusion as I am, I was not at all surprised when Jack (whom we had buried some few weeks previously) announced his presence at my threshold."[3] This opening ploy is meant to come as a shock to the reader, and the fact that it does indicates the extent

2. I could suggest two reasons for this, neither of which has anything to do with innate lack of panache on the part of Canadian fiction writers. The first is that the Canadian fiction tradition developed largely in the twentieth century, not the romantic nineteenth. The second is that in a cultural colony a lot of effort must go into simply naming and describing observed realities, into making the visible real even for those who actually live there. Not much energy is left over for exploring other, invisible realms.

3. "Visions before Midnight," in Garber, *Circuit* (Toronto: House of Anansi Press, 1970).

to which it is an exception to the usual Canadian realistic conventions.

The supposed lack of otherworldly dimensions, or even worldly ones, used to be almost routinely lamented by poets and other critics. Thus Earle Birney, in his much-quoted poem "Can. Lit.":

> we French&English never lost
> our civil war
> endure it still
> a bloody civil bore
>
> the wounded sirened off
> no Whitman wanted
> it's only by our lack of ghosts
> we're haunted

And, more severely, Irving Layton, in "From Colony to Nation":

> A dull people, without charm
> or ideas,
> settling into the clean empty look
> of a Mountie or a dairy farmer
> as into a legacy
>
> One can ignore them
> (the silences, the vast distances help)
> and suppose them at the bottom
> of one of the meaner lakes,
> their bones not even picked for souvenirs.

Fifteen years ago, this was Canada, or rather this was the image of it which everyone seemed to believe in: a dull place, devoid of romantic interest and rhetorical excesses, with not enough blood spilled on the soil to make it fertile, and, above all, ghostless. Unmagical Canada, prosaic as Mounties and dairy farmers appear to be before you actually meet some up close . . .

But is this a true picture of Canada or its literature,

and was it ever? Over the past fifteen years a certain amount of exhumation, literary and otherwise, has been taking place, which could be viewed as archaeology, necrophilia, or resurrection, depending on your viewpoint. The digging up of ancestors, calling up of ghosts, exposure of skeletons in the closet which are so evident in many cultural areas—the novel, of course, but also history and even economics—have numerous motivations, but one of them surely is a search for reassurance. We want to be sure that the ancestors, ghosts, and skeletons really are there, that as a culture we are not as flat and lacking in resonance as we were once led to believe. Prime Minister of Canada for more than twenty years, Mackenzie King, formerly a symbol of Canada because of his supposed dullness and grayness ("He blunted us," goes the F. R. Scott poem "W.L.M.K.," "We had no shape / Because he never took sides, / And no sides / Because he never allowed them to take shape . . ."), is enjoying new symbolic popularity as a secret madman who communed every night with the picture of his dead mother and believed that his dog was inhabited by her soul. "Mackenzie King rules Canada because he himself is the embodiment of Canada—cold and cautious on the outside . . . but inside a mass of intuition and dark intimations," says one of Robertson Davies's characters in *The Manticore*, speaking for many.

It is this talking-picture side of Canadian literature, this area of dark intimations, which I would like to consider briefly here. Briefly, because my own knowledge is far from encyclopedic, but also because Canadian fictions in which the supernatural and the magical appear are still only exceptions which prove what may soon no longer be the rule.

The North, the Wilderness, has traditionally been used in Canadian literature as a symbol for the world of the unexplored, the unconscious, the romantic, the mysterious, and the magical. There are strange things done 'neath the midnight sun, as Robert Service puts it. (There are probably stranger things done in Toronto, but they don't have quite the same aura.) So it's not surprising that a large number of Canadian monsters have their origin in native Indian and Eskimo myths. One of the earliest uses of this kind of monster in literary prose (I hesitate to call it fiction, although it probably is) is in a book called *Brown Waters and Other Sketches* by William Blake.[4] The narrator is fishing in "the great barrens that lie far-stretching and desolate among the Laurentian Mountains." He describes the landscape in exceptionally negative terms:

> So were we two alone in one of the loneliest places this wide earth knows. Mile upon mile of gray moss; weathered granite clad in ash-coloured lichen; old *brûlé*,–the trees here fallen in windrows, there standing bleached and lifeless, making the hilltops look barer, like the sparse white hairs of age. Only in the gullies a little greenness,–dwarfed larches, gnarled birches, tiny firs a hundred years old,–and always moss . . . great boulders covered with it, the very quagmires mossed over so that a careless step plunges one into the sucking black ooze below.

One evening the narrator's companion tells a story concerning the disappearance of a man named Paul Duchêne, a good guide, familiar with the wilderness, who wandered off and has never been found. He then mentions the belief of the Montagnais Indians:

> . . . strange medley of Paganism and Christianity,– that those who die insane without the blessing of a priest become wendigos,–werewolves, with nothing human but their form, soulless beings of diabolic strength and cunning, that wander for all time seeking only to harm whomever comes their way.

4. "A Tale of the Grand Jardin," in W. H. Blake, *Brown Waters and Other Sketches* (Toronto: Macmillan, 1915).

He goes on to speak of his journey the summer before to a place called the Rivière à l'Enfer, where he camps beside a lake with black water. His guides go back for supplies, and he is left alone, whereupon he experiences an "oppression of the spirit." "In what subtle way," he asks, "does the universe convey the knowledge that it has ceased to be friendly?" That night a tremendous storm blows up. Sitting in his tent, he hears an unearthly cry, which is "not voice of beast or bird." He bursts from the tent and is confronted by a creature—"something in the form of a man"—which springs at him. "And what in God's name was it?" asks the narrator. The storyteller replies, "Pray Him it was not poor Duchêne in the flesh."

The juxtaposition of the oppressive landscape, the storyteller's reaction to it as hostile, and the appearance of the wendigo indicate that this is a tale about the Monster as Other, which represents forces outside and, in this case, opposed to the human protagonist. Duchêne, child of the wilderness, has become the wilderness as seen by the narrator—the incarnation of an unfriendly natural universe. The storm is one aspect of this landscape; the wendigo, soulless and destructive, is the same landscape in human form.

The wendigo story in *Brown Waters* is short and simple as the folktale material from which it obviously derives. A more extended and much more sophisticated Monster as Other was created by Sheila Watson in her novel *The Double Hook*.[5] The novel begins, "In the folds of the hills, under Coyote's eye . . ." Coyote turns out to be a deity of sorts, part animal, part god, both below human nature and beyond it. At first, like the landscape he represents, he appears harsh and malevolent. He is Fate, he is retribution, he is Death, he is the nature of things; he is also called a "mischief-maker." But in fact he is double, like the hook of the title: "the

5. (Toronto: McClelland and Stewart, 1959).

glory and the fear," both together. His nature changes according to the vision of the perceiver, and the reader comes to know the various characters partly through their views of Coyote. "There's no big Coyote, like you think," says materialist Theophil. "There's not just one of him. He's everywhere. The government's got his number too. They've set a bounty on him at fifty cents a brush . . . This is a thin mean place, men and cattle alike." By the end of the book both Coyote and his landscape have become, if not exactly nurturing, at least more benevolent. He presides over the birth of a child and sings, in his rather Biblical manner:

> I have set his feet on soft ground;
> I have set his feet on the sloping shoulders
> of the world.

The wendigo and Coyote are both landscape-and-nature creatures, nature in both cases being understood to include super-nature. Neither is human; both can act on human beings, but cannot be acted upon. They are both simply *there*, as supernatural forces in the environment and as embodiments of that environment which must be reckoned with. They are objects rather than subjects, the "Other" against which the human characters measure themselves. The environment and its monster in *Brown Waters* are so overwhelmingly negative that the best thing the protagonist can do is run away from them, which he does. The environment and its deity in *The Double Hook* also provide an ordeal for the human actors, but both environment and deity are double-natured, and the proper response to them is not simple escape but further exploration resulting in increased self-knowledge. The one character who attempts escape ends by returning, and Coyote blesses him accordingly.

It is very difficult to make a completely nonhuman supernatural being the protagonist in a fiction, but in at least two Canadian novels the protagonist is a semihuman being. Such beings might be called "magic people" rather than monsters. They have magical powers and otherworldly attributes, but they are nonetheless partly human and can be acted upon by ordinary human beings. A case in point is the central character in *Tay John*,[6] Howard O'Hagan's potent and disturbing novel. Tay John is a strange creature, half white man and half Indian, half mythical and half "realistic." In the first third of the book, which is written in the form of a folktale or legend, we learn of his birth underground from the body of his dead and buried mother. He emerges and is seen wandering near the gravesite, an odd child with yellow hair, brown skin, and no shadow. After he has been lured into the land of the living by the elders of the tribe and given a shadow by a wisewoman, he is marked out to be the tribe's leader and potential savior. But first he must enter manhood by going apart to a place of his own choosing, to fast, to have a vision, and to acquire a guiding spirit.

Unfortunately he picks the wrong place. It is "a valley where no man went," and like the lake of Blake's Rivière à l'Enfer it has black water, with similar associations:

> The water that came down from that valley was turgid, dark, and flowed silently, with no rapids. It was said that if a man drank of that water he would lose his voice and go from the sight of his fellows, roaming the hills at night to bark at the moon like a coyote. The coyote men saw by day was not the same they heard by night, for the coyote they heard by night was the voice of a man whose hands had become claws and whose teeth had grown long and tusk-like, who sat on his haunches, lifted his head to the sky and lamented the human speech gone from him.
>
> The spirit of that valley was cruel. Men feared that one night, taking the form of a great white bear, it

6. (London: Laidlaw and Laidlaw, 1939).

would come down upon them in their sleep and leave them with a coyote's howl for voice and only a coyote's claws for hands, and each man would be for ever a stranger to his neighbour.

What the Indians fear most about the spirit of the valley is the power it has to divide the society, to make each man a stranger to his neighbor: "The boy says 'I'; the man says 'We'—and this word that the man speaks is the word of his greatest magic." But Tay John chooses to say "I." The valley of the wendigo-like were-coyote does present him with a sign, but it is an ominous one: he is visited by "an old bear, with snow-dust on his coat"; in other words, the great white bear of the myth. He is not changed into a coyote outwardly, but he brings back something that will have the same effect, a bag of sand from the river. The sand contains gold, which is not known to the Indians, but when a party of white prospectors arrives, it is Tay John they select to guide them to the valley, because he is the only person who has ever been there. From this time forward he has a new name, Tête Jaune (corrupted to Tay John), and is contaminated by the egocentric, individualistic spirit of the whites.

This trait emerges when Tay John wishes to marry. The tribe feels that, as magic leader, he should not marry. "The woman of Tay John is the people," they say. "He is a leader of the people and is married to their sorrows." But he will not accept this condition and leaves the tribe to seek out the world of the white men who have given him his name.

As might be expected, the encounter is disastrous. The remaining two sections of the book consist mainly of hearsay and eyewitness reports of the doings of Tay John—his hand-to-hand combat with a grizzly, his sacrifice of his own hand to gain possession of a horse. But he doesn't fit into the white world any more easily than he did into the Indian; in both, he is an exception. His tribe wished him to be a hero and leader, but all the whites can think of to offer him is a position as a guide or, worse, a tourist Indian, dressed up to meet the trains. He resists this tame fate and elopes into the mountains with a strange white woman, a "woman of the world" who leaves her rich protector to go off with him. Like Tay John's own mother she dies in childbirth, and Tay John is last seen pulling her corpse on a toboggan. The description reminds us of his magic origins:

> Tay John came on, more distinct now, through the curtain of swirling snow, entangled in it, wrapped in its folds, his figure appearing close, then falling back into the mists, a shoulder, a leg, a snowshoe moving on as it were of its own accord—like something spawned by the mists striving to take form before mortal eyes.
> "He seemed very big off there, shadowy like," Blackie said, "then again no bigger than a little boy."

When his tracks are followed, they lead nowhere:

> Blackie stared at the tracks in front of him, very faint now, a slight trough in the snow, no more. Always deeper and deeper into the snow. He turned back then. There was nothing more he could do. He had the feeling, he said, looking down at the tracks, that Tay John hadn't gone over the pass at all. He had just walked down, the toboggan behind him, under the snow and into the ground.

The semihuman hero has returned to the earth in much the same way as he emerged from it. His life, like the confused trails he makes in the snow, has been circular. Although he performs several acts beyond the range of most men and is generally regarded as singular, he has not used his gifts to benefit his people, and ultimately they do not benefit him either.

It is interesting to compare Tay John with the "magic" protagonist of a very different book, *The Sun and the Moon* by P. K. Page.[7] Kristin, born during an eclipse of the moon, is a visionary who can see things that aren't there. She can also "become" inanimate objects, seeing and feeling as they do: "She had only to sit still long enough to know the static reality of inanimate things—the still, sweet ecstasy of change in kind." As a child she likes doing this and finds people noisy and superfluous. But when she is seventeen she meets a painter named Carl; they fall in love and become engaged, and she finds herself "stealing" his essence by "becoming" him, much as she was once able to "become" a rock or a chair. Apparently, she discovers, she can "become" things in this way only by partially absorbing them. Kristin finds that she is draining away Carl's talent and even his personality by the sheer force of her empathy with him. He himself has no idea what is going on, but finds himself losing consciousness during what Kristin's father calls her "comatose periods." He awakens feeling drained and old and shaken; and when he tries to paint her portrait, he finds that it is in fact his own he has painted. (But badly; Kristin, who has temporarily taken him over, isn't much of a painter.)

Kristin wants Carl to play sun to her moon, to "predominate," as she puts it; she feels he will be strong enough to resist her inadvertent power. But it is doubtful whether or not Carl in fact possesses enough strength to justify her faith. " 'It is as if I have surrendered my being to an alien force and it has made me less,' " he thinks, just before one of these moments of "invasion." Kristin herself says of her love and her powers of metamorphosis:

> "If only . . . I turned into trees or stones or earth when I'm with him, it couldn't hurt him. But this way . . . I am like a leech, a vampire, sucking his strength from him—the moon eclipsing the sun . . . I cannot be

7. *The Sun and the Moon* (Toronto: Macmillan, 1944) was first published under the pseudonym Judith Cape.

with him without stealing into him and erasing his own identity."

On the eve of her wedding, she finds herself faced with an agonizing problem. She loves Carl and wants to marry him, but she feels she must find "a solution that would protect Carl" from her:

> As we are, if I marry him, it will mean the complete merging of two personalities. But the truth rushed to her out of the night: it will mean the obliteration of two personalities. That is, she thought slowly, the words like heavy sacks that had to be carried together to form a sentence, that is, if I have a personality of my own. For I am a chameleon, she thought, absorbing the colours about me and our marriage will submerge us, wipe us out as sun obliterates the markings of water on a stone.

The solution that she finds is worse than the problem. During the night, she allows herself to "become" the storm-tossed trees outside her window, projecting her soul into their substance, except that this time she does not return to her body. The woman Carl marries the next day is a soulless automaton, emotionless and almost idiotic, who goes through the motions of their life together with no joy and no pain. The "real" Kristin has become completely absorbed by the trees; to all intents and purposes she *is* a tree, and Carl—his talent destroyed by his harrowing experience, and still not knowing what has caused her to change—leaves her in despair. The book ends, not with a description of Kristin's reaction (for presumably she will have none), but with a cinematic cut to the external landscape, which we must by now presume to be the same as the inside of Kristin's head:

> The sun and a small wind broke the surface of the lake to glinting sword blades. On the far side, where the trees marched, unchecked, right down to the water's

edge, there the lake was a shifting pattern of scarlet, vermilion and burnt orange.

Kristin, like Tay John, has been absorbed back into the nature that produced her. But then, love affairs between men and the moon, or men and trees, or mortals and faery queens never did work out very well, if mythology and folklore are to be believed. It is odd to find a dryad in Canadian literature, even though she is disguised as a rather frothy socialite, but that is obviously what Kristin is. (All the objects she chooses to "become" are natural ones; she does not, for instance, ever "become" a motor car.[8]) Kristin and Tay John are both figures of this sort, demigods, with unusual births and strange attributes; like satyrs and their ilk, they are bridges joining the human world, the natural world, and the supra-natural world.

I have now mentioned four creatures, in four separate books: two, the wendigo and Coyote, are completely nonhuman, gods or devils, incarnations of their respective natural environments, and two, Tay John and Kristin, are semihuman but still strongly linked to nature. It would now seem proper to examine the next rung down on the hierarchical scale, which ought to be a priest figure if we are using an epic analogy, or a poet or artist if we are using a pastoral one.[9] Such a figure would be human but magical, and in twentieth-century Canada he is likely to be a magician, for what is stage magic but ritual from which the religion has been removed?

Two well-known Canadian authors have created magicians; they are, of course, Robertson Davies, in his Magnus Eisengrim trilogy,[10] and Gwendolyn MacEwen,

8. She does "become" a chair, but only on the level of its molecules.
9. Epic: gods, semidivine heroes, priests and oracles. Pastoral: nature, satyrs and such, singing shepherds.
10. *Fifth Business* (Toronto: Macmillan, 1970), *The Manticore* (Toronto: Macmillan, 1972), and *World of Wonders* (Toronto: Macmillan, 1975).

who creates a whole series of magicians who bear a strong generic likeness to one another. It would be hard to find two writers whose approaches to prose fiction are more different, yet their magicians have a few things in common. Both are artist figures, and both are in fact Canadian, although both disguise this plebeian origin under an assumed name. (The implication is that you can't be both Canadian and magic; or you can, but no one will believe in you if you reveal your dull gray origins.)

MacEwen specializes in magician as artist as Christ.[11] (In her first novel, *Julian the Magician*, the magician actually insists on being crucified, just to see if he can be resurrected.) Her characters are not only called magicians, they actually are; that is, they seem able actually to perform superhuman feats. Davies's Magnus Eisengrim, on the other hand, is a professional magician, the creator of a very good magic show based on the principles of illusion. But the reader is always left wondering whether MacEwen's magicians are really what they claim to be, or just clever frauds, or perhaps a little insane, whereas Davies weights the evidence in favor of the belief that Eisengrim may in fact have sold his soul to the devil.

Two of the stories in MacEwen's collection *Noman*[12] are attempts to reconcile the world of the Otherworld of the magical with the resolutely nonmagical world of Canada, which MacEwen spells with a *K*. In her earlier works these two places were always kept separate and opposed; the magic world was ancient Egypt, or the Arabian Middle East, or Greece; it contained miracles. Kanada was the place of bacon and eggs, of nonrevelations, and it had to be escaped from, either mentally or physically, if you wanted any vision other than the mundane. But in "Kingsmere," which is not really a story but a description, MacEwen explores the possibilities of

11. See her early poem "The Magician as Christ," in MacEwen, *The Rising Fire* (Toronto: Contact Press, 1963).
12. (Ottawa: Oberon Press, 1972).

what she calls "Noman's land": Mackenzie King's artificial ruins. What strikes her is the relationship between the remnants of the past (mostly European) and the landscape that frames them, or, rather, that they frame:

> He reassembled these broken bits of history to frame or emphasize certain aspects of the landscape. He made naked windows and doors for the forest and the hills.
> You stand on a terrace flanked by a row of unreal Grecian columns. You look through a classic arch and see, not Athens, nor Rome nor even Palmyra, but the green Gatineau hills of Kanada. You wonder if the landscape protests these borrowed histories, these imported ruins.

For MacEwen, Kingsmere is a time-travel place, a doorway between the past and the future:

> You walk farther down, toward the interior of the garden. Something isn't right. Into whose future are you moving? . . . You have spotted one very large arch at the far end of the field, and for a second you have an intense, blinding perception of the real nature of the place. This stone on stone, this reconstruction of a past that was never yours, this synthetic history. Only the furtive trees are real . . . Here there is a tension between past and future, a tension so real it's almost tangible; it lives in the stone, it crackles like electricity among the leaves.
> He tried to transplant Europe, to bring it here among the stark trees and silent trails, but
> *There, beyond the arch, is the forest.*

The narrator in "Kingsmere" is afraid to pass through this magic arch. Not so Noman, the central character in the story of that name. Noman is the magician as Kanadian; his name, in addition to being Ulysses' pseudonym, is probably intended to symbolize the famous Kanadian identity crisis. At first he pretends he cannot understand

English, and his friends construct all kinds of exotic nationalities and identities for him, "imagining a thousand possible tongues for him, for somehow it was incongruous that he could have worn so beautiful a coat, or danced so well in Kanada." He finally reveals the awful truth, and his friend Kali, who has been cooking exotic foods for him, calls him a monster and feeds him a can of pork and beans in disgust. He shares with Kristin the ability to become "whatever he encountered," and he seems to have worked in a carnival as a clown, an escape artist, and finally a dancer. With his thousand possible identities and his refusal to choose just one, he sets himself up (or is set up by his author) as Kanada incarnate. "Kanada," he sighs. "Paper-maker. Like a great blank sheet in the world's diary. Who'll make the first entry?"

As Kanada, he sets himself the task of solving his own identity crisis, and here he links up with "Kingsmere." He speaks to Kali:

> "Let's possess the future as surely as we possess the past!"
> "But you don't *have* a past," I winked at him in the mirror.
> "Yes I do, damn it! I'll tell you about it later. Let's become the masters of time, let's *move into* time!"
> "To pave the way for our descendants?" I laughed.
> "No," he said, and looked at me strangely. "For our *ancestors*. They're the ones who are trapped."
> I didn't feel like questioning him, so I let him go on.
> "We've inherited this great Emptiness," he said. "An empty door that leads into the forest and the snow. No man can get through . . ."
> "Can *you?*" I asked, though I wasn't sure what he was talking about.
> "Yes," he said, "I think I can."

He goes about this process, which will apparently make it possible to move into the future by rediscovering and releasing the past, in three stages. First he and Kali make love, and then sit applying metaphors to their bodies:

> We sat cross-legged like children proudly comparing the maps of our bodies—the birthmarks, scars, incisions, beauty-spots, all the landmarks of our lives, those we were born with and those we'd incurred. New trails broken in the forest, old signposts no longer used, footprints of forest animals who come in the night, places of fire, places of water, portages, hills.

The metaphors, which at the beginning of the story were resolutely polyglot European, are now just as resolutely Kanadian, although they are natural rather than the canned pork-and-beans Kanadian ones we have had earlier.

Next, Noman stages his own death, which is Kali's idea:

> "Noman, I have the answer to all your problems."
> "And what is it, Kali?"
> "You must die."
> "That's the answer to everybody's problem," he said.
> "No," I told him, "I mean you must stage a mock death, a brilliant scene in which we'll all participate. Then you can be born again, *maybe even assume a real name.*"[13]

Finally, after this fraudulent imitation of Christ, he and Kali go to Kingsmere, "Noman's land," and Noman peels off his clothes and makes it through the magic arch:

> He spotted an arch at one end of the terrace, like an ancient door that led into the forest, the final mystery . . .
> "Coming Kali?" he asked again, and when I didn't

13. The italics are mine.

answer he went on farther into the spooky grey-
ness . . .

"Noman, what are we *doing* here?" I cried. "Whose
past have we stolen? Into whose future are we moving?"

And he (swiftly removing his clothes) called back to
me—"Why, our own, of course!"

And blithely stepped, stark naked, through the arch.

We are not told what "real name" he will assume, what
the future is like on the other side of the arch, or what
becomes of Noman, but by the nature of the story, and
of MacEwen's "Kanada" itself, we can't know. It's interesting, though, that Noman's possession of himself in-
volves an entry into the forest; in fact the end of the
story is reminiscent of both O'Hagan and Page.

What we might call "the sacrificial fade-out" seems to
be typical of these Canadian demigods and magician
priests; their death or disappearance is chosen, and seems
to have some element of sacrifice in it, but unlike traditional sacrifices, such as Christ's, it doesn't save or even
benefit anyone else, and is more in the nature of an abdi-
cation or departure. The sacrificial fade-out is a Mac-
Ewen specialty. It's present in almost all of her magician
stories, including her two novels, *Julian the Magician*
and *King of Egypt, King of Dreams;* but it is most explicit, perhaps, in her short story, "The Second Coming
of Julian the Magician," a seriocomic treatment of the
dilemma of a real magic man in a nonmagical age and
country.[14] Julian materializes on Christmas Day, 1970, at
noon, at the top of a ferris wheel in "a second-rate carnival." The magic signs of his birth are "three white bal-
loons" in his left hand and "an inverted crucifix made out
of red and green tinsel paper" in the middle of his fore-
head. The left-handedness and the inversion are significant, as is the tinsel paper: Julian is a tacky upside-down
Christ, fated to be tacky and upside-down by the lack of

14. "The Second Coming of Julian the Magician," in *Noman.*

faith of his potential believers. He realizes that in this incarnation he has a choice of performing in carnivals or in "cheap burlesque halls" and that his iconography is contained only in comic books and people's dreams:

> In the comic books my cloak is red, green or yellow; there are little wings on my boots, little wings on my head, lightning bolts or sacred hammers in my fists. Only the children worship me now.

He is "Atman, his identity hidden only by a 'B' at the beginning of his name."

But even when he walks on walls or makes it rain or creates black fire, his audiences are only bored or uneasy, since they believe "it's all done with mirrors," his magic mere trickery. And a lot of it is. He's a student of Houdini and Blackstone, although he insists that even tricks and illusions are real magic as long as they are believed: "The Master of Illusions doesn't make you believe what he wishes, but what you wish." His failure is the failure of the audience:

> During my acts no-one swooned; no-one approached me afterwards with nervous diseases for me to cure. (How very different from my last life when the peasants regarded me as holy man, a healer. But then this is North America. Could Christ have taught in Rome?)

He quickly realizes that his "enemy" is the Twentieth Century itself, that Dr. Zero of the comics, the Power House of the city, the Machine. He had a terrible nightmare, in which a Fat Woman named Reality ("But you can call me Reali for short") grabs his magic wand and chases him with it. Reality and the city and the machine are one, and he refuses to be "tricked into reality." He decides to destroy the electrical city by blowing up the Power House where he has a job as night watchman, and he accomplishes this, in fact or fantasy. Then, observed only by the children who are his sole congregation, he performs an apotheosis, disappearing from the top of the ferris wheel in the same way he appeared. His encounter with reality has not been a pleasant one.

"Yet still I wave this wand like a sarcastic tongue at the universe . . . know myself to be both icon and iconoclast," says Julian in a speech that could have been made as well by Robertson Davies's Magnus Eisengrim. Eisengrim would have phrased it differently, however. For MacEwen, the magician is a poet, concerned with the transforming power of the Word; for Davies he is clearly a novelist, concerned with illusions produced by hard work and a meticulous attention to detail. Mac-Ewen's magicians want to control the universe, but Davies's creation contents himself with controlling the minds of the audience. Julian creates real birds out of mud, and nobody cares because nobody can believe he's really done it. Eisengrim gives them fake snow on a stage, but does it so well that it looks real. This is his magic: he's applauded, not for what he does—nobody *really* thinks he's magic—but for his consummate skill in doing it. Perhaps this is why he's a professional success and Julian is a failure.

Like "Noman," "Eisengrim" is a pseudonym. Davies's magician started life in a "Kanadian" small town of the pork-and-beans variety, narrow, puritanical, judgmental; his real name is plain Paul Dempster. His hatred of Canada stems from his persecution at the hands of this town and from its efforts to stifle his childish interest in magic. He is kidnapped by a figure paralleling Mac-Ewen's Fat Lady Reality, a cheap conjuror who abuses him sexually while subjecting him to a bitter apprenticeship in a carnival that is not just second-rate but third-rate. Here he learns a view of magic that is equivalent to the underbelly of God: cynicism, fraud and trickery, cunning as well as conjuring, exploitation, the audience as dupe. From these humble beginnings he works his way up in the world of international magic as, among other things, an escape artist and mechanical genius, with a stopover in the legitimate theater as a "double," and is finally able to create a distinguished magic show that brings him worldwide fame.

Although he is a consummate artist, he is also, curiously, a kind of nonperson, a Noman figure who is no one because he has the capacity to be everyone, as well as to be invisible. His first job in "Wanless's World of Wonders" is to crouch inside a mechanical monster named Abdullah, who is supposed to be a card-playing automaton but is really a trick worked from inside to defraud the customers. Of this period in his life he says:

> When I was in Abdullah, I was Nobody. I was an extension and a magnification of Willard; I was an opponent and a baffling mystery to the Rube; I was something to be gawped at, but quickly forgotten, by the spectators. But as Paul Dempster I did not exist. I had found my place in life, and it was as Nobody.

He lives under several pseudonyms from this time on; as the double of a famous actor, he takes the curious name of "Mungo Fetch," "fetch" being a Scottish word for an unlucky vision of yourself you see before you die. When he finally creates his own show, its *pièce de résistance* is a much more sophisticated version of Abdullah, a Golem-like oracular brazen head, which utters disturbing truths about members of the audience. Like Abdullah it's a fraud, although like Abdullah its effects on the audience are real and sometimes disastrous; Eisengrim's relationship to it is that of the invisible power. With both Abdullah and the brazen head, however, is some question as to whether Eisengrim is their master or their slave, controlled by the monsters he thinks he is directing and creating.

Eisengrim is "wolvish," a quality which has suggested his last assumed name. It's made clear that this ruthless quality is a result of his hideous early experiences and is responsible for his having survived them. It's also responsible for his success as a magician. Both he and the other characters in the book insist that he's both an artist and a genius, as well as a glorified trickster and fraud, a Master of Illusions. His "wolvishness" is linked to "an intensity of imagination and vision," and to what another character, quoting Spengler, calls "the Magian World View":

> It was a sense of the unfathomable wonder of the invisible world that existed side by side with a hard recognition of the roughness and cruelty and day-to-day demands of the tangible world. It was a readiness to see demons where nowadays we see neuroses, and to see the hand of a guardian angel in what we are apt to shrug off ungratefully as a stroke of luck. It was religion, but a religion with a thousand gods, none of them all-powerful and most of them ambiguous in their attitude toward man. It was poetry and wonder which might reveal themselves in the dunghill, and it was an understanding of the dunghill that lurks in poetry and wonder . . . Wonder is marvellous but it is also cruel, cruel, cruel.

And Eisengrim partakes of the cruelty as well as the magic. On one level Davies's trilogy is about spiritual vampirism, the exercise of sinister, devouring power over others. Eisengrim has been the victim in such a relationship, but he later becomes the devourer. On another level the novels are about retaliation, the justice rather than the mercy of the universe, and such justice is unpleasant, if not sinister. One of Eisengrim's friends says:

> The Devil is a setter of prices, and a usurer, as well. You buy from him at an agreed price, but the payments are all on time, and the interest is charged on the whole of the principal, right up to the last payment.

To which Eisengrim replies, "Do you think you can study evil without living it?" He implies that he has lived it, and this is certainly true. Eisengrim's public personality is a deliberate creation; he is, in a way, his own monster, with his own ego incarnate in the brazen head. The last word in the trilogy is "egoist," and it's an open question whether the religion for which Eisengrim acts as magician-priest is really a religion of wonder, as he sometimes claims, or merely a religion of himself, a form of devil-worship.

And this brings us to the last category of magician or monster I'll discuss here. I began with Blake's wendigo, a monster representing a destructive external environment, so it's fitting to end with the wabeno, a monster representing a destructive internal one. The wabeno appears in Wayland Drew's *The Wabeno Feast*,[15] a novel which cuts between two time-streams: a not-so-distant future in which Canada is dissolving into chaos, and the eighteenth-century past, at the peak of the Hudson Bay Company's power. The episodes from the past are told through the journal of a would-be factor, one MacKay, who journeys into the wilderness with his sinister double, Elborn. Early in the voyage, Elborn encourages the voyageurs to tell "tales of death and terror":

> They tell of the wendigo, a mythical creature of Indian lore, and each elaborates on the other's imagining until in his fantasy Elborn beholds a creature thirty feet in height, a naked, hissing demon whose frog-like eyes search out unwary travellers and roll in blood with craving to consume them! Another whispers that the creature lacks lips to cover its shattered teeth, and a third describes its feet like scabrous canoes on which it rocks howling through the swamps at evening.

MacKay refuses to pay heed to these stories. He is an eighteenth-century man, determined to be practical and rational and to make money; we learn that he has already renounced love and religion.

15. Wayland Drew, *The Wabeno Feast* (Toronto: House of Anansi Press, 1973).

MacKay does not meet the wendigo, the monster from without. Instead he encounters the wabeno, and in company with Elborn he is privileged to witness the singular ceremony staged by the wabeno and his followers on a nearby island. The wabeno is "the most powerful" of the Indian shamans, the translator tells them:

> Whether his influence be curative or pernicious he knew not, although he thought the latter. The wabeno, he said, would use any means to cure disease or to quench an unrequited love, and those who placed themselves in his influence and used his potions on themselves or on others must submit entirely their will to his, for the remedies might grow extreme . . . It was good, he added, that the power of the wabeno had declined, and that such sorceries as he practised so as to conjure an overturn of nature grew less common as the Company's influence spread.

The wabeno and his followers differ from other Indians in their height, the "military precision" of their tents, and their white garments. Their skins also are a peculiar shade of white.

The wabeno feast itself is an orgy which begins with murder and cannibalism, continues as a frenzied dance in which the performers leap through fire so that their sexual organs are burned away, and ends with the wabeno setting fire to the entire island. The wabeno and his band vanish, although no one knows whether or not they have died in the fire:

> Elborn maintained that they had fled, and that they would spread their dementia like a plague until the last had been run to earth; but for my own part I believe that we had heard the dawn crying of the loons, and that the shaman and his band had found that morning the death which they had sought so eagerly.

Although the wabeno makes only one appearance in the novel, he is its organizing symbol. The translator opposes the wabeno to the Company, but in fact they stand for the same things: the desire for power through the destruction of others, which in the end is the same as self-destruction. MacKay, who dedicates himself to the Company's goals of accumulating beaver skins by debauching the Indians so they will want trade goods, is insane by the end of the book. In fact he was probably insane at its beginning; his mocker and shadow, Elborn, appears to exist in his own mind only, and when he kills Elborn he is, like Poe's William Wilson, killing himself. MacKay's story counterpoints the twentieth-century half of the book; here we see the spirit of the wabeno infecting the whole of society. It is of course significant that the wabeno and his band are white; the only Indians in the book who are able to live in dignity and self-sufficiency, without drunkenness, murder, and disease, are those who have made a vow not to mingle with the white traders or use any of their goods,[16] just as the only twentieth-century characters who escape the destruction of society, both physical and spiritual, are those who choose to make a canoe journey alone into the wilderness.

It is usual for a critic to present some general conclusions at the end of an effusion such as this. I'm not sure that I have any to offer; as I noted, I'm a mere collector of Canadian monsters, and I present them so that their rarity and exotic beauty may be admired, not necessarily in order to interpret them. There are many more phenomena of a similar kind: ghosts, witches, talismans, time travelers, premonitory dreams, poltergeists, and affairs with bears (this latter seems to be a peculiarly Canadian interest, as I've collected three). But I've surely dredged up enough specimens to indicate that there is indeed "a

16. Compare also the story of Kakumee and the Tornak in Farley Mowat's nonfictional study *People of the Deer* (Boston: Little, Brown, 1952). Here also the spirit of the whites is seen as a demon, and its influence on the native people is entirely destructive.

mass of dark intimations" in the Canadian literary soul.

I have also arranged my specimens in a rough paradigm which, curiously, corresponds to the order in which their respective books were written. The wendigo and Coyote, which we may call "environmental forces" or Monsters as Other, come from quite early books,[17] as do the two demigods or "magic people" I've mentioned. The magicians, on the other hand, are creatures of the sixties and seventies and seem rather more concerned, symbolically, with man's relationship to his society and to himself, as opposed to his relationship with the natural environment. The final example, the wabeno, combines both concerns in a rather allegorical and very contemporary fashion. In the tradition of the horror movie, I've begun with a terrifying thunderstorm and ended with a man-made conflagration; that is, I've begun with a story which plays upon man's fear of natural power and ended with one illustrating the dangers inherent in his own lust for power. The connection between this pattern and the changes in Canadian society and outlook over the last sixty years is perhaps too obvious to be mentioned. In any case, such a critical pattern exists in the mind of the critic rather than in the external world. Perhaps the critic is himself a kind of magician, for, as Julian the Magician says, in his incantation for making an egg disappear:

> Like everything else in the universe its existence depends on your seeing it—that alone—and its existence is the gift of your inner eye.

And, in the face of this, who will say there are no wendigos, or that the picture of Mackenzie King's mother does not actually talk? There is more to Kanada than meets the eye . . .

17. Sheila Watson's The Double Hook, although published in 1959, was actually written a decade earlier.

V

Stephen Leacock

Douglas Bush

From 1910, the year of his first humorous book, *Literary Lapses*, Stephen Leacock (1869–1944) was by far the best-known Canadian author, both at home and abroad; indeed he became the best-known Canadian of any kind, except perhaps Mary Pickford. Doubtless it could not be said that his death eclipsed the gaiety of nations; there was little gaiety in the fourth year of the Second World War. Besides, Leacock had been more or less eclipsed by such younger American humorists as his admirer Robert Benchley, James Thurber, Ring Lardner, and others; the idle rich of P. G. Wodehouse pursued their Arcadian adventures in a never-never land not subject to time and change. But, though Leacock may have been relatively little read in recent decades, he is probably still, to the mass of American and British readers, the most familiar Canadian literary name. One can only hope that his best writings remain classics that are rediscovered by successive generations in an age which has nourished very little humor except the black variety. Modern criticism has made it clear, to those who needed illumination, that Leacock at his best was—like

Thurber and Lardner—not merely the funny man he was in his own time universally taken to be.

Among his most attractive writings are his personal reminiscences: the four chapters which make up *The Boy I Left Behind Me* (1946); the preface to *Sunshine Sketches of a Little Town* (1912); the account of "My Remarkable Uncle" (1942), that irresistibly engaging promoter of grandiose enterprises; and various incidental bits. We may recall some facts of his early life and assume that his public career is well enough known. Leacock was born in the Hampshire village of Swanmore; when he was six the family moved to Canada. His father, a scion of a prosperous stock of wine merchants, was a feckless being who, set up in turn on farms in Natal, Kansas, and Ontario, failed in everything except the begetting of children (eleven), drinking, and durability. Stephen's mother fully earned the devotion of her children. Remittances and legacies from England helped a good deal to keep the family uncertainly afloat. Stephen may have exaggerated hardships on the farm (near Lake Simcoe), "the damnedest place I ever saw," but life there was bleak enough. The mother, with her English consciousness of class (she came of a clerical and scholarly line), managed to remove the older boys from the public school and employ a tutor and then to send them to the excellent private school, Upper Canada College, in Toronto. The climax of family tensions came when Stephen, aged seventeen, drove his father to the station for what proved to be a final departure. As he was getting into the train, Stephen, white-faced, shook his whip (his brother reported) and said, "If you ever come back, I'll kill you." The incurable delinquent, taking another name and later a common-law wife, lived in sin in Nova Scotia to the ripe age of ninety-two.

Leacock entered the University of Toronto but after one year had to drop out to earn money. The least repellent road to that goal was a course of teacher-training at Strathroy Collegiate Institute. When the principal suddenly called on him to take over a class in progress, he—inspired by his gift for parody—closely mimicked the manner of his chief, whose rebuke made him, he said, feel for the first time the need of human kindliness as an element of humor.[1] After ten and a half years of very uncongenial schoolmastering, mainly at Upper Canada College, Leacock went to the University of Chicago to study political science and economics, married the daughter of a Toronto stockbroker, and achieved his Ph.D. in 1903. Part-time teaching at McGill University now gave place to a regular appointment. He consolidated his position with his first book, *Elements of Political Science* (1906), which was quickly adopted at many American universities, was translated into many languages, and eventually made more money than the most popular of his humorous books.

A few years later Leacock bought property on a lake near Orillia, north of Toronto, and by degrees built a house. There he was to spend most of his summers. The need for money recalled the humorous skits he had published in American magazines during the 1890s. A collection—declined by an American publisher—was, with a brother's zealous aid, got out in 1910 by a Montreal printing firm, and *Literary Lapses*, marketed at thirty-five cents, sold very rapidly. By good luck the publisher John Lane picked up a copy for shipboard reading and cabled an offer for an English edition. With that and an American edition in 1911, the book's success in Canada was quickly and greatly widened, and continued to be through many impressions of an enlarged edition. This

1. I am tempted to claim a tiny thread of connection with that well-beloved principal, James Wetherell (the epithet is Leacock's). He must have become the provincial Inspector Wetherell who later visited my school and gave me a pleasant glow by commending my use of Latin to explain a point in English grammar.

For biographical data, here and later, I am indebted chiefly to David M. Legate's *Stephen Leacock* (Toronto and New York: Doubleday, 1970).

first humorous book appeared when the author was forty—in the year of Mark Twain's death. There is no need of rehearsing the rest of Leacock's career. It is the story of some sixty volumes of various kinds; triumphant lecture tours—which had begun with his early mission around the British Empire—in England, the United States, and Canada; and the accumulation of money, honors, and general fame. The darkest experiences of his mature life were prolonged anxiety over his son's arrested growth, the death of his wife from cancer (1925), from which he did not soon recover, and—on a different level—the abrupt manner of his being retired from McGill in 1936, an action he bitterly resented.

If the humorous writing with which Leacock is identified was uneven in quality and excessive in quantity, we should remember that it was the by-product of an increasingly busy professional life. A pair of obituary articles in the *Canadian Journal of Economics* (10, 1944) carry a "Select Bibliography of Stephen Leacock's Contributions to the Social Sciences," which lists nineteen books, thirty-six articles, and four prefaces. Among the books were three on the beginnings of Canadian history (the *Chronicles of Canada* series), which were very readable summaries of current knowledge and speculation. A much more substantial work, on early "Responsible Government" in Canada, is a reminder that, as in his first book, Leacock was less concerned with economics than with political science, and, further, that a main motive of many writings long and short was his ardent imperialism. Even early in his own lifetime that term was becoming in some quarters a dirty word, but it never was in Leacock's passionate conception of the British Empire and its place in the world; he did not live to see the large shrinkage of that place.

When we think of Leacock's lifelong conservatism and Conservatism (he was asked by a prime minister of Canada to stand for a seat in parliament), it may seem odd that he had been drawn to the University of Chicago by the name of the noted radical Thorstein Veblen, whose *Theory of the Leisure Class* appeared in 1899; but critics have seen some strains of affinity, strains which are clear enough in *Arcadian Adventures with the Idle Rich*. Certainly *The Unsolved Riddle of Social Justice* (1920) showed Leacock's earnest concern with social injustice. He was angered by "the appalling inequalities of our human lot." "The palace is the neighbor of the slum . . . Inequality begins from the very cradle . . . An acquired indifference to the ills of others is the price at which we live." While the law of the jungle was done with for ever, Leacock saw no cure in socialism, "a mere beautiful dream, possible only for angels." And while he believed that the mass of industrial enterprise must be left to what is nowadays called the private sector, he went some way toward the welfare state: he demanded legislation to prescribe minimum wages, shorter hours of labor, work and pay for the unemployed, maintenance for the aged and infirm—matters he had touched briefly in the final section of his first book. The later work ends thus:

> The safety of the future lies in a progressive movement of social control alleviating the misery which it cannot obliterate and based upon the broad general principle of equality of opportunity. The chief immediate direction of social effort should be towards the attempt to give to every human being in childhood adequate food, clothing, education and an opportunity in life. This will be the beginning of many things.

Such convictions do not seem to support the opinion apparently held by some fellow economists (an opinion possibly sharpened by envy of Leacock's popular fame) that his contributions to the dismal science were only a branch of his comic fiction.

When in the 1890s the young man was publishing in American magazines of humor the skits that were to become part of *Literary Lapses*, he probably had no motives beyond enjoying himself, winning a little kudos, and especially adding a little money to his meager resources. His chief equipment, apart from his inborn comic talents, probably consisted in his strong liking for Dickens and Mark Twain and contemporary humorists. We may suppose that he did not begin writing with much of the conscious theory that he expounded in books of the 1930s—not that he was very profoundly analytical in them.

In popular biographies of his two great favorites, *Mark Twain* (1932) and *Charles Dickens* (1933), Leacock enlivened facts and conventional ideas with humor and his warm personal devotion. He admitted Mark Twain's most obvious faults, from prejudiced ignorance of European history to "the garrulousness of self-indulgent old age" (a phrase which Leacock's own humorous books had begun to deserve); but he extolled, in writing of *Innocents Abroad* and *A Connecticut Yankee*, the penetration of the "innocent" eye that exposed outworn traditions and the power to make words impress that vision upon readers. *Huckleberry Finn* must be "the greatest book ever written in America"—as it may be, though *Moby-Dick* had not yet come into its own.[2] But it seems odd to declare Mark Twain the first great "American" author while counting Hawthorne among those who "wrote English literature in America." The lesser fact that most earlier American humorists were far inferior to Mark Twain was made very clear in Leacock's anthology, *The Greatest Pages of American Humor* (1936). One of his editorial comments is of a kind worthy of Mark Twain at his worst and too often manifest in Leacock. Granting that Artemus Ward was

2. If I may illustrate the garrulousness of self-indulgent old age with another reminiscence, when I was a freshman or sophomore in 1915 I wrote an essay on Leacock in which I pronounced him better than Mark Twain. This piece somehow—I never knew how—got into the *Toronto Star* and led to Leacock's correcting my error by sending me an inscribed copy of *Huckleberry Finn*.

"a purely historical product," he says, "But so too, for those candid enough to admit it, are the works of Homer and the *Chanson de Roland*, and dare we say Milton— and does someone murmur Shakespeare. Ward is in good company." In view of Leacock's other remarks on these poets, we cannot assume that his logic here is merely facetious.

Charles Dickens embodied high admiration, humor, candor (up to a point), various signs of hasty composition, and the old-fashioned view of the novels which was soon to be turned upside down. We cannot, to be sure, blame a slapdash critic, relying on his memories, for not having the insight of George Orwell and Edmund Wilson, who were to inaugurate the modern view of the great and always growing artist whose later works far surpassed the early ones in breadth and depth and controlled power and subtlety. Leacock saw the novelist most people had long seen, one whose supreme achievement was the great "characters" of the earlier books and who in his later years "still drove his pen ahead with a tired brain and an exhausted imagination that substituted mechanism for inspiration." (In a review of 1865, reprinted in *Views and Reviews* of 1908, Henry James had said the same thing about *Our Mutual Friend* and Dickens's work of "the last ten years," including *Bleak House* and *Little Dorrit*.) *Pickwick Papers*—the only book in the canon, says Leacock, that disputes the primacy of *David Copperfield*—really begins with Alfred Jingle, a cheat and a crook turned into a charming character (a small-scale literary prototype, we might say, of Leacock's "Remarkable Uncle"):

> It is as if the world itself were transformed and its worst sins seen in the light of a kindly and amused tolerance that is higher than humanity itself. This is the highest quality of Dickens's work; beside this, all his comic humour, his melodramatic climax, and his fountain of tears are as nothing.

This pronouncement has its truth—more truth than, say, Orwell's angry view of Micawber as "a cadging scoundrel"—and it suggests the quality of *Sunshine Sketches*, but it quite ignores the fierce and righteous intolerance of Dickens's comprehensive arraignments of English society and institutions. Leacock's book ends with an assertion that would give pause to the most fervent Dickensian: "In due time it will be known that the works of Charles Dickens represent the highest reach of the world's imaginative literature." Yet to turn from that to *The Greatest Pages of Charles Dickens*, which Leacock edited in 1934, is to be somewhat disconcerted: many of the chosen pages and related comments might make one ask how and why even the "old" Dickens had won his great fame.

Leacock's ideas about humor were set forth more at large in "American Humour" (*Essays and Literary Studies*, 1916), *Humour: Its Theory and Technique* (1935), *Humour and Humanity: An Introduction to the Study of Humour* (1937), and in parts of the mainly unfortunate *How to Write* (1943). His central ideas remain constant, with some variations in emphasis or examples. He sees the essence of humor in "the kindly contemplation of the incongruities of life, and the artistic expression thereof"—a definition that excludes unkind or angry satire, from which, happily, Leacock himself did not altogether abstain. Historically, he sees humor moving from cruelty to horseplay, from horseplay to wit, from wit to the humor of character, "and beyond that to its highest stage as the humor of life itself. Here tears and laughter are joined, and our little life, incongruous and vain, is rounded with a smile." "It is born, as it were, in perplexity, in contemplation of the insoluble riddle of existence." All but the analytical may be content with such a classification of levels of humor in any age. But Leacock sees humor, indeed all literature, as—with occasional "sports"—steadily improving, like machinery, from the primitive to the refined, thanks to man's growing humanity. Aristophanes had the wit of "a village cut-up" and is not to be named along with humorists from Dickens and Mark Twain to A. P. Herbert, Robert Benchley, and Leacock himself. We might have expected to find Chaucer on the highest level of humor and humanity, but he is not: "He told dirty stories well." Rabelais seems to be left out altogether, though we should have thought Leacock, of all men, would exult in the quest of the Holy Bottle. Humor of the highest type first appears in Shakespeare, Cervantes, and Molière, and Shakespeare is barely admitted; his power seems to be confined to Falstaff (there is no mention of that supreme example, Lear's Fool), and Shakespeare is said to be far less humorous than Irvin S. Cobb. The humor of humanity, growing in the eighteenth century, reaches its zenith in the nineteenth, in Mr. Pickwick, Huckleberry Finn, and Daudet's Tartarin; among other humorists celebrated are Lewis Carroll, Sir William Gilbert, Wodehouse, and Lardner. One thing that confounds us, even if we allow for a radical change of opinion in the course of our century, is Leacock's extravagant and repeated praise of O. Henry. In the list of American humorists from Franklin and Irving up to and beyond "Mr. Dooley" (F. P. Dunne), Hawthorne and Mark Twain have the larger view of life, "and, perhaps more than all, the work of O. Henry, whose name will stand in retrospect among the greatest . . ." Leacock's joining of tears and laughter, however valid in general, had its dangers. So, too, in his own humorous writing, did his common appeal to "laughter," a more visceral kind of response than that evoked by the fusion of what he called sublimity and pathos.

As for the techniques of humor, the general principle of incongruity embraces various modes and levels from play with words to play with metaphors, ideas, and emotions, with burlesque and parody, with English understatement and American exaggeration, with situation and character, with ironical presentation of plain truth and exposure of absurdity through the writer's pose of ignorant naiveté. The humorous juxtaposition of unrelated ideas can bring out a new significance. The best humor needs not only character and situation but "that elusive element called atmosphere," of which the greatest master is Dickens. Thus fine humor requires in both writer and reader a degree of literary appreciation, and that—said Leacock in 1916—had not in North America been commensurate with other aspects of social growth: "Our ordinary citizen in America is not a literary person." The judgment is probably less true now than it was in Leacock's time, but, as regards the growing refinement of humor, we may question such evidence as *Portnoy's Complaint* and the performances of Lenny Bruce. At any rate Leacock's own early audience must have embraced a high proportion of the nonliterary, though it also included such young devotees as the elegant Cyril Connolly and the waspish Wolcott Gibbs.

Leacock's spectrum of humorous writing extended, as we have seen, from verbal ingenuity to the kindly contemplation of the incongruities of life, born of the perplexing riddle of existence. One end of that spectrum was represented, the other approached, in the two pieces that first made Leacock known long before they appeared in *Literary Lapses*. "Boarding-House Geometry" (1897) was a neatly diverting application of geometrical language to the pains of a mode of life the author had fully experienced as a student: "A single room is that which has no parts and no magnitude"; "A pie may be produced any number of times." But far above these brisk jokes was the kindly humor of character and situation, born of perplexity, which had a simple but unforgettable beginning in "My Financial Career" (1895). Perhaps the best tribute one can pay to this sketch is to say that one instantly sees it acted—with the necessary dialogue—by Charlie (or must one say Sir Charles?) Chaplin. Here is the "little man" bewildered and cowed by the big alien world. With this I at least would link the purely descriptive but also unforgettable biography of John Smith, the neglected "ordinary common man," the salesman whose life—which included marriage, nine untalented, long-eared sons like himself, and increasing "hydrophobia"—carried him by degrees from the ribbon counter all the way up to gents' fancy shirting and then down through the same degrees to the ribbon counter, dismissal, and death. For all the humor it is pretty grim; one may remember the sentence pronounced by a fellow apprentice of H. G. Wells's Kipps: "I tell you we're in a blessed drainpipe, and we've got to crawl along it till we die." And again there is no sentimentalizing. Some other pieces have been praised as still alive, but one may think that in the main *Literary Lapses* has lost the captivating sparkle it had two generations ago.

The same thing must be said of *Nonsense Novels* (1911), which has no such redeeming gems as its predecessor. *Literary Lapses* had included one nonsense novel and several pieces which burlesqued other literary genres, though "The Life of John Smith" did much more than make fun of official biographies of the great. The title of the new book indicated its unified contents, and all the items were of recent vintage, not—like the better part of *Literary Lapses*—dug out of the author's early files. *Nonsense Novels* burlesqued more or less familiar types of popular fiction of an older day. The stories were not at all the kind of subtle parodies of eminent novelists enshrined in Max Beerbohm's *Christmas Garland* (1912); Leacock was not writing for connoisseurs. In *Humour and Humanity* he was to recall two earlier models, Thackeray's *Novels by Eminent Hands* and Bret Harte's *Condensed Novels*. The chief promoter of *Nonsense Novels* was Theodore Roosevelt; he gave universal currency to the hero of "Gertrude the Governess" who "flung himself from the room, flung himself upon his horse, and rode madly off in all directions." In one serious satire, "The Man in Asbestos," Leacock apparently had in mind H. G. Wells's science fiction, Edward Bellamy's *Looking Backward* (a book he attacked elsewhere), and his former instructor, Veblen; he condemned the living death with which a socialist and technocratic utopia would replace the vital joys and sorrows of mankind. *Nonsense Novels*, which had some forty printings in thirty years, seems to have been Leacock's best-selling humorous work. We may regret that mainly slapstick burlesque appealed so strongly to his and his publishers' literary and financial instincts; he was to carry it on, for better or worse, in other collections. When *Winsome Winnie* (1920), in which the humor was perhaps less elementary than in *Nonsense Novels*, encountered a now reluctant publisher, Leacock vehemently declared it the best thing he had done since that book of 1911, passing over what critics agree are his two finest achievements. At these we have now happily arrived.

Leacock's masterpiece, *Sunshine Sketches of a Little Town* (1912), holds a unique place in the canon and in Canadian literature. It was one of two large-scale canvases, the other being the complementary urban masterpiece, *Arcadian Adventures with the Idle Rich* (1914). It was not a novel (Leacock's talents did not stretch to that), but a group of related sketches or stories written around central figures who are more or less visible throughout and who are encircled by a flock of minor but not pallid characters. The result is that, vivid and amusing as individuals are, the principal character is the little town itself. (Leacock was to say, in *Humour and Humanity*, that the best thing about *Tartarin* is the broad way in which whole villages are satirized at once.)

It is hard to believe the author's avowal that he "wrote this book with considerable difficulty." "I can," he said, "invent characters quite easily, but I have no notion as to how to make things happen to them . . . Such feeble plots as there are in this book were invented by brute force, after the characters had been introduced. Hence the atrocious clumsiness of the construction all through." This is quite unjust. Nearly all the funny happenings serve admirably for the display of characters in speech and action. The introductory chapter, after a sketch of the little town and its ways, tells of the crisis in the affairs of the hotel proprietor, Josh Smith, who is about to lose his license on account of selling liquor after hours: through a disastrous oversight the bar had been closed one night with Judge Pepperleigh outside of it! Other potential or actual catastrophes of equal or greater magnitude supply the drama of the ensuing chapters: the financial rise and fall of the barber, Jeff Thorpe; the sinking of the *Mariposa Belle* on the annual excursion of the Knights of Pythias; the deeper sinking of Dean Drone and his church under its long accumulation of debt, the failure of the Whirlwind Campaign for its relief, and the final extinguishing of both the debt and the well-insured church through the nocturnal exploit of Josh Smith with a can of kerosene; the apparently hopeless passion of Peter Pupkin, the bank teller, for Judge Pepperleigh's daughter, so happily brought to fruition after the mysterious bank robbery and the false report of Peter's heroic death. The only episode that unduly exceeds the limits of comic credibility is the great election (about reciprocity with the United States). Granted political ethics on a par with those of the Eatanswill election in *Pickwick Papers*, we really cannot conceive of the crude and illiterate (though shrewd and not unlikable) Mr. Smith as winning a seat in parliament.

It is a minor, indeed irrelevant, but not uninteresting fact that Leacock set in the town of Mariposa some well-known figures of Orillia who were readily recognizable. His prefatory disclaimers (put in, it seems, at the insistence of his mother, a resident of the town) did not suffice to ward off resentment. In the first version, in the *Montreal Star*, the original of Josh Smith retained his actual name, but no doubt he had a thick skin. Some other men were given names very little disguised and coupled with their real occupations. A lawyer friend of

Leacock playfully threatened a libel suit on behalf of the injured. One prominent victim, a Canon Greene, the model for Dean Drone, was, said Leacock's mother, the most beloved man who had ever lived in Orillia (which readers can well believe), and he manifested unresentful Christian charity. In concentrating on his fictional characters and not thinking of their living prototypes who had feelings to be hurt, Leacock perhaps forgot the lesson of kindly humor that he later said he had learned at Strathroy Collegiate Institute; later, too, he censured Dickens for just such treatment of living persons. However, even if these characters—caricatures, some would say—had been purely imaginative creations (if that is ever possible), they do exist substantially as small-town types, as the author truly asserted. Moreover, if some persons were made more or less foolish or worse, Leacock's presentation of them does not quite deserve to be called unkind; they all, even the unscrupulous Josh Smith, have a heart that can be touched. The barber, after the collapse of his paper fortune, slaves at his trade to reimburse a friend his example had led into speculation. The explosive Judge Pepperleigh, while no ideal embodiment of the law, cherishes the memory of his son, killed in South Africa; he has never been told that his image of his noble son is a delusion. Most of all, Dean Drone, who has his unworldly oddities and is so much better at making mechanical toys than at preaching or understanding finance, is goodness itself. The book very rarely approaches sentimentality, but it has touches of legitimate sentiment and pathos that do much, along with the humor, to create the kind of "atmosphere" Leacock found so essential and so supreme in Dickens. At the end of the preface he was only telling the truth (not merely obliging his mother) when he said that if his portrayal had failed the fault was rather in "an art that is deficient than in an affection that is wanting."

Not being a disciple of Henry James, Leacock did not worry about "point of view." His omniscient narrator can indeed combine contradictory roles. As the agent of the author's enveloping irony, he must be far enough above Mariposans in sophistication to make gentle fun of naive simplicity that poses as sophistication and to explain things a stranger might not understand. A visitor from New York, for instance, might think Mariposa the sleepiest of country towns, whereas it is actually "a mere mad round of gaiety." But the superior role shifts easily into and out of that of a typical Mariposan who shares the limited outlook of most of his fellow citizens. Now and then he touches a cultural nadir, as when he reports that on the excursion boat Lilian Drone and Miss Lawson, the teacher, have "a book of German poetry,— Gothey I think it was." But when Dean Drone has heard one of his flock say that "the Church would be all right if that old mugwump was out of the pulpit" and has been cut to the heart by the mysterious word, the narrator—who can report that he has "seen" the Dean searching the encyclopedia and has "known" him to turn over *Animals of Palestine* in vain quest of the deadly creature —the narrator rises above even his own superior level to remark that "It must have been unknown in the greater days of Judea." Quite often the tone of an item is such that it may be taken as either superior irony or irony veiled as Mariposan simple-mindedness: Pete Glover, the hardware dealer, "was a Presbyterian, till they ran the picket fence of the manse two feet on to his property, and after that he became a freethinker." The author could hardly have achieved the rich, mellow flavor and atmosphere that pervade the book if the narrator had not thus been allowed to shift his two or three masks with entire freedom—somewhat like the men of Mariposa, who all belong to all fraternal organizations, including the Orange order, and celebrate with equal gusto the days allotted to national saints, St. Patrick, St. Andrew, and St. George, and the Fourth of July as well. The last sentence of the book, as we shall see, gives a clue to the narrator's real status—and to his use of the spontaneous speaking voice which so largely sets the tone of the whole.

A very few Mariposans have some intellectual pretensions, still fewer have any intellect. One marginal exception is that "complete eggnostic," Mallory Tompkins, the young man who works on the *Mariposa Times-Herald* and is a great reader. He is always buying huge encyclopedias on the installment plan and is an expert on anything beginning with the letter *A*, because the volumes are always reclaimed by the salesman before reading has got any further. Another intellectual is Dr. Gallagher, who, looking out from the *Mariposa Belle*, thinks of the journeys of Champlain, while Dean Drone, beside him, thinks of the wonders of creation and of Xenophon's long march; the one wishes that he could have known Champlain, the other that he could have known Xenophon.

Other people have less disinterested dreams, some fulfilled (for Peter Pupkin and Josh Smith), some not (for Mallory Tompkins and Jeff Thorpe). Dean Drone is a special case. Through years of preaching in the little old church he had hoped "to rear a larger Ark in Gideon, . . . to set up a greater Evidence, or, very simply stated, to kindle a Brighter Beacon." The dream was in time fulfilled, though it brought that ever-worsening nightmare of debt which haunted the Dean's mind. He is surely Leacock's richest creation; he yields continual amusement, yet all his weaknesses are viewed by the author, and hence by us, with a benevolent, indeed an affectionate, eye. One would like to quote every word said by and about him.

The Dean's dream may be not wholly unrelated to the less exalted dreaming of the people whose civic pride and ambition aspire to the size and standing of a city, a status achieved in inflationary talk, in spite of the census. Jeff Thorpe's speculative enterprises (undone by rascals in New York), the idea—which the bank manager brought back from the city—of the Whirlwind Campaign to pay off the church's debt, the shady doings in everyday life of such a mastermind as Josh Smith, and his and his opponent's tactics in the election—these endeavors attest the more energetic citizens' craving to emulate urban ways and become bigger than they are. Even small, backward Mariposa was stirred by the Canadian "boom" of the period. In the remote Maritime Provinces Peter Pupkin's father, the builder of a far-flung financial empire, could cherish conflicting dreams. He had such a longing for the simple life that "He often bought little old farms, just to try them, but they always turned out to be so near a city that he cut them into real estate lots, without ever having had time to look at them." Yet, on his flying visit to Mariposa at the time of the bank robbery, this giant of finance quickly became "one of the boys."

The attractions of littleness and bigness come together, and move apart, in the last chapter. "*L'Envoi. The Train to Mariposa*" is both a fond farewell to the little town and a sort of anticipation of *Arcadian Adventures*. For the fact is that the tycoons of Toronto and Montreal had been boys in Mariposa and are always thinking of going back to see the old place. As the train approaches the town and the passengers begin to recognize the once familiar scenes, they forget the rat race of money-getting in the city and grow chummy with the conductor and brakemen. But all this is nostalgic dreaming. The passengers, the dreamers, are really "sitting here again in the leather chairs of the Mausoleum Club, talking of the little Town in the Sunshine that once we knew"—"we," for the narrator, who has such intimate, loving knowledge of Mariposa, is an urban émigré too. If the reader, who fully shares such nostalgic bewitchment, would not care to live out his life in what the harsh light of common day reveals as a cultural desert, it is none the less a far more attractive one than the Plutoria Avenue of *Arcadian Adventures*.

But before we come to that book, which is set in the

United States, we may ask a question, less easy to answer than it seems, about the unmistakably Canadian quality of *Sunshine Sketches*. Anyone who grew up in such an Ontario community in the early 1900s can attest that, for all the bits of farcical extravagance Leacock could never resist, in spirit and most of the time in data the book is thoroughly authentic, so far as it goes. This last proviso is put in because, as the word *Sunshine* indicates, Leacock's portrait allows no really disfiguring warts. Comic realism there is in abundance, but not the sober realism of, say, the smaller Ontario village recreated in Robertson Davies's *Fifth Business*. Mariposa is nearer, if not very near, to Thornton Wilder's "Our Town" than to Sherwood Anderson's Winesburg—and a world away from Masters's Spoon River. Some of Leacock's characters and incidents could perhaps have appeared, with little change, in a picture of a small town in the United States, but, although he normally wrote with an eye on the American scene and the American market, *Sunshine Sketches* was in countless ways so essentially Canadian that, outside Canada, it seems to have had far less appeal than *Nonsense Novels* and other books mainly compounded of crackling foolery.

One may be hard put to it to define the meaning of "Canadian" in general or in regard to *Sunshine Sketches*. In an area where many and more informed people than I have not, so far as I know, had much success, I could not hope to do much better than Dean Drone in his vain efforts to write a letter of resignation. To raise the problem to a higher level and a greater theologian, I find myself in the same situation as St. Augustine when he sought to define time: "What is time then? If nobody asks me, I know: but if I were desirous to explain it to one that should ask me, plainly I know not." One may indeed doubt whether, in the early 1900s (or now, for that matter), Canada was or is a sufficiently old, stable, homogeneous, and cohesive nation to have a definable national character. It would be—or rather, in the early

1900s it would have been—easier to define the varying characters of the nine provinces. Ontario had, we may be sure, many little towns like Leacock's Orillia, but we may also be pretty sure that there were few or none in any other province. Except perhaps in its eastern and northern extremities, Ontario was predominantly Anglo-Saxon and Protestant. This most populous and prosperous province had many descendants of United Empire Loyalists, that is, people who had left the American colonies rather than support the Revolution; it had had also a steady stream of emigrants from Britain (including the Leacocks) who perpetuated British ways, from class consciousness down to cockney accents and "fish and chips." Toronto, now so large and multinational, was, in its own conception, almost the heart of the Empire, and most towns and villages were more or less proudly if dimly conscious of Canada's filial relationship: "Daughter am I in my mother's house, / But mistress in my own"—an attitude much altered in later years. "Everybody remembers," says the narrator in *Sunshine Sketches* (and I remember), the Canadian tour of the Duke of York (later George V). Mariposans regretted that he would get such a false idea of the town from seeing only the railway station and the lumber yards; in their loyal address they considerately refrained from alluding to the trouble over the town wharf and the row about the location of the new post office. Aged Canadians have too a different kind of memory: of the general response—outside Quebec—to the South African war and, above all, the crusading spirit of multitudes of young men who volunteered for a better cause, the First World War. And Canada joined at once in the Second—we may recall Colonel Lindbergh's protest.

As for peacetime activities, painting and music and little theaters flourished in Toronto and lesser cities and some towns. Imaginative writing was, with a few notable exceptions, inadequately nursed by patriotic and parochial sentiment, and such products could make small headway against the flood of American publications. Since those days, sophisticated writers have multiplied and Canadian literature has gained a place—a modest place, to be sure—in the contemporary world.

In small towns politics and religion were of much more general concern. In politics there were the two traditional British parties: to adapt Sir William Gilbert's words, every boy and every gal born in Canada alive was either a little Liberal or else a little Conservative. (In Mariposa party spirit ran high around election time. Even the pacific Dean Drone preached from such texts as "Lo! is there not one righteous man in Israel?"— which was "a signal for all the Liberal business men to get up and leave their pews." On the other hand the Presbyterian minister, denouncing "the elevation of the ungodly into high places in the commonwealth," proceeded "to show from the scriptures that the ancient Hebrews were Liberals to a man, except those who were drowned in the flood or who perished, more or less deservedly, in the desert.") The emotions I recall did not reach that feverish intensity; and I might say that my own town engendered one of Ontario's premiers, Sir James Whitney, a man of complete honesty far above Leacock's Josh Smith or John Henry Bagshaw.

The religious spectrum was much wider than the political. My very small town, hardly half the size of Mariposa, had thriving Anglican, Methodist, Presbyterian, Lutheran, and Roman Catholic churches. After a particularly destructive fire the colorful Catholic priest, anathematizing from his pulpit the primitive fire brigade, declared that "a couple of little dogs could have done as much." The Anglican church was a massive, handsome stone edifice, without a shadow of debt, thanks to a large congregation and a zealously active rector. Every summer he chartered a steamer for a money-making excursion on the St. Lawrence, an event attended by the prolonged whistle-blowing and other phenomena (except sinking) that Leacock records of the excursion on the

Mariposa Belle. Ecumenical spirit was in advance of its time: parades of the Knights of Columbus had the use of the Orangemen's drum (or perhaps it was the other way about). I recall a kindred display of civic magnanimity: on the death of a rich and prominent alcoholic, our town council toured New York State in quest of a model for a drinking fountain to be put up in his honor.

In little Ontario towns many people had an old-fashioned, wholesome steadiness, integrity, and dignity, a good share of what bourgeois intellectuals now stigmatize as "bourgeois virtues." And, whatever the cultural deficiencies, gentility was not altogether lacking: matrons of standing had their "day" for receiving callers (armed with cards), and some elderly husbands wore silk hats and Prince Alberts to church—as Leacock's Peter Pupkin does, though I never beheld a young bank teller in such attire. In general there was, so to speak, a mixture of the sedate proprieties of, say, Mrs. Gaskell's Cranford and the raw, contagious energies of Canada's mighty neighbor; both strains contribute their incongruities to the overflowing humor and comedy of life in Mariposa. Possibly, to echo Leacock's phrase again, the self-indulgent garrulousness of my reminiscences may help a bit to confirm if not to define the Canadianism of *Sunshine Sketches.* The book should have been and should be, outside as well as inside Canada, the uniquely beloved work in the Leacock canon because its account of people and their ways is a very funny, very warmhearted Canadian or Ontario version of humanity as it was in almost any small town in the Western world.

Arcadian Adventures with the Idle Rich, Leacock's second-best work of fiction (to grade it on his own prime principle of humor), was set in the United States and in a large city and dealt with people and activities at once very different from and akin to those of *Sunshine Sketches.* The American setting was made quite explicit in the last chapter and was evident elsewhere in scattered references, including some to Canada as another country. The Mausoleum Club and everything else are now American. There was doubtless more than one reason for the change of scene and material and tone. If there was to be, instead of kindly humor, mainly sharp-edged satire on rapacity and hypocrisy, clearly the United States offered bigger and better targets than Canada—although Canadians, caught by the spirit of expansion, had been assimilating American smartness with all deliberate speed: witness even Mariposa's small efforts in that line. Also, Leacock's youthful experience had nourished a natural and strong desire for a comfortable income and mode of life (he had, no less than, say, Dickens or Bernard Shaw, a keen eye for royalties, an instinct not incompatible with the social conscience of all three), and his largest public was in the United States, where *Sunshine Sketches*, with its wholly Canadian flavor, had, as we noticed, been much less popular than its greatly inferior predecessors. (Not long ago I happened to observe that a notably excellent college library in the United States contained a goodly number of Leacock's poorer books but neither of his two best ones.)

Probably a third reason for the American setting was strategic disguise of the material at hand in Leacock's familiar Montreal, which on the level of big business and society provided a sufficient parallel with large American cities. The financial barons of Plutoria Avenue and its Mausoleum Club had models in those of Sherbrooke Street and the Mount Royal Club. The little old Concordia College—from which young men had gone to join Washington's troops and the Army of the Potomac—was akin to the Toronto University and McGill of earlier days; and they were now beginning to catch up with the huge supermarket, Plutoria University, which Concordia College had become under its hustling President Boomer. The merger of the rival churches had had a recent precedent in Montreal.

The first and last chapters of *Arcadian Adventures* are good enough as glimpses of a Gilded Age in action, though they evoke fewer laughs or smiles than the six chapters between them. The opening description of Plutoria Avenue includes a not altogether comic bit which anticipates the angry utterance quoted earlier from *The Unsolved Riddle of Social Justice:*

> In fact, if you were to mount to the roof of the Mausoleum Club itself on Plutoria Avenue you could almost see the slums from there. But why should you? And on the other hand, if you never went up on the roof, but only dined inside among the palm-trees, you would never know that the slums existed—which is much better.

The story of the first chapter concerns the cutthroat efforts of the piratical Lucullus Fyshe to outwit a supposedly rich visitor, the Duke of Dulham, and then—since the Duke has come not to invest but to borrow—to unload the barren prospect on a financial rival. The last chapter, "The Great Fight for Clean Government," is more serious and less funny than the account of the Mariposa election. Mr. Fyshe leads a successful campaign to replace the corrupt city council with a board headed by himself which—unlike the contemptible small-time grafters of the council—will approve large, long-term contracts of great profit to Mr. Fyshe and his friends.

Satire is enriched with the humor of humanity in the tale of the simple rustic, Tomlinson, who has wealth suddenly thrust upon him through the discovery of gold on his farm. The attempts he and his wife make to get rid of the burden always backfire, since his "bad" investments are so productive that he is celebrated as "the Wizard of Finance"—which incidentally suggests the general craziness of the economic system. Just when, under the expert tutelage of Dr. Boomer and a colleague, Tomlinson learns that he can give his whole fortune to the university, the bubble bursts. A company had been floated after the "salting" of some real ore, authenticated by a geologist, in what further tests have shown to be worthless ground. (This phenomenon the unworldly scientist interprets as meaning a revolutionary hypothesis in geology.) When the news spreads, Mr. Fyshe and his fellows rush to bestow their stock on various charities. The innocent, bewildered Tomlinson and his wife—and their half-spoiled son, now cured by adversity—return to the contentment of their Middle Western farm. They and the geologist embody the decency and the pathos that belong to the humor of character. Indeed Tomlinson takes us back to "My Financial Career"; he is another "little man" who cannot cope with the hard-headed world's complexity—complexity now including corporate fraud.

One would like to linger with Mrs. Rasselyer-Brown and her salon and her husband and his domestic saloon and with her sponsorship of the Yahi-Bahi Oriental Society (we have gurus still with us); and with "The Love Story of Mr. Peter Spillikins," in which that wealthy, brainless, and amiable young man is loved by and comes to love "the Little Girl in Green" but is captured by a predatory widow with four sons. Yet the rivalry of the two churches, the Episcopalian St. Asaph's and the Presbyterian St. Osoph's, is such a brilliant satire on commercialized religion that it must have priority. The note is sounded in the first paragraph. The young milk-and-water rector in his Lenten noonday sermons warns against the sins of a commercial age, and the rows of bald-headed businessmen in front of him wear "faces stamped with contrition as they think of mergers that they should have made, and real estate that they failed to buy for lack of faith." That, needless to say, is more than verbal humor.

St. Osoph's has been going downhill under the ministrations of the aged professor-minister, Dr. McTeague, a sort of philosophical Dean Drone, but when he has a stroke, his successor, Dr. Dumfarthing, wins away growing crowds from St. Asaph's with his hellfire sermons, which provide a novel thrill. A solution for the crisis is proposed by the astute Mr. Fyshe: since one or both "concerns" will go under, they must be merged. Financial terms are easily arranged, and business and legal acumen simplifies doctrinal problems:

> Should any doubts arise, on or after August first proximo, as to the existence of eternal punishment, they shall be settled absolutely and finally by a pro rata vote of all the holders of common and preferred stock . . . But no form of eternal punishment shall be declared valid if displeasing to a three-fifths majority of the holders of bonds . . . all other points of doctrine, belief, or religious principle may be freely altered, amended, reversed, or entirely abolished at any general annual meeting.

The hellfire preacher, it must be added, has, no less than the businessmen, an acute consciousness of the present life. Having received an offer they could not meet, he notified them, as one of their number reported, "that he would remain in his manse, looking for light, until 2:30, after which, if we had not communicated with him by that hour, he would cease to look for it."

This story contains one exemplar of warm human feeling for others, the frail old Dr. McTeague, but his mind, it is freely admitted, is quite gone. In the whole book, in its affluent world of greed and corruption and pretentious cultural fakery, McTeague and Tomlinson and the geologist represent the kind of incongruity by which that world is judged. If there seems to be no Swiftian indignation boiling below the cool ironic surface, it is because anger and disgust are submerged in comedy. And if my account of these two books has not reached critical analysis, it attests Leacock's power to cast a spell that can foil the most earnest intentions.

"Humour and disillusionment," said Leacock, in his preface to *The Garden of Folly* (1924), "are twin sisters. Humour cannot exist alongside of eager ambition, brisk success, and absorption in the game of life. Humour comes best to those who are down and out, or who have at least discovered their limitations and their failures. Humour is essentially a comforter, reconciling us to things as they are in contrast to things as they might be."

We may partly agree, and Leacock, like Dickens, Mark Twain, and other humorists (and people in general), had his strains or moments of skeptical, even cynical, disillusionment, melancholy, and bitterness. At the same time—like Dickens, Mark Twain, and other humorists—he did not lack ambition or brisk success or stay out of the game of life (if his phrase includes a strong interest in money), nor did he and other humorists reconcile themselves or their readers to things as they are.

Of the countless topics Leacock wrote upon, we can look, briefly, at only two. On education he had much wisdom to offer, and some unwisdom. One firm principle was that education must be seen as a lifelong process, not merely as a phase of youth. Leacock's fundamental conservatism ensured his concern with central and substantial knowledge and ideas on all levels. Having had full experience on the low and the high rungs of the pedagogical ladder, he could speak with authority, if not always without prejudice. Like many other people, he at first held schoolteaching in low esteem and endured it for ten years only to make enough money to escape; he came in time to urge that it should not be regarded as a means to other ends or as a dead end but should be raised to the status of an honorable and properly rewarded profession. The best teacher he himself had ever had, he said, was his boyhood tutor (who, having become a high-school principal, gave his old pupil his first job).

As for higher education, in his best-known discourse, "Oxford as I See It" (*My Discovery of England*, 1922) and elsewhere, Leacock ridicules or denounces curricula designed either to produce uneducated experts or to lure the unintellectual into meaningless busyness. Oxford tutors, on the other hand, concentrate on the able and with minimal machinery somehow turn out educated, civilized minds—in spite, it appears, of despising science. Leacock was to say later that the rise of scientific education had barely saved Canada from "the dead weight of the classical tradition" (*Last Leaves*, 1945). If he had lived two or three decades longer he might have found that scientific education was not enough to prevent the lowering of intellectual standards, in the United States and Canada, to accommodate hordes of unqualified students.

About the tribe of professors, to which he was always proud and happy to belong, Leacock had much to say, chiefly in his humorous writings; his remarks varied greatly with characters and occasions. He satirized professors as timid, fussy, lazy moles or as aggressive "operators"; he also honored their unworldly dedication to learning and teaching at the cost of comparative poverty; and he contrasted their solid knowledge with the veneer affected by the habitués of Mrs. Rasselyer-Brown's salon. The name reminds us of Leacock's discussions, in the Oxford piece and other places, of the proper education and sphere of women. His views would now evoke the strident cry, "Male chauvinist pig"; and that would draw, from the semi-Victorian gentleman, a pungently un-Victorian response.

In the preface to *The Garden of Folly* Leacock gave a tip in regard to the methods of his humor and his humorous-serious essays: "I have always found that the only kind of statement worth making is an overstatement. A half truth, like half a brick, is always more forcible as an argument than a whole one. It carries further." We should doubtless keep this principle in mind when or if we are irritated by some of Leacock's opinions. We have already encountered specimens in the way of literary judgments, even on his own work, and he is especially outrageous in his unceasing war against the Greek and

Latin classics. Near the end of his life he could, apparently not in fun, speak of himself as presumably still the specialist in Latin, Greek, and modern languages that he had been when he qualified as a secondary-school teacher; and some critics have paid tribute to his classical training and classical taste. However thorough his training may have been, its later fruits were worse than barren. Of course his humorous writings for a mass audience largely forbade display of his classical remnants —though the hapless Tomlinson could be riddled by the Latin cross fire of Dr. Boomer and Dr. Boyster. The chief single item, "Homer and Humbug" (*Behind the Beyond*, 1913), might, with straining, be taken as the sportive diversion of a real devotee who amuses the man in the street by pretending to support him; at any rate no one could object to the mockery of sham raptures. And we all relish Dean Drone's somewhat vague attachment to Theocritus.

But the serious assertions in the two books on humor and in *Too Much College*, whether they are bricks or half-bricks, compel us to pronounce Leacock guilty, if not of ignorance then of almost incredibly crass philistinism. Both Greek and Latin languages and literatures, he tells us, belong to primitive stages of man's evolution. Greek humor was "pretty primitive and clumsy," partly because of the "heavy and cumbrous language." We noted Leacock's estimate of Aristophanes as only "a village cut-up," far inferior to modern humorists, including himself. The drama of Aeschylus, "with just two people on the stage," is about as exciting as the dialogues that used to be spouted at entertainments in the little red schoolhouse sixty years ago. The Greek language is for philologists and Apostles, and the world has no time for Greek literature, which is only for the fortunate few who go to college and stay there for ever. The Latin language is immensely useful for the mastery of English (one nugget of wisdom), but "Latin literature, apart from its setting in history, amounts to very little." We don't need to go further. But, since Leacock rarely descends to particulars, I will add one: Lucretius, he says, "thought it entertaining" to watch a man drown—either a carelessly forgetful or a willful perversion of the opening of Lucretius's second book.

However, as Keats said, every man can be cut to pieces on his weakest side, and I cannot end without recalling the many-sided Leacock's central strength. He was not a great writer, but for many years he was the buoyant entertainer of multitudes throughout and beyond the English-speaking world, and he left behind him two enchanting books and a number of small pieces which are surely lasting contributions to Canadian literature. Without any sentimental blowing-up of Leacock beyond his proper dimensions, we can say that, while providing choice amusement, these writings in their way and degree encourage a sane view of an irrational world, that they nourish our humanity, our sympathy with the misfits in such a world, with the feeling heart against the scheming head. And if we have thought of Leacock as only a professional clown, we might listen to one of his few bits of serious self-revelation, however woefully Victorian it may sound: "If religion is what I think it is—a communing of the spirit with the unseen, an imminent sense of life beyond death and of duty laid upon us—I don't see how you can take a 'course' in it, unless you don't believe in it. Human life itself is the only course in religion." Perhaps, to keep the balance even, we should recall the conclusion of *Humour: Its Theory and Technique*, where Leacock gave his version of the once fashionable attitude of cool cosmic despair in the face of the ultimate extinction of man and the world: looked at from a sufficient distance, life dissolves itself into humor, and "All ends with a cancellation of forces and comes to nothing; and our universe ends thus with one vast, silent, unappreciated joke."

VI

Is There a
Canadian Drama?

Brian Parker

I have borrowed my title from Douglas Bush, who in 1929 was already throwing off oracular sparks in all directions, including an inflammatory shard for the *Commonweal* of November 6 entitled "Is There a Canadian Literature?" "Propounding and discussing this great question," Bush begins, "has been for years a favourite pastime among Canadian literati"—a comment no less relevant nearly fifty years later. He then gets off some pleasant squibs about Mounties, villainous trappers, and totem poles, and he ends with the following, I think crucial, remark: "The best Canadian writing is moving away from the local and parochial to the local and universal, and it can be increasingly judged by other than domestic standards."

Bush's distinction between the "local and parochial" and the "local and universal" is the nub of the matter, and of my argument here, which will suggest a way of interpreting the terms "local and universal" and demonstrate the suggestion by reference to three plays by the ranking Canadian dramatists of the moment: *Forever Yours, Marie-Lou* by Michel Tremblay of Montreal (which I shall cite in the translation by Van Burek and

Glassco), *Colours in the Dark* by James Reaney of London, Ontario, and *The Ecstasy of Rita Joe* by George Ryga, once of Alberta and now of Summerland, British Columbia.[1]

First, let me sketch the development of Canadian theater since about the 1920s. Before that time there was no real Canadian drama to speak of, nor even what may properly be called Canadian theater. True, there was continual theater activity of a kind, right from the performance of a marine masque called *Le Théâtre de Neptune* as early as 1606, forty years before *Ye Bare and Ye Cubb*, and true, there was a steadily increasing number of Canadian plays written, heavily dependent on poor European models, but stretching out to accommodate at least some part of the Canadian experience. However, these examples are interesting only historically, rarely intrinsically, even to Canadians.

The very situation of Canada was inimical to drama. The country was too big and too sparsely populated for a medium that is essentially an art of developed cities. It lacked any truly metropolitan centers until after World War II. Its early settlers were puritans who distrusted the theater, and from the first its culture was split into warring traditions—French, English, and, very soon, American too. Canada has been a nation for only 110 years, scarcely more than a single lifetime, and it has always tended to define itself in relation to its parent countries. It lacks an imaginative myth of itself, any ideal such as the "American Dream" or the "frontier" or even "democracy." Or at least it has never had a myth around which dramatic work could cluster.

I make this qualification because the myth that critics have claimed as central to much Canadian nondramatic

1. *Forever Yours, Marie-Lou*, trans. Van Burek and Glassco (Vancouver: Talonbooks, 1975); *Colours in the Dark* (Vancouver: Talonbooks, 1971); *The Ecstasy of Rita Joe* (Vancouver: Talonbooks, 1970).

writing—in the essays of Northrop Frye, for instance, or in Margaret Atwood's study *Survival*—is the individual's confrontation with raw nature: the "stark terror" that Frye says grips men confronting "the frightening loneliness of a huge and thinly settled country," where men's "thrifty little heaps of civilized values look pitiful beside nature's apparently meaningless power to waste and destroy on a superhuman scale,"[2] where the melancholy isolation of the creative mind can produce an almost Anglo-Saxon sense of bleak endurance. Canada's frontier was and is the North, largely unmapped and resisting all attempts to humanize it.

Like many, I have experienced the feeling Frye speaks of. Two years ago I flew back to Canada from England by the northern route because it was late in the fall and there were storms over the central Atlantic. I was in a peculiarly receptive state of mind, I suppose, for I was returning from my mother's funeral, and when we reached Greenland in crystalline sunshine and I looked down on the monstrous glaciers of the coastline, merging on one side into the frozen sea and on the other into a sky as blindingly white as the ice itself, so that all sense of distance, all differentiation was lost, I had a strong experience of what William James called "vastation," the sense of personal annulment before the immensities of time and space. (The experience was emphasized by the stewardess's choosing that moment to offer me Canadian Club whiskey in a miniature bottle.)

However, true though the experience may be, most of Canada's population no longer face it directly. They live in cities strung out along the American border, and their attitude to the wilderness is the romanticizing one of sports fishermen or summer cottagers. There was always a streak of this pastoralism in Canadian literature, of course (as how could there fail to be in the heyday of Romanticism?), and with the recent

2. Northrop Frye, "Canada and Its Poetry," in Frye, *The Bush Garden* (Toronto: House of Anansi Press, 1971), p. 138.

concern about pollution, about the inhumanity of cities, and about the depletion of natural resources, the romantic view is now more prevalent than forlornness. Fear of the wilderness, in fact, has been replaced by fear of the city. The latter can be dramatized because what it comes down to is fear of people, but the experience of the land, whether horrific or romantic, is one that drama, because of its very nature, finds it difficult to cope with.

Of course, there have been attempts to do so: long descriptive passages in nineteenth-century verse tragedies, depictions of rural deprivation and loneliness in Merrill Dennison's plays of the twenties or Gwen Pharis Ringwood's in the thirties, the "Group of Seven" drama of Herman Voaden, or, more recently, Michael Cook's drama about the outports of Newfoundland with their dwindling populations and tireless, insistent sea. The success of these plays is very limited, however, in comparison to what has been done in poetry and the novel, because the experience of the empty land just does not lend itself to a nondescriptive medium that can only convey reactions to experience, not the experience itself. The central Canadian myth, in other words, is antidramatic, so it is not surprising that Canadian drama has had to wait for a more widespread, diverse, and traumatic urban experience in order to begin to develop more fully. The two world wars helped to create this experience.

When the great touring system of the "road" collapsed after World War I, because of costs and the competition of the movies, the gap was filled in Canada by a growth of amateur little theater, and the hundreds of groups which sprang up in the twenties were organized in 1932 into the Dominion Drama Festival. Not only did these groups train most of the current Canadian theater professionals, but their demand for homespun plays was sufficient for Samuel French to publish a special Canadian Playwrights series, although the plays it included make tedious reading today. A more professional stimulus came from the government's decision to nationalize radio as a tool for unifying the still very disparate country. Canadian Broadcasting Corporation drama grew steadily through the late twenties and the thirties to what has been called its golden age in the early forties, when each Sunday night Andrew Allan's "Stage" series was listened to from sea to sea. The best of these Sunday plays were satirical in kind, a third noteworthy aspect of the period between the wars. Satirical revue clearly appealed to a certain wry feeling in Canadians, a feeling of being at the edge of things,[3] uncommitted but also rather out of it. The most important manifestation of this humor was the appearance of Gratien Gélinas in Quebec, developing his "Fridolin" vaudeville sketches into sad urban folk comedy which cracked the highminded traditionalism clamped on Quebec theater until then by the classical colleges and the Catholic church.

As World War I stimulated amateur theater, World War II was followed first by the growth of professional theater of high quality, then by an enormous increase in Canadian drama. To simplify, five main influences should be borne in mind. First, the addition of television to radio began to provide enough bread and butter to enable Canadian theater professionals to survive without drifting over the border to find work, so that by 1969 *Variety* was listing Toronto as the third major talent pool on the continent, not far behind New York and Hollywood.[4] Then there was the Shakespeare Festival which Tyrone Guthrie was brought over to start in 1953 in a tent outside the little town of Stratford, Ontario. The festival is now so successful and firmly established that it is criticized as being part of the conservative establishment, but its effect in raising Canadian acting

3. Millar MacLure, "Smith's House of Fame," *Tamarack Review*, 17 (1960), p. 64.
4. See Ontario Arts Council Report, *The Awkward Stage* (Toronto: Methuen, 1969), p. 6.

and production values to the highest international standards can hardly be overestimated, and its success encouraged the foundation of many other theaters and festivals across the country. Two years before Stratford opened, a royal commission had warned that Canada was in danger of becoming culturally dependent on the United States, and in 1957 this warning bore fruit in the Canada Council, a federal subsidizing body which has transformed the Canadian theater scene. Besides funding individual artists and productions, the council has helped build up a chain of regional repertory theaters across the country, culminating in 1969 in the National Arts Centre in Ottawa. An extra boost was then given to this activity by the 1967 centennial celebrations. And, finally, in response to the drug and dropout problems of the late sixties, the federal government introduced yet another level of grants—the Opportunities for Youth and Local Initiatives Program grants—which helped launch an exceedingly vigorous alternative-theater movement on the off-off-Broadway pattern. At first this movement was too dependent on its model, but by 1970 the alternative theaters were concentrating almost exclusively on original Canadian drama, so that in looking down the Toronto Live Theater list it has been common in recent years to find fifteen or sixteen of its twenty-odd theaters showing indigenous plays.

What may we conclude, then, from this rather breathless survey? Clearly, from a purely quantitative point of view the answer to the question in my title must be a resounding Yes. After the first trickle of new playwrights in the forties and fifties—Gélinas, Marcel Dubé, and Jacques Ferron in Quebec; Robertson Davies, John Coulter, and Mavor Moore in Ontario—there has been a spate, a deluge in the late sixties and in the seventies. In the two seasons 1971–72 and 1972–73, for example, no fewer than two hundred Canadian plays received professional productions.

However, qualifications must be made about all this bustle. What about quality? And is the drama in any way distinctively Canadian?

To start with, the quality of the work is uneven, usually evanescent, and often quite silly. Moreover, other countries had a similar flood of theater in the sixties. For whatever complicated reasons, it was part of the times and was international, not especially Canadian; it is therefore slippery ground on which to build one's hopes for a national tradition. In Canada, moreover, theater was stimulated by government grants, and as the new austerity has cut the Opportunities for Youth grant and Local Initiatives Program, the alternative theaters have begun perceptibly to falter.

More disturbing still, from a scholarly point of view, the new drama has become involved in a shrill, self-conscious nationalism. There is still real cause for alarm at the danger of Canada's being flooded with American advertising and mass media. The Canada Council was founded on this premise, and the government has recently thought it necessary to restrain the rapid American absorption of Canadian publishing houses and to impose "Canadian content" quotas on the news magazines and Canadian commercial television. Taking their cue from this approach, the militant dramatists have demanded that the government also impose a "Canadian content" quota of 50 percent on all theaters receiving a public subsidy, and, as usual, the most strident demands are from by no means the best playwrights. Fortunately the demand has so far been resisted, although this battle is still being waged.

The situation is further complicated in Quebec because there the cultural threat is not just America but *les Anglais* in general; in addition, the last two decades have seen a much more drastic social, educational, political, and sexual revolution in that province than in any other. This revolution began when the corrupt conservative Union Nationale of Maurice Duplessis was at last displaced in the 1950s, but with the life-style of the counterculture flooding in on one side and a revolutionary ideology from the Third World pressing in on the other, change ran riot in Quebec of the late sixties. Politically, it took the form of separatism, with the guerilla tactics of the Front de Libération Québécois (FLQ) as its most extreme form. Culturally, its achievements have been consistently more numerous, more adventurous, and several years more advanced than those in English Canada, but ideologically they have been correspondingly extreme. Just as there has been a separatist movement among American blacks, with a political distinction made between the terms "negro" (or "colored") and "black," so there are dramatists in Quebec who distinguish between "French Canadian" and "Québécois,"[5] giving the latter a separatist emphasis and claiming, like the Black Arts movement, that they write only for their own people and wish to be intelligible only to them. *Joual*—the elided, mispronounced, part-English argot of the Quebec working class—which in the past was regarded as culturally regressive, has now acquired the same political cachet in Quebec as have the American blacks' "jive" and "soul" in the United States.

Thus we return with a vengeance to Douglas Bush's distinction between "local and parochial" and "local and universal," and the value judgment this distinction implies. I am, of course, on Bush's side, but there are further distinctions to be made before we turn to particular plays. In the first place, let us admit that, although it always runs the risk of overvaluing the mediocre, the "local and parochial" in literature can have its own value, as long as it accurately reflects the life around it and does not give itself unsuitable airs ("being world famous right across Canada," as Mordecai Richler puts it). Much of Canadian literature, and its drama in par-

5. cf. Michel Belair, *Le Nouveau Théâtre Québécois* (Montreal: Dossiers Leméac, 1973).

ticular, comes off poorly by international standards, but those are not the only standards that matter. "If evaluation is one's guiding principle," says Northrop Frye, "criticism of Canadian literature would become only a debunking project, leaving it a poor naked *alouette* plucked of every feather of decency and dignity."[6] "The critic of Canadian literature," he says, "has to settle uneasily somewhere between the Canadian historian or social scientist, who has no comparative value-judgments to worry about, and the ordinary literary critic, who has nothing else."[7]

Without going to the lengths of separatism, then—or even mild chauvinism—it is justifiable to defend mediocre drama as "culture" in the wider, anthropological sense, the sense in which E. K. Brown speaks of it in his influential study of Canadian poetry: "One of the forces that can help a civilization to come of age is the presentation of its surfaces and depths in works of imagination in such a fashion that the reader says: 'I now understand myself and my milieu with a fullness and clearness greater than before.' "[8] Or as the playwright James Reaney puts it, shifting the emphasis significantly, "the feeling of place is a power within us." In all great art the universal rises from the particular; good literature, like good wine, needs a specific locality. Obviously, understanding one's local condition will be even greater if the work of art cuts down to universal levels—Brown's "depths" as well as "surfaces"—but what is it that we mean by "universal" in the Canadian context? Surely not the opinion of the New York or London critics.

Two recent critical answers to this problem have been pluralism and internationalism, neither quite the same as what traditionally we have understood by "universal."

6. "Conclusion to a 'Literary History of Canada,' " *The Bush Garden*, p. 213.
7. "Preface to an Uncollected Anthology," ibid., p. 163.
8. *On Canadian Poetry*, rev. ed. (Toronto: The Ryerson Press, 1944), p. 12.

"One of the blessings of the Canadian way of life," says the historian W. L. Morton, "is that there is no Canadian way of life, much less two, but a unity under the crown admitting of a thousand diversities."[9] An analogous point (without Morton's royalism) was made by Harry Levin in his address to the Canadian Comparative Literature Association in 1972, in which he pointed out that a lack of a specific national identity may, in fact, be culturally enriching, as Thorstein Veblen argued was the case with European Jewry.[10] This view overlaps interestingly with Frye's recent theory that, coming on the world scene so late, Canada is inevitably committed to a modern international art style, which he characterizes as spatial rather than linear, imaginative rather than rational, and "in process" (and thus involving) rather than finished. It presents an admittedly limited structure for coordinating and integrating experience and is concerned neither with representing actual facts nor with universal hypotheses; in short, its focus is neither local nor universal, but somewhere in between. "Complete immersion in this international style," Frye says, "is a primary cultural requirement, especially for countries whose cultural traditions have been founded since 1867, like ours."[11] The particular level of integration that Frye himself is most interested in is, of course, that of Jungian archetype and mythopoeia, where object and subject, outer and inner realities imaginatively combine, so that, for example, horror of the empty land both produces and expresses one's personal nausea before Not-Being. This level of perception, says Frye, then dictates "the structural principle of the poem itself," so that "the

9. "The Relevance of Canadian History," in Eli Mandel, ed., *Contexts of Canadian Criticism* (Chicago: University of Chicago Press, 1971), p. 68.
10. "Literature and Cultural Identity," *Comparative Literature Studies*, 10 (1973), 139–156.
11. *The Modern Century* (Toronto: Oxford University Press, 1967), p. 57.

poet's quest is for form not content"—a comment to remember.[12]

As a principle, however, the idea of an imposed but tentative organizing pattern can obviously have more applications than that of Jungian myth. It fits in well, for example, with Marshall McLuhan's theory of a modern sensibility so changed by electronic technology and speed of communication that it sees things always in terms of simultaneous pattern, what McLuhan calls mosaic, or crystalline, perception. And I would suggest that this theory may be peculiarly appropriate to the present Canadian situation, not only because of the nation's newness, its extreme regionalism, and its utter dependence on communication networks, but because of its political nature—a loose confederation, under law, but without a constitution; second, because of the huge proportion of its recent immigration, which is not being homogenized in the melting pot but is officially encouraged to retain its cultural differences; and, third, because the two most typical Canadian art forms are the documentary—in film, the novel, and the long narrative poem —and the cycle or sequence of short poems that are autonomous yet loosely connected. The suggestion (and it is no more than a suggestion) is, then, that—in drama at least—this international structure may appeal to the same Canadian experience of loosely controlled space that Frye talks of in terms of the wilderness, but in a formal rather than thematic way.

It is this combination of precise local detail with a spatial, nonlinear form that I wish now to examine in plays by Tremblay, Reaney, and Ryga. Whether or not it is a distinctively "Canadian" combination does not really bother me; it suffices that it should be revealed in the most interesting Canadian plays of the seventies, and its success as art will depend, I suggest, on the relation it manages to establish between Canadian "content" and

12. "Preface to an Uncollected Anthology," p. 194.

international "form," which is how I would (for the moment) transmute our two terms "local" and "universal" in order to use them for analysis.

First, some facts about Michel Tremblay. The most important is that he was and is of the working class, a part of the deprived and sometimes squalid life of Montreal's East End about which he writes and where he was born in 1942, in an overcrowded house, to parents already in their fifties. He turned down a scholarship at one of the classical colleges because of its social elitism and worked as a typesetter while he learned about plays from listening to the radio and watching television. He won the Quebec Young Authors Award in 1964, when he was twenty-two, and the following year wrote *Les Belles Soeurs.* This play was unanimously rejected on first reading by a jury of the Dominion Drama Festival, and Tremblay had to hawk it round for two and a half years before it was at last given a workshop reading by the Centre d'Essai des Auteurs Dramatiques. On the strength of this reading it was produced by Montreal's Théâtre du Rideau Vert, and from its opening on August 14, 1968, it was an immediate *succès de scandale,* "probably the most important single event in the history of Quebec theatre," according to the *Encyclopaedia Canadiana.*

Les Belles Soeurs is a funny-sad piece about a slum woman who wins a million trading stamps in a contest and gives a party for her female relatives and neighbors to help her paste the stamps into discount books. During the chat and comic by-play the desperate sadness of each of these women is revealed. They end by stealing most of the books for themselves and leave bellowing the national anthem as stamps rain down from the ceiling. What made the play explosive, however, was not its social commentary but the fact that it was written in *joual.* Gélinas, Dubé, and Roger Lemelin had already established that realistic plays could be written about the

Quebec working class, but they had used a modified and very cleaned-up version of slum language. The Théâtre du Nouveau Monde had also used mild *joual* to translate parts of Shaw's *Pygmalion* and Shelagh Delaney's *A Taste of Honey*. But Tremblay's language was the thing itself, obscene, uncouth, mispronounced, and ungrammatical. To no one's surprise, the literary establishment disowned the play completely, to the extent that when Jean-Louis Barrault wanted to take it to Paris, the Quebec Minister of Culture refused the necessary subsidy on the grounds that Tremblay's language made the play an unworthy representation of the province's culture abroad.

Correspondingly, the separatists welcomed Tremblay as one of their own, ascribing his use of *joual* to nationalism. His real reasons for using it, however, are not so simple. Like Harold Pinter (whose use of English met with much the same objections earlier), Tremblay uses *joual* negatively to show cultural fragmentation, the breakdown of communication. In this he can be aligned with theorists writing for the journal *Parti-Pris* in the mid-sixties, who urged that *joual* could be used in literature to reflect the alienation of French Canadian society. But this is not the only reason he uses it. In spite of its grim crudity, *joual* can also be very funny, in a vaudeville, folk fashion, again very like Pinter. An example from Tremblay's *Forever Yours, Marie-Lou* is the husband and wife's absurd argument about the relative cost and merits of two brands of peanut butter, "le peanut crunchy" and "le peanut smoothy," an argument reflecting comically their actually bitter antagonism. Moreover, like Pinter, Tremblay achieves extraordinarily subtle effects by repetition, juxtaposition, and counterpoint. Thus his *joual* can be related both to social and psychological realism—the "local" aspect of his art—and to his innovative musical structure—its "international" form.

The story of *Marie-Lou* is very simple. Two sisters,

Manon, a sickly, religious introvert, and Carmen, a singer of cowboy songs in a seventh-rate bar, discuss their parents, who died ten years before. The father, Leopold, was a coarse, bitter factory worker who drank to forget the nullity of his life; the wife, Marie-Louise, was frigid and religious. They quarrelled endlessly about money and their sexual incompatibility, each rancorously blaming the other. Manon sides wholly with her mother and broods obsessively over the past, indulging in her mother's sense of martyrdom. Carmen defends her father, but really wants to forget and leave the old life behind. The arguments and memories of the sisters are interwoven with the past itself, so that the play ends with a double climax, Carmen's final rejection of her sister's morbidity coinciding with Leopold's invitation to Marie-Lou to take the car ride on which he killed them both.

Several aspects of the play are common to all Tremblay's work. In many of his plays the combination of financial stress, religiosity, and sexual ignorance makes the family a trap in which, instead of finding companionship, each member feels more isolated. "I was reading in the [Catholic] *Digest* the other day," says Marie-Louise, "that a family is like living in a cell, that each member's supposed to contribute to the life of that cell. Cell, my ass! It's a cell all right, but not that kind. When people like us get married, we end up alone, together. The whole bunch of us, alone, in prison, together." Typically also, Leopold seeks relief at the nearest bar, but even there he stays alone, sitting behind a table covered with drinks, hoping for company which never joins him. Moreover, he knows that the drink is betraying him to an inherited streak of insanity, with which his wife continually taunts him. The violence built up in him by his miserable present and future finds an outlet in his unjustly beating his little son, Robert, who never appears in the play but who is taken with his parents on the suicidal trip in which that violence finds its ultimate release. And by his suicide Leopold hopes not only to release himself and his family but also, somehow, to sabotage the society that has helped to ruin them:

> We're like gears in a great big machine [he says in the imagery of his alienating work] . . . And we're afraid to stop it 'cause we think we're too small . . . But if a gear gets busted, the machine could break down . . . Who knows . . . All of a sudden the machine just stops . . . Christ, what a big machine . . .

Marie-Louise is also typical of Tremblay's characters. She perpetuates the mistakes of her mother and passes them on to her daughter Manon. She married to escape the misery of her parents' home; she was sexually ignorant, her mother having told her that women could not enjoy sex; and her husband proved equally ignorant, and drunken and brutal as well. In their long marriage they have had sex only four times. Each time it has happened against her will, with Leopold drunkenly raping her; each time it has resulted in a child, driving them further into debt. It is Marie-Louise's disclosure that she is now pregnant for a fourth time which precipitates Leopold's final decision. Marie-Louise, moreover, is that Québécois archetype the *mère martyre*, wallowing in self-pity and projected guilt, and all these attitudes Manon has learned from her and will broodingly perpetuate. Even the other sister's escape, as an entertainer in a bar, is linked with Tremblay's frequent depiction of show business as false glamour, a "dream" (as Carmen herself admits) little more reliable than a miraculous fall of trading stamps. Its sleaziness is emphasized by the ridiculous cowgirl costume that Carmen wears throughout the play. *Marie-Lou*'s vision of slum life is not very different from that of the plays of Paul Zindel and Tennessee Williams which Tremblay has translated, but another strong influence (which has not been sufficiently recognized) is the European existentialism and absurdism which dominated Québécois writing in the fifties. Behind the family trap, behind the theme of reenactment, lies Sartre's *Huis-Clos*, with its comment that "hell is other people." And multiple influences can also be traced in the form of the play. The nonlinear, disjunctive, intercut nature of Tremblay's structure, with its dependence on monologues, develops partly from the vaudeville tradition of Gélinas, sophisticated by the lessons of radio and television montage. But there is also a strong influence from the absurdists and, in this piece particularly, I think, from Beckett's play called *Play*.

The orchestration of individual alienations can be seen most clearly in another Tremblay play, *En pièces détachées*, where the title itself sums up both the theme of isolation and the play's fragmented form. In that play, as in his musical comedy *Demain matin, Montréal m'attend* and his more recent *Bonjour, la, bonjour* (1974), the speeches are actually identified musically as duets, trios, quartets, quintets, and choruses. The same musical effects are also in *Marie-Lou*, but they are presented more obliquely.

The set of *Marie-Lou* (which closely resembles that of *En pièces détachées*) itself reveals separate lives held spatially in tension. At the center is the kitchen in which the two girls talk in the present. The action of the past also took place in this kitchen, Tremblay tells us, but to emphasize the separation of the characters involved in it, he has placed Marie-Lou in her sitting room, surrounded by religious bric-a-brac, constantly knitting and looking at her television. Leopold is in his bar, waiting muzzily behind six glasses of beer. The action is overhung by a huge enlargement of a snapshot of Marie-Lou at eighteen, which she gave to Leopold with the sentimental, now bitterly ironic, inscription *"A toi, pour toujours, ta Marie-Lou.*

The separateness of the characters is emphasized, because, the opening stage direction tell us, "the characters never move, never look at one another. They stare straight ahead. Marie-Louise and Leopold will only look at one another during the last two lines of the play." The likeness of this vision to Beckett's play called *Play* is increased by the beginning of the dialogue, as the four separate, contradictory voices gradually emerge, incrementally, from the silence:

Marie-Louise.	Tomorrow . . .
Carmen.	Wow . . .
Leopold.	Yeah . . .
Manon.	Still . . .
Marie-Louise.	Tomorrow . . .
Carmen.	Wow . . .
Leopold.	Yeah . . .
Manon.	Still . . .
[*Silence*]	
Marie-Louise.	Tomorrow we gotta . . .
Carmen.	Wow, it's already . . .
Leopold.	Yeah, I know . . .
Manon.	Still, it feels . . .
[*Silence*]	
Marie-Louise.	Tomorrow we gotta eat at mother's . . .
Carmen.	Wow, it's already ten years . . .
Leopold.	Yeah, I know. . . What a pain in the ass.
Manon.	Still, it feels like yesterday.

There are no chorus effects in this play as there are in *Les Belles Soeurs* and *En pièces détachées,* just very subtle counterpoint and two crucial monologues—"arias," perhaps, to keep the musical terminology: one by Leopold, in which he speaks of the alienating effect of factory work and of feeling himself to be a mere wage slave; the other by Marie-Louise, in which she speaks of the sexual trauma of her relations with Leopold.

The counterpoint effects are made possible by the very complex time relationships of the play. Basically, what we have is double time. The conversation of the daughters is interwoven with the arguments of the parents ten years before, with eerie and ironic echoings of phrase—for example, the striking non-English idiom of putting one's eyes in butter (or grease) as a metaphor for seeking pity, or Carmen's complaint to her sister, "Then why don't you answer? You know how I hate that, when you start to say something and don't finish," which is echoed a few moments later by Marie-Louise, speaking ten years before. There are also constant forebodings and foreshadowings of the final disaster. (I counted eleven of them, but there are probably more.) This double time is complicated by the single-time flashbacks, indicated by a change of lighting, when all the conversation is in the past and the daughters revert to their girlhood characters—Manon constantly spying and exclaiming with horror, Carmen not interested, trying to avoid trouble, but always being blamed. The stage directions instruct that "it is very important that the spectator feel that Marie-Louise and Leopold are in the early 1960s, while Carmen and Manon are in the 1970s. It is also important (perhaps through a change in lighting) that the audience realize when Carmen and Manon become characters in the past, in other words, girls fifteen and sixteen years of age."

This complex, flexible shape gives extraordinary intensity and dramatic tension to the basically simple and squalid events. It also gives an important ambiguity, because we see things through a double focus—Manon's vision and Carmen's vision. Leopold's motives, for example, in killing not only himself but also his wife and son are left ambiguous. Was it hatred, a final explosion of the violence building inside him? Or was it a kind of love, an attempt to release them all from intolerable recurrence? There is enough vestigial tenderness in his reminiscences of the past (reinforced by the overhanging photograph with its sentimental inscription) to warrant at least some belief in the second motive, and he uses the diminutive "Marie-Lou" (not his usual "Marie-Louise") when he proffers the invitation to go for a ride. Then there are Marie-Lou's reasons for accepting the invitation, and the meaning of the single, enigmatic glance they finally exchange at the end. Is the Québécois critic Michel Belair correct in asserting that Marie-Lou is calling Leopold's bluff?[13] (After all, as he points out, she *has* said she wants the new baby.) Yet is there not also a finality in the way she at last stops knitting after a particularly brutal insult from Leopold and, turning for the first time to look at him, replies "You'll never know how much I hate you"? Like her jeers about his insanity, her words seem deliberately provocative. When Leopold immediately responds with his ironically wooerlike invitation, "You want to come for a ride in the car with me tonight, Marie-Lou?" the stage directions indicate, "After a long silence, Marie-Lou gets up." The pause suggests to me that she knows what she is doing.

Most enigmatic of all is the author's attitude toward Carmen. Michel Belair argues that Carmen marks a new positive turn in Tremblay's basically pessimistic drama.[14] Leopold, indeed, tells his wife at the end, "There aren't many like us left, Marie-Louise . . . Thank God for that . . ." and Carmen leaves knowing that, although singing cowboy songs is not great art, it is something she likes and can do well enough to be happy in. Such an interpretation is backed up, perhaps, by the endings of two of Tremblay's more recent plays: the homosexual lovers' recognition and acceptance of their real personalities in *Hosannah*, and the new, tender relation to the ineffectual father and acceptance of incest as an authentic relationship in *Bonjour, la, bonjour.*

However, just as these positive interpretations are obviously very qualified (particularly in the latter play, since *bonjour* means "goodbye" as well as "hello"), so too is Carmen's escape. Tremblay has specifically said that he considers the Québécois craze for Western music

13. In the Introduction to *A toi pour toujours, ta Marie-Lou* (Montreal: Editions Leméac, 1971), p. 27; see also his *Michel Tremblay* (Montreal: Collection Studio, 1972).
14. Introduction, *A toi pour toujours, ta Marie-Lou*, pp. 20ff.

ridiculously inappropriate to French Canadian life,[15] and his depiction of show business in his other plays represents it as a pantomime of sexual desperation. Moreover, Leopold's comment on the lovelessness of his marriage being exceptional is contradicted by a remark by his wife: "When you look around, it's the same everywhere . . . Your brothers and sisters who all married for love, what do they look like after twenty years? Corpses."

As the play progresses, moreover, our initial impulse to identify Manon negatively with her mother and Carmen more positively with her father becomes increasingly impossible. The mixture is more complex. Not only are Leopold and Marie-Lou equally at fault (as Carmen says), but the girls, too, share characteristics of both parents. Although she would like to resemble only her mother, it is emphasized that Manon has many likenesses to her father, spiritually as well as physically. (Tremblay says he spent most of his time creating this character.) And Carmen, too, has disconcerting touches of her mother—especially in her refusal to accept the fact of her father's suicide and in her open admission that she prefers to live in a dream world, if reality is unpleasant. As a character says in *Demain matin*, "You can take a girl out of the East, but you can't take the East out of the girl." An uncomfortable parallelism remains between Leopold's final decision, with its mixture of motives, and Carmen's departure to entertain in a bar like the one in which her father sat alone, drinking himself to insanity.

The play is a triumph of complex structure, and it is much too ambiguous for nationalists to equate Carmen with the emergence of the FLQ and an independent Quebec, as they have tried to do. Because of its basic humanity and its involving, sophisticated form, the play operates at a universal level. His aim, says Tremblay, is an "exorcisme collectif," a "thérapie de groupe." His at-

15. See Belair, *Michel Tremblay*, p. 75.

titude is compassion, not the "miserablisme" of which he has been accused, and he has no specific political intention. True, he was constantly stopped and searched by police during the FLQ crisis of 1970; but true, also, that he wept when he first saw *Marie-Lou* performed.

James Reaney's work is completely different from that of Tremblay. He is rural where Tremblay is urban, centrifugal where Tremblay is centripetal, comic where Tremblay is despairing. Reaney comes across like the offspring of Thornton Wilder and Grandma Moses, that is, as a very sophisticated primitivist whose concern is with the apocalypse of the ordinary. Like Wilder, he wants to show the mystical value and interconnectedness of ordinary living, to induce epiphanies and demonstrate (in his own phrase) that "everything is something." Basically he is a poet who on the stage makes verbal imagery visual within a complex frame of Jungian philosophy.

On the surface Reaney's life has been unspectacular. He was born in 1926 into a grimly evangelical family on a mortgaged farm outside Stratford, Ontario. He graduated from the University of Toronto, taught briefly at the University of Manitoba, returned to Toronto to work with Northrop Frye on a thesis about Spenser and Yeats, and then joined the English department of the University of Western Ontario, where he has been ever since, close to the farm where he was born. While still an undergraduate he began to win prizes for poems with a uniquely antipastoral, "gothic" vision of Ontario, in which innocence, creativity, sex, and childhood are shown as luridly perverted by provincialism. Later, under the influence of Frye and his own study of Spenser, Blake, and Yeats, he came to believe that art can transform such meanness by reinterpreting it in terms of human myth—Frye's mythopoeia. He founded a journal called *Alphabet* to explore this fusion of realism and imagination—which he calls "documentary" and "myth"

—and, while still winning prizes for poetry, began increasingly to experiment with children's theater, both for itself and for the effects it might have on adults (including himself) by putting them into the child's ambience of "play." Thematically, his preoccupation with ruined innocence swung to an exploration of whether a return to "childhood" could rewaken in adults their natural and mental creativity, setting the powers of sex and the word against society's sterility:

> And the darkness gave me
> Two boneless wands or swords:
> I knew not their meaning then
> Whether traps or rewards.
>
> One was the vorpal phallus
> Filled with jostling army,
> Henhouse and palace
> Street crowds and history.
>
> Two was the magic tongue
> Stuffed with names and numbers,
> The string of song,
> The waker from fallen slumbers.[16]

Childhood then, and man's development in relation to it, have become Reaney's central myth: "Babe and child represent perfectly sound objective symbols for a part of man's existence that does not, since he can be reborn, always coexist with the actual state of babyhood and childhood."[17] And he tries to discover a form of drama that will recover for adults the child's free sense of play:

> The one thing we never imitate enough is games, play . . . imitation itself. The instinct just to "have fun" . . .[18]

16. From *One-Man Masque*, in *The Killdeer and Other Plays* (Toronto: Macmillan, 1962), p. 176.
17. *Alphabet*, 2 (1961): 1.
18. "Production Notes," *Listen to the Wind* (Vancouver: Talonbooks, 1972), p. 117.

Children's games—all their activity—are potentially very important and perhaps much more worth watching than adult games and activities.[19]

I want a society where directing a play is not equated with the stage-managing, where the important rehearsal is not the technical rehearsal, where the lighting, costumes, all that money can buy disappear and what we have instead is so much group skill and sense of fun in imagining out things that richness reappears all over the place for nothing.[20]

At first Reaney could not find a suitable dramatic structure for this impulse, and his early plays take the form of elaborately symbolic yet deliberately childish melodramas. Gradually, however, influenced by collaboration on musical collages for radio and by a memorable Canadian visit of the Peking Opera, he has developed an increasingly plotless, mosaic structure in which the verbal imagery is replaced by "theatricalist" stage effects built around symbolic props. He describes how he developed this form at his Listeners' Workshop in an essay entitled "Ten Years at Play": "My latest theatre has been working on the Book of Genesis with no script, simply a list of images and turning points nailed up on a post where both the actors and myself go occasionally to see what is coming next . . . and a prop table filled with the things you need to put on Genesis with."[21]

This approach has led him to many techniques similar to those of Thornton Wilder. Journeys, for instance, are conveyed by chanting the names of the places passed through—a favorite Reaney device used twice in *Colours in the Dark*. Jane Crofut's address in *Our Town*, which begins with her name and ends with the universe (echoing, you will remember, Joyce's Stephen Dedalus), has its equivalent in the family-tree chant, on

19. *Alphabet*, 2 (1961): 1.
20. "Ten Years at Play," *Canadian Literature*, 41 (1969): 55.
21. Ibid., 53.

which Reaney plays variations throughout *Colours in the Dark*. To make one child, he says,

It takes
Two parents
Four grandparents
Eight great grandparents
Sixteen great great grandparents
Thirty-two great great great grandparents
Sixty-four great great great great grandparents
One hundred and twenty eight great great great great

and so on. This chant is laid out as a pyramid on the page, and on the stage it is chanted antiphonally. Most of all, Reaney tries to achieve the air of spontaneity, of creation right before the audience's eyes, that Wilder tries for (less successfully) in *The Skin of Our Teeth*. The beginning of *Colours in the Dark*, for instance, is a family party at which the family plays musical chairs, and each night of the performance it is a *real* game with both adult and child actors making a competition of it. And again as with Wilder, there is a profound philosophical purpose behind this stage immediacy, a belief that theater is itself an epiphany, a transfigured present ("In the theatre it is always now," says Wilder), whose unrealism relates it to universal themes and creates for performers and audience alike a "peaceable kingdom" where metaphor *is* reality ("A flower *is* a star," the children chant), where life imitates art.

Colours in the Dark is Reaney's most elaborate version of this free form, very difficult to analyze conceptually because of its theatricalism and fractured structure, and much less rewarding to read than to see. It has forty-two discrete scenes, each highly metaphorical, with an almost continuous musical and sound accompaniment. These scenes form a collage of selections from the playwright's own poetry of the previous twenty-five years, brought together for the Stratford Festival's 1967 centennial celebration in a mosaic form based on Paul Klee's painting *Magic Squares*. The patch work effect is represented on stage by a cross of independent movie screens on which different series of images are projected, while the cast of six actors, four singers, and a versatile chorus of children act out the episodes presentationally on the bare stage in front, with simple props and much doubling. In his introduction Reaney calls the work a "playbox" or "Christmas concert" in which there is a new play every two minutes, because, he says, "life could be an endless procession of stories, an endless coloured comic strip, things to listen to and look at, a bottomless play box."

Nonetheless, there *is* a structure and a thread of continuity in the scenes. In the opening birthday games, the blindfolded father is able to guess colors and explains that he learned how to do this as a child when he was kept in a dark room for forty days with his eyes bandaged to prevent damage from the measles. The rest of the scenes conjure up the memories not only of that child but of the grown man's subsequent experience, internalized into mythic form by blindness, memory, and childlike imagination, and ending with the removal of the blindfold as a symbolic rebirth. The sequence follows the events of Reaney's own career, as reflected in his successive books of poetry: encounters with nature and rural eccentrics on the Stratford farm of his childhood (including a funny sequence in which the schoolchildren are marshaled to watch the king of England go past in a train at sixty miles an hour); struggles against intellectual abstraction and skepticism at the University of Toronto; near-defeat in the winter provincialism of Winnipeg; increased revolt against the city squalor of Toronto on his return; but then marriage and escape and the happy birth of children; followed by a relapse into the morbidity of death consciousness, expressed in poems from his emblematic sequence *The Dance of Death in London, Ontario* and reflecting, perhaps, his feelings at the death of his own son; and finally a triumph over death manifested by the chorus of children in a game in which they deliberately attract the lightning—the inspiring danger of life, which is a sign of grace. The play ends with a final recitation of the family tree, now inverted so that, instead of the child widening out to his ancestors, the one thousand twenty-four great-great-great-great-great-great-great-great-grandparents now funnel down to just one child. The play's "backbone," Reaney tells us, is the myth "of a person growing up, leaving home, going to big cities, getting rather mixed up, and then not coming home again but making home and identity come to him."[22]

The hero's developing sensibility is traced by a recurrent "existence" poem, spread throughout the play in five stages. At first the child has a pure sense of everything's uniqueness:

Existence gives to me
What does he give to me
He gives to me   [*antiphon*]   a pebble
He gives to me   a dewdrop
He gives to me   a piece of string
He gives to me   a straw
      Pebble   dewdrop   piece of string   straw

Experience then darkens this vision; existence becomes a problem:

The pebble is a huge dark hill that I must climb
The dewdrop is a great storm lake that we must cross
The string is a road I cannot find
The straw is a sign whose meaning I forget.

Further experience seems utterly to obliterate the vision by encounters with the mysterious Tiger, Balloon, Prostitute of Snow, and Gorgeous Salesman. But Tiger turns out to be Christ, Balloon is Buddha, the Prostitute

22. "Production Notes," *Colours in the Dark*, p. 5.

of Snow is Emily Brontë, and Gorgeous Salesman the Emperor Solomon, "who sang of the foot in the doorway." So the childlike vision returns:

But love and patience do quite change the scene
Now the mountain becomes a pebble in my hand
The lake calms down   to a dewdrop in a flower
The weary road   to a string around your waist
The mysterious sign   is a straw that whistles home
Pebble   dewdrop   piece of string   straw

This kind of symbolism raises the sequence from mere autobiography to a more universal level. In a stage direction Reaney comments: "Dimly we realize that not only are we going through the hero's life and stories he has heard as a child, but we are going through Canada's story —glacier and forest, also the world's story." Specific Canadian history is mythologized into an Indian vision of storm-bearing sundogs chasing away the bear of winter; of maple trees driving out the firs; of the settlers' ships coming up the Saint Lawrence; of the Indian chief Tecumseh dying and crawling through a log to become his totem animal, the tortoise; of King George V whizzing past the children's Union Jacks in the heyday of the empire; and of the depersonalization that has come with industrialism and the growth of cities. This last element, however, is really more of a general condemnation of cities, typical of the 1960s, than a specifically Canadian comment, in spite of its local place names; and it is on this level that I feel the play works least well. The Canadian historical reference is only intermittent, and drops out completely before the end of the play.

On the other hand, the archetypal "world" level is much more successful. Jung's four characters, the crone, the wise old man, the young man questing, and the girl who is at once his protector and goal, are here divided among three generations to become the play's six principals: Gramp and Gram, Pa and Ma, and Son and Niece.[23] The multiple roles that each plays thus have always several levels of meaning. "Granny Crack," for instance, played by Gram, is an old beggar woman who terrorized the Stratford urchins during Reaney's childhood; she also represents the inevitability of personal aging and death, as realized by the growing boy; and at a further level she is Jung's crone—the threat of external nature as mirrored in our own minds. And reinforcing this sense of universality, the play moves through the seasons of the year from spring through summer, autumn, winter, and back to spring again, but with a curious hiatus just before the return to spring, when there is a brief reversion to Hallowe'en. A similarly interrupted cycle can be found in Reaney's earlier *One-Man Masque* and presumably represents the final trial before the paradisal goal.

Finally, and most obviously, the scenes are knit by the film projections into eight stages, each associated with a day of the week (from Sunday through Saturday to "Someday"), each with a plant, with letters of the alphabet (moving from A to Z), and with appropriate colors, flowers, and songs. It would be tedious to list all eight stages but one example will give an idea of the technique. Tuesday is orange, Mercury, midsummer, the lily, the songs "Beulah Land" and "Lillibullero," and the letters *F*, *G*, *H*, and *I*; it is the heyday of the empire spirit; and the boy is twelve, beginning to ponder life and death. There are scenes of the Orange parade of the Ulster settlers and of quarrels between children of Catholic and Protestant descent; the boy watches the king's absurd train ride through Stratford and writes a letter to his father about it; a song about Little Orphan Annie establishes his identification with the early-1930s

23. See Michael Tait, " 'Everything Is Something'; James Reaney's 'Colours in the Dark,' " in William H. New, ed., *Dramatists in Canada* (Vancouver: University of British Columbia Press, 1972), pp. 140–144.

radio serial; then, walking the roads with his father, the boy meets "Granny Crack" and is prompted to ask questions about life and death. This scene moves into a charming sequence set in the local country store in which a customer leaves (through the audience) with her parcel still tied to the store's big ball of string; they reel her back so slowly that they find only a skeleton at the end of the line; they then do it too fast and find she has reverted to a child. Finally, on his walk the boy reaches a bridge where a girl/swan makes him hesitate to cross; the pebble-dewdrop-string refrain returns to reflect a world grown problematical to him; the Bear (Gramp) and Lady of Death (Gram) seek to drag him back; and as the family pyramid forms, irregularly, to conclude Act I, it funnels down to a child, who, turning, exhibits the mask of Adolf Hitler, ushering in the troubled forties when the boy leaves home.

It is difficult to describe *Colours in the Dark*. It is a symbolic poem almost wholly translated into stage emblems (like the recent work of Robert Wilson in New York). Its essence lies in the suggestiveness of its particularity, and no summary can do justice to the charm, humor, and emotion of its individual scenes. The material is extremely local, even personal in some respects, but its significance and the organizing principles of the whole are profoundly and consciously universal.

In fact, *Colours in the Dark* was too universal for some of the Canadian theater critics, but, speaking as a nonCanadian (but also, I suppose, as an intellectual) I found the play luminously clear in production and utterly delightful—a genuinely life-enhancing experience.

Finally, we turn to George Ryga's *The Ecstasy of Rita Joe*, a tragedy of the North American Indian in which "international" form is made to reflect not only the confusion of the heroine, Rita Joe, but also the nonlinear thought processes of Indians in general.

Ryga himself is of Ukrainian Catholic origin, born in

1932 and raised on a marginal homestead in northern Alberta. After only seven years' schooling and a variety of laboring jobs, he began to write for radio and television and has been successful enough as a playwright to transport himself and his large family to the Okanagan Valley in British Columbia, where he now lives. Certain aspects of Ryga's drama, both thematic and formal, stem as clearly from his background as the plays of Tremblay and Reaney do from theirs.

Most obviously, there is a much stronger, more committed element of social criticism in Ryga's writing than in that of Tremblay and Reaney, a championing of the dispossessed, the workers, and the "stunted strong." It is an attitude skeptical of reform and far too radically individualistic to ally itself with any party platform; its ideals are, rather, family love and personal responsibility, a "parenthood" that rejects state welfare and mechanical charity. However, in the early plays it is complemented by a strong sense of man's unity with nature, so that although formal religion is eschewed (Ryga has lapsed from Catholicism), social protest is balanced against an almost mystical sense of tragic acceptance. The tension between these responses, one social, one quasi-religious, with their common denominator in personal relations, is at the very center of his drama.

The Ecstasy of Rita Joe reflects Ryga's outrage at the fact that some twenty Indian girls like Rita Joe perish each year in Vancouver alone, first prostituted, then killed, because white society will accept them only in the role of dependents. Although the form of the play is complex, the plot is very simple. Most of the play is taken up with the trial—or, rather, trials—of Rita Joe before a city magistrate for successive charges of vagrancy, prostitution, and theft. These overlapping trials are intercut with flashbacks and premonitions and also with ballads sung by a "white liberal folklorist" whom the stage directions describe as Rita Joe's "alter ego." Rita Joe remembers life on the reservation with her younger sister, Eileen, and her father, David Joe, who refused to sell her as a child, even for a thousand dollars; she recalls encounters with a succession of white authority figures, prefiguring her final encounters with the magistrate; and she remembers life in the city, where she was seduced by her employer, harassed by the police, and condescended to by the social worker. Too poor to settle down with her childhood sweetheart, Jaimie Paul, she stubbornly stayed on rather than return defeated to the reservation like her sister, Eileen. The spiral of degradation established by these memories and indictments is continually threaded by premonitions of the outcome: Jaimie Paul's murder in front of a railway train (based on an actual incident at Kamloops) and Rita Joe's own death in a rape-murder. And, moving out of the courtroom, the action concludes with an inner circle of Indians and an outer circle of whites left mourning the victims they have each in their different ways betrayed.

Ryga's major themes are easily traced in the play. The theme of inadequate "parenthood" is there in the magistrate's anecdote of a four-year-old Indian girl lost in the Cariboo, a vignette with rich implications. At a literal level, the child may perhaps be Rita Joe's own, as the magistrate suspects. The incident also reflects Rita Joe's unfulfilled desire for a family with Jaimie Paul, and, more profoundly, it reflects Rita Joe herself, lost in the white man's world, and, beyond her, the childlike Indians in general. The anecdote also relates to an incident in which Rita Joe and her sister were lost in the bush as children and Rita Joe had to act prematurely like a grown-up; it also reflects her favorite story of how, when she was four years old, her father refused to sell her—unlike another Indian, Clara Hill, who gives her children away to welfare agencies, as the magistrate advises Rita Joe to do.

For David Joe children are life itself ("You never forget you are alive with children"), but he is inadequate to meet the contemporary demand for Indians to change, "scared" before the demand to adapt so completely. The surrogate parents with whom society replaces him do not care personally enough: the kindly but ineffectual priest; the prudish schoolmarm; and the settlement worker, Mr. Homer, who, like all Ryga's welfare agents, is contemptuous of the people he assists, wanting, as Jaimie Paul points out, to keep them as subservient children. Finally, the benevolent magistrate of the play, with "all the rambling confidence of the detached authority," forgets his vision of the lost Indian child in disgust with the lost woman, until his questions about venereal disease become merely an excuse for isolating her further. Like the sweeper from Tom-all-Alone's in *Bleak House*, the Indians are society's guilt which may strike back as disease, in the fear of which all compassion for them disappears.

However, the play is not merely a simple tract about the mistreatment of Indians. Their own limitations are recognized too. Ryga's rival standards of nature mysticism and social reform occur in the conflict between David Joe and Jaimie Paul, the one standing for the "old stories" of family love and sympathy with nature which he knows no longer assure survival, the other, with his scheme for an Indian berry industry denied, wasting his energy on assertive brawls and gestures of defiance, the farcical nature of which Ryga carefully emphasizes. The element of "Red Power" was expanded by Ryga in revision so that, at the end of the later version of the play, the younger Indians in the inner mourning circle "rise one after another facing the outer [white] circle defiantly." However, although this movement adds an interesting complication to the conclusion, it is not in this that the final statement of the play is to be found.

The strongest final impression is of the heroine's personal integrity. All the false guardians are more concerned with rules than persons ("You got rules here that was made before I was born," says Rita Joe), and their advice is always to conform ("There is no peace in being extraordinary," "There is nothing special here," "We are a melting pot"). Both Eileen Joe and Clara Hill, with whom Rita Joe is implicitly compared, conform in their different ways, but Rita Joe will not, although her integrity is fatal. Rather than surrender her "child," she tells the magistrate, she will kill it; and toward the end she deliberately allows herself to be caught for stealing. It is this state of mind that explains the "ecstasy" of the play's title. As with the heroes of Genet, authenticity for Rita Joe entails self-destruction,[24] so that in a perverse way her rape and death are the "ecstasy" of a martyr, and, despite disaster, the last act can be subtitled "Survival."

This twist of values overlaps interestingly with aspects of the form. As in Reaney and, more particularly, Tremblay, the structure of the play is circular and repetitive. The several trials of Rita Joe are intermingled until they all seem the same trial, recurrent throughout Act I and recapitulated, with an almost musical effect, in the penultimate scene of Act II. Similarly, the climactic rape and deaths are heralded from the first, and this circularity is emphasized by the circular ramps of the playing area (and further by the staging of the original production). Linearly, events are linked by Rita Joe's memory and emotional associations; their causal relations become clear only through repetition, like the development of a theme in music. Often the normal sequence of cause and effect is reversed to delay this understanding; thus we learn that Rita Joe let herself be caught stealing a sweater before we see the scene in which Jaimie Paul advocates the theft, forbidding her to accept a charity sweater from Mr. Homer; or, more subtly, Rita Joe con-

---

24. Cf. Lionel Trilling, "Violent meanings . . . are explicit in the Greek ancestry of the word 'authentic' . . . *Authentes:* not only a master and a doer, but also a perpetrator, a murderer, even a self-murderer, a suicide" (*Sincerity and Authenticity* [Cambridge: Harvard University Press, 1972], p. 131).

veys her lost happiness by a dream of children chasing chocolate paper, and only later do we see Jaimie give her chocolate in a scene in which she realizes they cannot afford to start the family she longs for. The play as a whole has a similar movement, from the bewilderingly intercut memories, premonitions, and clues of Act I to the relatively simpler selection of subsequent events in Act II. The effect is of a slowly clarifying gestalt, with the gradual falling of pieces into place creating a sense of inevitability and universality.

The form of the play differs from that of Tremblay in two main ways, however. First, in *The Ecstasy of Rita Joe* the form is far more closely keyed to the state of mind of its protagonist. There are a few touches of Brechtian distancing: the "workmanlike and untheatrical" entrance and exit of the cast while the house lights are still on, for example, and two occasions when the audience is blamed directly for the Indians' plight. But outweighing such techniques of "alienation" is a much more thorough attempt to draw the audience into Rita Joe's thought processes, to make it share in the confusion of a mind where the past is more real than the present, which has the unreality of a nightmare because of hunger and exhaustion. Lighting effects establish the rapid flow of a feverish stream of consciousness, and the stage directions refer constantly to "memory," "reverie," "dream," and "mood" as keys to the sequence of events. Moreover, it is several times emphasized that such thinking is also typical of the intuitive Indian mind, which communicates by fragments of reminiscence and imitation, not by abstract concepts—as in David Joe's stories of the geese and dragonfly or in Jaimie Paul's comic mimes of Mr. Homer's incompetence in a canoe.

The final effect is deepened further by Ryga's second major difference from the other playwrights we have considered. "International" form is combined in *The Ecstasy of Rita Joe* with a much older ballad tradition. The effect of this combination is complex because the ballad influence functions on two levels at once, an inadequate level and a true one. The inadequate level is the singing of Rita Joe's "alter ego," "a white liberal folklorist with a limited concern and understanding of the ethnic dilemma" whose sentimentally cynical ballads are meant to contrast with, as much as to complement, the emotions of the heroine. The cynicism is seen most clearly in the conflict over the fate of Jaimie Paul, when Rita Joe's stubborn optimism is countered by the singer's uncritical balladic assumption that he is doomed. The sentimentality becomes blatant at the end of the play when the singer's description of Rita Joe's death as the flight of a bird that has found its wings is deflated by Eileen Joe's comment, "When Rita Joe first come to the city—she told me . . . the cement made her feet hurt."

Beyond the use of inset songs, however, is a truer, more general influence of ballad technique. This influence can be found in the play's anecdotal sense of character, which does not explore motivation but builds up a "myth" of personality by accumulating characteristic incidents; similarly, its method of narration focuses on typical events without bothering to tell the whole story, and it adopts the ballad's use of emotional analogy, which conveys the feeling of a scene obliquely by referring to anecdotes or vignettes not otherwise related to the main action. Most important of all, there is a balladic sense of destiny, the compression of social realism into a pattern of fate in which disaster is offset by the recognition of human dignity *in extremis*.

Because of these ballad influences the final impression of *The Ecstasy of Rita Joe* is not as pessimistic as that of *Forever Yours, Marie-Lou*, although the content is equally sordid and the structure has the same circular inevitability. The lack of pessimism is not to be traced to the final gesture of "Red Power" as much as to the integrity of the heroine's sensibility, presented in a form that reflects and thus confirms it. The pattern is finished and inevitable, but it does not convey the impression of a totally closed world because the form here embodies the heroine's integrity equally with her fate.

Tremblay, Reaney, and Ryga, then, use local—even personal—material in the "international" form, although their structures differ widely and serve quite different ends. It would be possible to examine similar experiments in Herschel Hardin's *Esker Mike and His Wife Agiluk*, which tries to trace the rhythms of Eskimo thought, or in such "group creations" as *The Farm Show* or the theatrical anthology of the depression, *Ten Lost Years*. There is no longer any question that there is a Canadian drama quantitatively; it has caught up with Canadian poetry and fiction in this respect. Inevitably much of the work is weak, as is true of drama in all countries; and its involvement with Canadian nationalism has had very ambiguous results. Nevertheless, an increasing number of Canadian plays are interesting to read and, especially, to see. In my opinion, the best of these combine local subject matter with various experiments in spatial form. Whether we define this as "universal" or merely "international," one thing about the plays is certain. Their combination of intense particularity with a sense of arbitrary pattern is typically Canadian.

VII

Quebec Literature in Its American Context

Marine Leland

The literary critic Desmond Pacey defined a Canadian as "one who is increasingly aware of being American in the *continental* sense without being American in the *national* one." It is in this continental sense, in the sense of the Americas, north and south, above and below the equator, that I am using the term "American." By viewing the development of French Canadian literature, or Quebec literature as it is increasingly called, in relation to the evolution of other American literatures, which also stem from Europe, my purpose is to place it in its proper perspective.

Notwithstanding the profound and striking individual characteristics—geographic, racial, historical, religious, and political—which distinguish the countries of this hemisphere from one another, they have a great deal in common that is basic. All of them have a colonial past. All were originally extensions of one of four great European colonizing nations, Spain, Portugal, France, and England, which, in the sixteenth and early seventeenth centuries, transplanted to the Americas their language, religions, laws, and systems of education as well as the cultural and literary ideas and ideals which education fosters. In the course of the colonial period these European roots sank so deep in American soil that, although they were gradually modified, neither time nor revolutions nor conquest destroyed them.

In the second half of the eighteenth century and in the early nineteenth, the American colonies shared another experience, that of being separated from their mother country. In all cases except that of New France and Brazil, this separation was effected through revolutions and resulted in independence. Brazil evolved into independence. As for the French colony, it had been separated from France by the Peace of Paris in 1763, when it became a British colony. Yet, in spite of the profound difference in the manner in which these separations from the mother country took place, the cultural mold in which France had set its American colony turned out to be as lasting as the patterns imprinted by Portugal, Spain, and England on their colonies proved to be durable after these territories became independent.

Thus, viewed in its American context, the preservation by French Canadians of their cultural traditions and the steady development of an individual civilization based on these traditions are normal phenomena, typical of all American civilizations. What *is* remarkable about Quebec is that these normal phenomena, notably the existence and growth of an indigenous literature, occurred under exceptional circumstances. The Mexican writer Octavio Paz has remarked that "colonial society was an order built to endure." Quebec's civilization provides impressive proof of the truth of this statement.

The history of every American literature is an account of the long and arduous struggles of the American writer to define the identity, the self, of the people to which he belongs, and to portray the unique character of his country. The struggle began very early in the colonial period. Its starting point was the colonists' awareness that the New World created a new type of Englishman, Frenchman, Portuguese, and Spaniard.

What we find in early American writings is the affirmation of the colonists' identity in contradistinction to the identity of the inhabitants of the mother country, whichever it might be. While this affirmation certainly does not imply disloyalty on the part of the writer, it is accompanied, more often than not, by a jubilant statement to the effect that everything in that part of the New World which he calls home is as good as in the mother country—unless, of course, it is better. Very early in the seventeenth century a Mexican writer described Mexico City as superior in every way to Madrid. A few years later, in 1627, Brother Vincente do Salvador, who was born in Bahía, produced a *History of Brazil* in which he criticized Portugal and affirmed his love for his native land.

One of the finest examples of what may be termed "incipient nationalism" is Pierre Boucher's little book *Histoire véritable et naturelle des moeurs et productions de la Nouvelle France vulgairement dite Canada* [A true and natural history of the customs and products of New France commonly called Canada]. Printed in 1664, this is the first Canadian book. As its title indicates clearly, it is not a literary work. Pierre Boucher, the founder and seigneur of Boucherville across the Saint Lawrence from Montreal, was a plain man, a self-made man of the New World, with no literary aspirations whatsoever. He had come to Canada with his family (farmers from Normandy) in 1634 when he was twelve years old. Intelligent, courageous, able, and honest, he was to earn for himself, in the course of the next twenty-five years, the confidence and respect of his fellow colonists and of the administration. In 1661, when the news reached Canada that the young king, Louis XIV, had formally assumed power, Pierre Boucher was governor of Three Rivers. M. d'Avaugour, governor of New France, chose him to go to France to ask the king for military aid in fighting the Iroquois and to explain to him and his ministers the crucial need for more colonists.

During his sojourn in France, Boucher was struck by the general ignorance of Canada which prevailed. Far from humiliating him, it had amused him and, on occasion, excited his scorn. It had also made him realize, as nothing else could have done, the *identity* (as we say today) of Canada, an identity distinct from that of France although like it in many ways, an identity which resulted from the blend of the old and the new, of Europe and America. A loyal Frenchman, Boucher was also essentially an American, a Canadian. In his eyes, everything in New France was as good as in old France —except when it was better.

When he returned to his modest home in Three Rivers, he wrote a handbook that would provide future colonists with useful, practical information regarding New France. His picture of Canada is realistic, not idealized. His avowed aim was to attract only good sturdy colonists, people who, like his family and himself, were willing to face hardship and to work for what they were sure to get *if* they worked. And he stuck to his resolve. He lists conscientiously and describes faithfully the dangers, the hardships which awaited the future colonists: the wily, ferocious, and ever-lurking Iroquois, the myriads of black flies and mosquitoes in summer, the long, bitter-cold winters. Even so, on practically every page of his businesslike and most valuable report we find expressions of the national spirit which was to be expressed much later in both French and English Canadian literatures.

"It is true," he writes, "that the winters in Canada are long and extremely cold, and that there is a great deal of snow. But the cold here is gay, and the snow is less troublesome than the mud in France. Besides, the air here is extremely healthy at all times, but particularly in winter. Sickness is seldom seen in this country."

Always intent on giving an unadorned picture of Canada, Boucher reverts to some of its less attractive aspects, and it is precisely here that his love for it is most movingly expressed. "It is true," he admits again, "that there is something forbidding in the aspect of the approaches to this country called New France, for the sight of the Island of Newfoundland, on which is Placentia, of Saint Pierre Island, of Cape Ray, of Saint Paul Island, and of the mainland at the entrance of the Gulf of Saint Lawrence (the land that God gave to Cain), inspires terror and an inclination to keep away from Canada rather than a desire to come and live in it. Therefore, I am not surprised that this country was so long without inhabitants. Yet, I can assure you that there are few of those who have settled here, who have any intention of returning to France, unless called there by affairs of *the greatest* importance; so true it is that New France has something attractive for those who know how to appreciate its delights."

The difference in character, social attitudes, social mobility, and general outlook which distinguished the inhabitants of the New World from those of the Old never failed to surprise Europeans, either agreeably or otherwise. What impressed them most in the colonists was their individual spirit of freedom as well as the egalitarian attitude it engendered, which in turn led to a deplorable disregard for the established rules which governed the European social hierarchies. In 1576 a Spanish woman was deeply shocked when her own brother, Lorenzo de Cépeda, who had made a large fortune in Ecuador, returned to Spain, and, as she writes, "allowed himself to be called 'Don' as it was the custom to call him in America." In 1720 the Jesuit Charlevoix observed that the Canadians breathe from birth "the air of freedom and this makes them very agreeable in social intercourse." He also noted, "Rusticity, whether in manners or language, is unknown there even in the most remote settlements." But he adds that this air of freedom which the Canadians breathed from birth made them very poor servants, as each of them was convinced that he was the equal of everyone—a little "more equal" as we say today.

Almost forty years later, in 1757, Bougainville, who was far less well disposed toward the Canadians than Charlevoix had been and who, as an officer, had been constantly irked by the "caractère indiscipliné" of his men, was nevertheless favorably impressed by at least one aspect of the egalitarian attitude which distinguished Canadian society from that of France. "The simple *habitans* [settlers]," he reported in one of his memoranda to the home government, "would be insulted if they were to be called peasants. As a matter of fact, they are of better stuff, brighter and better educated than the peasants of France." This, he explains, is because the *settlers* "pay no taxes, . . . have the right to hunt and fish wherever they please and . . . live in a kind of independence."

I have mentioned only the most striking traits of the American identity. There were others less readily discernible today. A number of these were peculiar to the individual colonies and represented, in greater or lesser degree, modifications of the characteristics of the mother countries.

Despite the colonists' awareness of their distinctive identity and notwithstanding the satisfaction and the pride which their country excited in them, few if any serious attempts appear to have been made anywhere in the Americas during the colonial period to express these feelings in literature. The reasons for this general reticence have been stated time and again, in virtually identical terms, in histories of the American literatures whatever their language. The gigantic undertaking, we are told in English, French, Portuguese, and Spanish, of opening up a continent to civilization, the back-breaking, the sinew-straining task of hewing down the forest primeval or the jungle, as the case may be, and the endless contest with the Indians who inhabited these, absorbed the colonists' energy and left them neither strength nor time to produce literature of their own.

"Under the French regime," wrote Camille Roy in 1939 in his *Manuel d'histoire de la littérature canadienne de langue française*, "the laborious colonization of our vast regions, the arduous process of setting up our economic organization, the almost incessant warfare with the Indians and with our New England neighbors used up all the resources of our activity. Add to this that the absence of a printing press during the entire French regime could only contribute to the delay of a literary production." Champlain's *Voyages*, the *Letters* of Mère Marie de l'Incarnation, the *Jesuit Relations*, Pierre Boucher's *Histoire véritable et naturelle* and many other works were printed in France.

While the printing press was also absent from Brazil, it was not lacking in most of the Spanish colonies. In Mexico a printing press was established in 1533, less than fifteen years after Cortez had settled in Mexico City. In New England the printer Stephen Day opened his shop in Cambridge in 1639, within twenty years of the Pilgrims' landing at Plymouth. Even where printing presses existed, however, there is little evidence that educated colonists seriously tried (much less succeeded) to express in a literary form the special identity of the colony in which they had been born, where they were living and which they so deeply loved.

Another important reason is also generally invoked to explain the absence of Americanism in the American colonial literatures. This reason lies in the European systems of education which had been transplanted here. Trained in a European intellectual atmosphere, educated Americans were grounded in the classics and imbued with the literary ideas and standards of Europe. American writers sought with meritorious zeal to emulate the writers of the mother country.

"Our ancestors," wrote Walter C. Bronson in *A Short History of American* [U.S.] *Literature*, "imported poetry, essays and novels from England just as they imported fine fabrics and other luxuries." He adds, "Next to the inferiority of American literature, the most conspicuous fact is the imitation of English models. Throughout its whole course it runs parallel with the literature in the mother country, although usually lagging about a generation behind. In America as in England, the heavy prose of the seventeenth century is succeeded by lighter and more orderly prose in the eighteenth. The 'metaphysical' poetry of the Jacobean and Caroline periods is solemnly echoed from the rocky New England coast. The didactic and satiric verse of Dryden and Pope feathers the shaft of the American satirist in regions which not long before knew only the whiz of the Indian's arrow." Bronson's observations on the literary tastes of the cultivated New England colonists apply to the same class of readers in Portuguese and Spanish America and in New France.

In 1646 Father Germain, a professor at the Jesuit college which had been founded in Quebec eleven years earlier, wrote in the *Jesuit Relations*, "Everything is done here as it is done in our houses in France." As a result, the very few and very short samples of literary efforts which have come down to us (in manuscript, naturally) show the influence of writers in France. In other words, Americans everywhere were conscious of their special identity except as writers or cultivated readers. In these respects, they were still Europeans.

The revolutions of the late eighteenth and early nineteenth centuries changed all that. In the thirteen colonies and in Spanish America the prolonged and bitter struggle for independence produced in the colonists an aggressive realization of their identity and a burning desire to express this identity in a literature which not only would reflect it but would affirm and demonstrate its distinctness from that of the former mother country and thus complete the political independence they had just achieved. "The United States must be as independent in literature as they are in politics," declared Noah Webster. In his 1955 study *The Literary Emancipation of Mexico*, the Mexican critic José Luis Martínez not only mentions the efforts of Mexican, Chilean, Venezuelan, and Peruvian writers to bring about the literary independence of these countries and to de-Hispanicize their literatures, but also stresses that these efforts assumed at times the form of a collective and dynamic movement which embraced almost all of Spanish America. "In Spanish America," he writes, "no subsequent undertaking was ever to attain the power and the drive of this struggle to conquer our literary emancipation."

The birth of French Canadian literature was not accompanied by such fireworks nor was its subsequent development. In Canada the separation from France was marked by grief, dismay, and exhaustion, not by anger. Other factors also account for the calm with which the transition from the French to the English regime took place. Two and a half years were to elapse between the departure of the French army after the fall of Montreal in 1760 and the signing of the Treaty of Paris in February 1763. During those years the ultimate fate of Canada remained in doubt, and the British government forbore making radical changes in the institutions of a colony which might be returned to France. Another factor was the humanity of the military governor, James Murray. Hence, when the terrible news of the definitive transfer of the French colony to Great Britain reached Quebec in May 1763, the blow was somewhat softened by the reassuring experience of the preceding two and a half years. However, this relative peace of mind was to be shattered within the next few months. The royal proclamation of September 7, 1763, made it clear that the government in London fully intended to lose no time in transforming the former French colony into an English one. It abolished the French criminal and civil laws and replaced them with those of England. The change in the criminal laws was accepted without murmur, but the abolition of French civil laws, including, of course, the property laws, not only aroused the French Canadians' fears and indignation, but also excited the indignation of jurists in England, notably that of William Murray, Lord Mansfield, chief justice of the King's Bench. "Is it possible," he wrote to Lord Grenville, secretary of state, "that we have abolished all [the Canadians'] laws and customs and forms of judicature all at once?—a thing never to be attempted or wished. For God's sake learn the truth of the case, and think of a speedy remedy." These feelings were shared by Governor Murray as they were to be by his successor, Sir Guy Carleton. The battle lasted a decade. We shall return to it briefly.

In 1764 many among the Canadian seigneurs who had left Canada in 1760 with their French regiments, as well as other members of the Canadian upper classes who had gone to France in 1763 (a number of them to settle their affairs with their French business associates), were beginning to return to Canada. Thus, contrary to what has been stated both long before and long after Parkman, "the peasants and poorer colonists" were not "left alone to begin a new life under a new flag."

In 1764 also a printing press was established in Quebec, and on June 21 of that year a weekly newspaper began to appear. Although privately owned, it was used by the government for the publication of its proclamations and other official notices. As the population was more than 99 percent French-speaking, *The Quebec Gazette/La Gazette de Québec* was bilingual. Its owners-editors, William Brown and Thomas Gilmore, encouraged their readers to submit for publication essays and poems in English or French. These invitations were accepted. For the first time in their history, *Canadien* would-be writers enjoyed the experience of seeing themselves in print, and their readers had the pleasure of perusing a newspaper on the day it was published.

In 1766 Governor Murray was recalled to England and Sir Guy Carleton was appointed lieutenant governor with special instructions to look forthwith into the matter of the civil laws. On December 24, 1767, Carleton wrote Lord Shelburn, the then secretary of state,

> To conceive of the true State of the people of This Province, so far as the Laws and Administration of Justice are concerned, and the Sensations they must feel, in their present situation, it is necessary to re-collect, they are not a Migration of Britons, who brought with them the Laws of England, but a Pop-ulous and long established Colony, reduced by the King's Arms to submit to his Dominion on certain conditions: That their Laws and customs were widely Different from those of England, but founded on Natural Justice and Equity as well as these. . . . All these arrangements, in One Hour were overthrown . . . and Laws ill-adapted to the Genius of the Cana-dians, to the Situation of the Province, and to the Interests of Great Britain, unknown and unpublished, were introduced in their stead; a sort of Severity, if I remember right, never before practiced by any Con-queror.

And the struggle went on.

Today, with the wisdom of hindsight, the ill-advised attempt to abolish the French civil laws may be viewed as a blessing in disguise for the French Canadians. It led to the passing in 1774 of the Quebec Act which rein-stated French civil laws. These are still the civil laws of the Province of Quebec. In other words, within eleven years of the Treaty of Paris, the ethnic and cultural identity of the French Canadians was officially recog-nized. Seventeen years later, the Constitutional Act of 1791 reinforced this basis immeasurably by the establish-ment of a House of Assembly, thus enabling the French-speaking majority to play a normal role in the affairs of the province in the very city where the French Canadian traditions had originally taken root.

Like other American colonists, the *Canadiens* had a strong sense of their own identity, a sense that is at the root of any national literature. However, a national literature cannot be created, let alone grow, in a political vacuum. For the French Canadians, this void was filled by the Quebec Act, their Magna Carta, and by the Constitutional Act of 1791.

Although a number of French-language newspapers came into being early in the nineteenth century, it is generally agreed that French Canadian literature began in the 1830s. In the course of its development it met with precisely the same difficulties and problems that the literatures of Latin America and of the United States encountered in theirs.

The revolutionary spirit which had achieved the political independence of the English and the Spanish colonies did not manifest itself in the cultural field. Education was untouched by it, and as a result postrevolutionary writers persisted both in their traditional adherence to the thought of the mother country and in their servile imitation of its literature as if nothing had happened.

In 1837 Ralph Waldo Emerson referred indirectly to the content of United States education in *The American Scholar:* "The millions that around us are rushing into life," he declared, "cannot always be fed on the sere remains of foreign harvests . . . We have listened too long to the courtly Muses of Europe . . . The spirit of the American free man is already suspected to be timid, imitative and tame." Just as Emerson deplored the overwhelming influence of the past on the thought and literature of the United States, Spanish Americans bewailed its enduring authority in the intellectual and social fields. In 1847 in Chile, Victorino Lastarria declared with sorrow, and with anger as well, "The despotism of kings has fallen; but the despotism of the past still stands in all its vigor." Like Emerson and many other writers in the

United States, Spanish American writers were determined to de-Europeanize their respective literatures.

Early French Canadian writers were free both from this hatred of the mother country and from any impatience with the persistent sway which their French past exercised over their thinking. With regard to France, they expressed feelings of nostalgia. Moreover, isolated as they were on the American continent, educated French Canadians not only welcomed but sought every opportunity to keep in touch with the intellectual and literary activities of France. Toward England they felt no animosity; their attitude as expressed in early writings is one of sincere respect and trust.

Hatred, on the rare occasions on which it appears, is expressed with singular moderation and is aroused either by the age-old adversaries across the border or by the enemies within Canada, English Canadians, whose avowed aim is to deprive their French-speaking fellow citizens of their rights. Fortunately, England is watching over these. "Albion veille sur tes droits . . . Respecte la main protectrice d'Albion, ton digne soutien," counsels a would-be French Canadian poet in 1829.

The theme which recurs constantly in early French Canadian writings is love for Canada. What is most striking about these declarations is that they are never accompanied by the aggressiveness which so often denotes a lack of self-confidence. The French Canadian writer is so sure that Canada is his *patrie*, that he belongs to it as it belongs to him, that he takes his attitude toward it for granted and therefore experiences no need to express his feelings stridently. For France, his affection is deep. It is the country from which his ancestors came and to which he owes the traditions which have become his own. England, under whose rule he is destined to live, he respects and trusts. But both France and England are foreign countries. *La patrie* is Canada, first and last.

"Avant tout, je suis Canadien," sang an anonymous

poète d'occasion in 1832. To him, as well as to his audience, this affirmation is so self-evident that he can afford to be humorous about it. In fact, he adapted his words to a tune entitled "La pipe de tabac." France and Spain, he sang merrily, have their wines, Italy its cloudless skies, England its admirable laws and constitution. Europe produces daily masterpieces in all fields. "Should Canada," he asks, "not recognize the Old World's superiority?" The reply is a firm No.

In carrying out this grand design of producing an original literature which would rival that of the Old World in beauty and yet reflect the special and original identity of the New, French Canadian writers were faced with the same literary problems as those which harried writers everywhere in the Americas. Among these difficulties, two are basic: lack of technique and, paradoxically, in view of the goal which Americans desired most ardently to attain, lack of originality.

Regarding the first, little need be said. Barring the accident of genius or extraordinary literary talent (and in these respects, the Americans were not accident-prone), every poet, novelist, and playwright has to master the rules of his art, and, above all, he must have experience. In short, he needs a certain amount of leisure. He also needs the encouragement of writing in an atmosphere in which his efforts to write are recognized for what they are—work—and one in which his writings are accepted as valid and, better still, as valuable contributions to the progress of the society of which he is a part.

In the Americas, early and not-so-early poets, novelists, and writers found neither the leisure they required to become professionals rather than remaining amateurs nor the acceptance by their fellow-citizens of the validity, the respectability, of their chosen calling.

In 1825 Thomas Jefferson, who like Noah Webster had believed that an independent literature would soon follow political independence, admitted ruefully that conditions in the United States did not favor American writers. "Literature is not yet a distinct profession with us," he remarked in a letter to a friend. "Now and then a strong mind arises, and at its intervals of leisure from business, emits a flash of light. But the first object of young societies is bread and covering; science [i.e., study] is but secondary and subsequent."

In the Province of Quebec not so long ago the rejection of the writer by a philistine society used to be summed up in the saying, "Ce jeune homme ne fait rien, il écrit." If the "jeune homme" in question was poor (and he often was), he soon found himself obliged to give up his chosen calling and to "do something," that is, "work," in the accepted and acceptable meaning of this verb, "earn one's living." This situation accounts in very large measure for the amateurish character of much of French Canadian literature. Until the 1930s, a great many writers in Quebec, perhaps the majority, were "one-book" authors, and this one book was usually written when its author was young, dedicated, often gifted, and always inexperienced.

The second difficulty which retarded for many, many years the progress of every American literature is closely connected with the first, but it is far more fundamental: lack of originality, the inability to see, to discern, and to capture what was characteristic, typical, distinctive—original, in a word—about the American scene in its various aspects, natural and human, and to depict these in a style which would give readers at home and abroad a vivid sense of the identity of the New World.

Some thirty years ago the French Canadian writer François Hertel analyzed this problem which still besets some of the "new literatures" on the American continent as elsewhere. "French Canadian literature, observed Hertel in *Le Beau Risque* [The splendid risk], "is often reproached for having no style. The reason for this is that we *don't see*. We don't dare to allow ourselves to see the reality which surrounds us, and to conform to what it presents. We look with old, bookish, *French* eyes at things which we should sense through every pore of our Canadian flesh."

In the nineteenth century American critics everywhere recognized this lack of originality in the literature with which they were individually concerned. A few even wondered "whether the muses, like the nightingales, are too delicate to cross the salt water, or sicken and mope without song if they do." Many attributed this lack of originality to the persistent intellectual and literary hold of the mother country on its former colony. For others, the failure of their poets, novelists, and playwrights to produce vigorous, original, and truly American works was due to their writing, perforce, in the language of the mother country, a European language unsuited to the expression of American feelings or to descriptions of the American scene. Everyone was aware, of course, that this European language, whichever it might be, had been modified by the American environment and that, as a spoken language, not only had it acquired new words, but, far more important, it had undergone a number of changes in accent, intonation, and rhythm. Yet this awareness and the "linguistic nationalism" which it produced in the United States, in Latin America, and in Canada were not sufficiently widespread to affect the written language, which, unlike the spoken language, had not changed. As in all countries with a colonial past, the literary language, which imitated the literary language of the mother country, was proving ineffectual in expressing the national identity or even in describing American landscapes.

In desperation, certain critics, such as Walter Channing (who surmised that "a national literature is the legitimate product of a national language") went so far as to state that, since the language of England was too "enfeebled by excessive cultivation" to do justice to the vigor of the American spirit and to the grandeur of the American scene, writers in the United States should revert to the "language of the Indian." The "language of the Indian," Channing argued in 1815, "is elevated and soaring, for his image is the eagle; precipitous and hoarse as the cataracts among whose mists he is descanting," whereas English is so "tame" that it is suited to describe only "the falls at London Bridge or the Thames River," not Niagara Falls or the Mississippi.

A half-century later a French Canadian poet, Octave Crémazie, expressed the same idea. He had certainly not read Channing, and he knew as little about Indian languages as Channing did, but he was filled with the same pessimism regarding the possibility of producing an original literature in the language of the former mother country, and he offered the same solution. "The more I meditate on the destiny of French Canadian literature," he wrote in 1867, "the less I think it has a chance of leaving any trace in history. What Canada lacks is a language of its own. If we spoke Iroquois or Huron, our literature would survive. Written in one or the other of these virile and vigorous languages which were born in the forests of America, our poetry would be steeped in an authentic atmosphere, and the productions of our writers would attract the attention of the Old World. Unfortunately . . . we write, and rather poorly, it must be admitted, in the language of Bossuet and Racine. Whatever we may say or do, and even though Canada should become, someday, independent, we shall remain nonetheless, simple literary colonists."

Fortunately, time was to prove that such pessimism was not justified. American writers have succeeded in communicating—in English, French, Portuguese, and Spanish—their American origin and originality, without resorting to the radical means suggested by Channing and Crémazie in a spirit of despondency rather than as a practical solution. Nevertheless, the belief that "a national literature is the legitimate product of a national language" is anything but a dead issue in several parts of this continent. In 1949 César Garrizurieta delivered a lecture in Mexico City in which he affirmed, much to the displeasure of some members of his cultured audience, "It is imperative that we fight for the conquest of our literary independence." This literary independence could be achieved, he argued, only "If the popular language, the Mexican vernacular, with all its wealth of expressions and nuances, is the basis of the national linguistic wealth." In 1952 Santiago G. Flores asked in his *Introduction to Mexican and Ibero-American Literature*, "Is there a Mexican literature which is not a reflection of Spanish literature?" His reply reminds us of the ideas expressed by Channing and Crémazie. "Yes," he said, "as far as we can judge from the translations of Indigenous poetry," that is, the poetry of the Aztecs. As for Mexican poetry written in Spanish, he observed that "Spanish as spoken in Castile is energetic and has a special accent and pronunciation, none of which is suited to Mexican poetry."

In Quebec, discussions and polemics have been going on almost continuously for over one hundred years on the subject of which language, the French spoken in France ("universal French") or the French spoken in Canada, should be used in literature. In a lecture delivered at the University of Montreal in 1964, "Les grandes options de la littérature canadienne-française," Professor David Hayne of the University of Toronto gave an overall view of these discussions. I shall here mention only a few of the opinions expressed by French Canadian writers, critics, and scholars.

"The French language exists," affirmed Marcel Dugas in 1929; "there is *no* French Canadian language." That same year (1929 was marked by epic exchanges of opinions on the subject) the French Canadian novelist Harry Bernard declared, "Everybody's French language is *not* our language." This view was echoed by the excellent critic Albert Pelletier: "Parisian French is not our language."

In 1933 Claude-Henri Grignon, the author of *Un Homme et son péché*, warned with characteristic pungency, "If we persist in writing in a language which is spoken fluently by French writers, we shall never succeed in producing books that are superior to theirs, and no one on earth will read our works whether they are about the soil or not."

In 1953 Professor Roch Valin of Laval University, whose field is linguistics, denounced as "narrowly chauvinistic, presumptuous, childish, and suicidal" the very idea of comparing French and French Canadian. Three years later Professor René de Chantal of the University of Montreal tried to pour oil on these turbulent waters: "Our French Canadian speech would enliven our regional literature, but the books of international significance . . . will be written in French."

So much for the trials and tribulations which attended the creation of national literatures in the Americas. I turn now, for a moment, to the path which these literatures followed in the nineteenth century, namely, to the enormous influence which romanticism exerted on their progress.

In the Latin countries of Europe, especially in France, romanticism was a revolution against the outworn classical tradition. "Le romantisme," proclaimed Victor Hugo, "c'est la Révolution dans la littérature." This is not the character which it assumed in the Americas. On this side of the Atlantic, romanticism, with its predilection for nature, local color, national history, Indians, legends, folklore, and the expression of personal and national feelings, was a God-given gift. It gave the American writer the opportunity to write on subjects that were familiar to him and about which he cared. "Romanticism opened to every national or regional group the road to self-expression," affirmed an Argentine critic. Furthermore, it renewed or awakened everywhere the hope of creating a national literature that would reveal the distinctive identity of the group.

This hope, alas! was not immediately realized, and

Spanish American critics, notably, were not slow in pointing out that American writers had only exchanged one European influence for another. Even so, romanticism played a major role in establishing the American literatures on a firm basis, one on which they would grow.

In Quebec, in the course of the sixty-odd years which had elapsed betweeen the establishment of a printing press in 1764 and the appearance of romanticism in the early 1830s, a great deal of writing had been going on. In 1806, *Le Canadien*, the first truly French Canadian newspaper was founded. Within the next twenty years, many periodicals appeared in the French language. While these provided space needed for French Canadians with literary inclinations to publish their conscientious imitations of Voltaire, Florian, and Rousseau, whose works were taught at the Petit Séminaire (a boys' school in Quebec City), the taste for such exercises gradually diminished. Newspaper editors preferred essays in prose or verse dealing with topics, chiefly contemporary, which interested the majority of their subscribers. Moreover, booksellers in Quebec City and Montreal were importing the works of Chateaubriand and Lamartine as well as those of Scott, Byron, and Wordsworth. In other words, romanticism did not come to Quebec as a thunderbolt any more than it did to other American civilizations.

French Canadian romanticism began in the 1830s and lasted into the twentieth century. It is generally agreed that its long history falls into two parts, the second beginning about 1860. Liberalism was characteristic of the first part and conservatism of the second. This division rests on the political and psychological climate peculiar to each period rather than on purely literary considerations, for in both periods the chief concern of novelists and poets, regardless of their individual temperament or political leanings, was the creation of a national literature, and in both periods very nearly all the works they produced in their attempts to achieve this goal were inspired by the literary themes associated with romanticism and developed with more or less success (less rather than more) in the *couleur locale* of a Quebec setting.

The earliest years of French Canadian romanticism coincided with political agitation. Louis-Joseph Papineau, the speaker of the Quebec House, and the *Patriotes*, as his most ardent followers were called, were strongly in favor of responsible government, as were the Upper Canada Reformers, including William Lyon Mackenzie, Robert Baldwin, and George Brown. Moreover, the *Patriotes* were vigorously opposed to the British government's plan to unite Upper and Lower Canada, now Quebec and Ontario, under one legislative assembly. In 1837 a rebellion broke out in both provinces. Its leaders, Papineau and Mackenzie, fled to the United States.

An outstanding characteristic of Papineau and his young followers was their liberalism, a liberalism which was not limited to the political field but included a lively belief in the freedom of conscience and the freedom to think, to learn, and to speak. It explains their anticlericalism, an attitude which the position of the higher clergy in political matters served to accentuate. Although neither the agitation of the 1830s nor the liberalism of the *Patriotes* is reflected in the literature of the first period of Quebec romanticism, liberalism was widely felt, and its influence, while intermittent, proved to be a lasting one.

The first French Canadian novel, *L'Influence d'un livre, ou Le Chercheur de trésors* [The influence of a book, or The treasure-seeker], appeared in 1837. Although its youthful author (he was twenty-three), Philippe Aubert de Gaspé fils, gave it as a subtitle *Roman historique* [historical novel], it is based on folklore, a field in which Quebec is extremely rich. The treasure-seeker of the title is influenced in his quest by a book, *Le Petit Albert*, an ancient handbook of sorcery which enjoyed great popularity among the Quebec *habi-*

tants as it did with peasants in France whence it had come with the early colonists. Although correctly written, the novel is awkwardly constructed as were so many novels in the Americas, and the "love interest" fails to interest the reader partly because of the innumerable hair-raising adventures (straight out of Alexandre Dumas's and Eugène Sue's best-sellers) which block the lovers' path to happiness. On the other hand, the Introduction, in which the novelist expresses his scorn for French classical literature and his enthusiasm for French romanticism, is both lively and interesting.

In 1846 Patrice Lacombe's *La Terre paternelle* [The homestead] and P. J. O. Chauveau's *Charles Guérin* broke deliberately with the mind-boggling plots of romantic novels and replaced them with situations familiar to their readers, situations and events connected with life in the country. In so doing, they initiated the rural novel, a genre that was to enjoy unrivaled popularity for a century, until the almost simultaneous appearance of Roger Lemelin's *Au pied de la pente douce* (published in English as *The Town Below*) in 1944 and Gabrielle Roy's *Bonheur d'occasion* (published in English as *The Tin Flute*) in 1945.

Except for a number of poems of the late 1830s which were inspired by the tragic events of the political agitation, the poetry of this period indicates that the poets, like the novelists, were far more interested in French romantic literature than in current local events. The most striking example of this attitude is the work of Octave Crémazie, who was to be known by generation after generation of French Canadians as "notre poète national." Crémazie, who with his brother owned a bookshop, was a learned and cultivated man. Between trips to England and France to buy books he kept in touch with European intellectual trends and happenings. He was a true follower of the French romantic poets, Lamartine, Vigny, Musset, and, above all, Victor Hugo. Like Hugo, he found inspiration for some of his poems in exotic lands—Italy, Spain, Egypt, Turkey, Arabia, India —and also in certain important contemporary events which occurred in those remote regions. A great admirer of England and passionately loyal to his French and Canadian ancestors, he experienced a special joy in celebrating the victories of the Crimean War, in which France and England shared. Stimulated and enchanted though he was by his intellectual excursions to exotic lands, it is Canada that aroused his most passionate and profound feelings.

Notwithstanding the importance of early fiction and poetry for the study of early French Canadian literature, the intellectual quality and the liberal climate of this period are to be found in neither of these but in the scholarly works it produced and in the activities of certain associations, notably The Literary and Historical Society of Quebec (founded in 1824), which included both English- and French-speaking members, and the Institut Canadien de Montréal, which was established twenty years later. Such is the profusion of scholarly books, pamphlets, and essays which appeared in Quebec City, Montreal, and even far less populous localities such as Three Rivers and Saint-Hyacinthe that only the most important, and few of even these, can be mentioned here.

In 1837 the first essay on Canadian bibliography appeared, the *Catalogue raisonné d'ouvrages sur l'histoire de l'Amérique et en particulier sur celle du Canada.* Fifteen years earlier the author of this descriptive catalog of historical works, Georges Barthélemi Faribault (1789–1866) a good lawyer, had given up his law practice to take a post in the Legislative Assembly that would allow him more time to devote to historical and bibliographical research. The 669 books and documents listed in the *Catalogue* were those he had collected for the assembly's library.

The most important work in any field which appeared in this period and for many years to come was *Histoire du Canada depuis sa découverte jusqu'à nos jours* (published in English as *History of Canada, from the Time of Its Discovery till the Union Year*, 1840-1) by François-Xavier Garneau (1809–1862), the four volumes of which were published in French successively in 1845, 1846, 1848, and 1852 and in English in 1860. Based on sound research and a broad knowledge of historical writings, and agreeably readable (a quality it has retained to this day), it was also the first history of Canada worthy of the name to appear in French since 1744 when Charlevoix's *Histoire et description générale de la Nouvelle France* was published in Paris. Moreover, the first three volumes are remarkably impartial. In writing of the French regime, he scorned idealizing it; he weighed both its strong points and its weaknesses, thereby inviting the indignation of some of his chauvinistic readers. Parts of the fourth volume, those in which he recounts events which he had witnessed and concerning which he had formed firm opinions, are understandably less so.

It is believed by many that Garneau began to work on his *Histoire du Canada* in 1840 and that he wrote it as a reply to Lord Durham's *Report on the Affairs of British North America*, published in February 1839. This may be true. There is no need to reiterate the deserved praise which Lord Durham's celebrated report has received. Its treatment of French Canada, however, is its major weakness. The *Report* indicates clearly that in the course of his five-months' sojourn in Canada Lord Durham had met few, if any, intellectual French Canadians and that he had listened only to the English Canadians in Quebec City and Montreal whose eagerness for the union of the Canadas led them to exaggerate the numbers of French Canadians who had taken part in the political agitation as well as the extent of the racial antagonism which existed between French and English Canadians. The *Report* also suggests that Lord Durham had no idea of the unofficial but continuous intellectual relations which existed between Quebec and its former mother country. He thought of the French Canadians as forever deprived of this stimulus, sinking slowly and permanently into the abyss of ignorance unless they were anglicized. Anglicization, he argued, would enable them to learn, through English publications, of activities and developments everywhere in all fields. "There can hardly be conceived a nationality," the *Report* states,

> more destitute of all that can invigorate and elevate a people, than that which is exhibited by the descendants of the French in Lower Canada, owing to their retaining their peculiar language and manners. They are a people with no history, and no literature. The literature of England is written in a language which is not theirs; and the only literature which their language renders familiar to them is that of a nation from which they have been separated by eighty years of foreign rule, and still more by those changes which the Revolution and its consequences have wrought in the whole political, moral and social state of France. Yet it is on a people whom recent history, manners and modes of thought, so entirely separate from them, that the French Canadians are wholly dependent for almost all the instruction and amusement derived from books: it is on this essentially foreign literature, which is conversant about events, opinions and habits of life, perfectly strange and unintelligible to them, that they are compelled to be dependent.

In a moment of optimism, Lord Durham added, "In these circumstances, I should be indeed surprised if the more reflecting part of the French Canadians entertained at present any hope of continuing to preserve their nationality." Returning to his own solution of the problem, he concluded, "I repeat that the alteration of the character of the Province ought to be immediately entered on, . . . that in any plan, which may be adopted for the future management of Lower Canada, the first object ought to be that of making it an English Province . . .

and that the ascendency should never again be placed in any hands but those of an English population."

Lord Durham left for England in November 1838; he arrived in London on December 30. On February 8, 1839, the London *Times* began to publish the text of the *Report*. In England it was much criticized by the Tories and even by the Whigs. In Canada, on the contrary, it was well received by both English and French. All the French Canadian newspapers except one supported its policy of responsible government. The *Patriotes* had been opposed to union but in favor of responsible government; hence, if the latter could not be obtained without union, they accepted union. Moreover, some of the Upper Canada Reformers lost no time in getting in touch with those in Lower Canada and made plans with them to push for the rapid introduction of this form of government. As to the majority of French Canadians who had never manifested opposition to the union of the Canadas, they naturally accepted it.

The second period of French Canadian romanticism began around 1860 in an atmosphere of calm, prosperity, and conservatism. The union of Lower and Upper Canada, which was now twenty years old, had proved to be neither what Lord Durham had hoped nor what the French Canadians had feared, a means of bringing about their anglicization. On the contrary, in 1848 Section 41 of the Union Act which limited the use of the French language in Legislative Assembly business had been repealed. Thanks to the influence of the governor, Lord Elgin, a son-in-law of Lord Durham, the French Canadians "were given full scope for the use of their language."

Moreover, from 1840 on Upper Canada Reformers and Lower Canada *Patriotes*, who were also reformers, worked together. In 1842 Robert Baldwin, a moderate Reformer, and Louis Lafontaine, a *Patriote* who had been forced to flee from Canada in 1837, formed the first

Baldwin-Lafontaine ministery; a second one was formed in 1848. In 1853 another former *Patriote*, Georges-Etienne Cartier, who had fought in 1837 at the battle of Saint-Charles against an English detachment and fled to the United States, was chosen by the leader of the Tories to form the MacNab-Cartier ministry. In other words, the young intransigent liberals of earlier days were well on the way to becoming elder statesmen. They no longer looked upon the higher clergy as enemies, but as allies.

The second manifestation of romanticism is sometimes referred to as L'Ecole patriotique de Québec. Patriotic its members undoubtedly were, but a school it never was. It began with informal meetings of a group of intellectuals in the city of Quebec, where a favorite meeting place was the Crémazies' bookstore. Several members had already published, including Garneau (whose *Histoire du Canada* had just gone into its third edition), Faribault, and Chauveau, who was to become the first premier of the Province of Quebec under confederation.

Among the members of this distinguished literary group three stand out, each for a different reason. Philippe Aubert de Gaspé (1786–1871) was the oldest by many years. Moreover, he was the father of the author of the first French Canadian novel, *L'Influence d'un livre, ou Le Chercheur de trésors*. But most important of all, in 1863, at the age of seventy-six, he published his first and only novel, *Les Anciens Canadiens*, the first French Canadian novel to become a classic. A second edition was brought out in 1864, and that same year the first of two English translations appeared under the title *The Canadians of Old*. The plot of *Les Anciens Canadiens* is not hair-raising, as was the case with *L'Influence d'un livre*, but it can scarcely be described as stark realism. Both father and son were interested in folklore. In its presentation and use, however, the father is far superior to the son. Finally, both were influenced by romantic literature and both, especially the elder, had read widely in French and English literatures.

A second outstanding figure was Abbé Henri-Raymont Casgrain. At the age of twenty-nine he assumed, unconsciously no doubt, the role of *animateur* or moving spirit of the group of intellectuals he had recently joined, a role for which his passion for a national culture, as well as his exuberant temperament, suited him perfectly. He was interested in literature, and he wrote about Quebec literature. He also published a number of biographies of his contemporaries: Garneau, Crémazie, and Francis Parkman. His chief interest was the history of New France, and it was as an historian, of course, that he corresponded with Parkman. For Americans, certainly, this correspondence, which lasted twenty-eight years, is of special interest.

In March 1866 Parkman, who through his research had kept abreast of the publicatons that appeared in Quebec, wrote to subscribe to the journal *Le Foyer Canadien*. Abbé Casgrain, the editor of the review, replied by return mail; he had read *The Conspiracy of Pontiac*, and as a token of his admiration he was sending to Parkman the complete file of past issues. Thus began a correspondence which would not end before 1892, the year before Parkman's death. In the course of these years, Abbé Casgrain, a more than ardent Catholic, and Parkman, who was extremely critical of the role of the church in New France, and especially of the Jesuits, did not always see eye to eye. Each expressed his opinions and convictions in terms at times far from friendly. Yet the friendship and the exchange of letters and information continued. Abbé Casgrain furnished Parkman with documents from Faribault's collection and other Canadian repositories, and Parkman always heeded and responded to Abbé Casgrain's requests.

No French Canadian writer ever received such recognition and so many honors as did Louis Honoré Fréchette (1831–1904). In 1871 he was the first French

Canadian to be honored by the Académie française. A disciple of Crémazie, he received the Prix Montyon for his collection of poems entitled *Fleurs boréales* [Northern flowers]. In 1881 two Canadian universities, McGill and Queen's, bestowed on him the degree of doctor of letters. In 1888 he received the same degree from his own university, Laval, and in 1900 the University of Toronto followed suit. That same year, he was elected president of the Royal Society of Canada, of which he was a charter member.

Like all Quebec romantics, Fréchette worshipped Victor Hugo, and his adoration occasionally took the form of open imitation. Hugo had published successive parts of his *La Légende des siècles* [The centuries' legend] in 1859, 1871, and 1883; Fréchette's *La Légende d'un peuple* [A People's legend] appeared in Paris in 1883. Fréchette's fame rested chiefly upon his poetry, but to the modern reader it seems dated. His prose, on the other hand, has stood the test of time. In his collection of tales *La Noël au Canada*, translated into English by Charles G. D. Roberts under the title *Christmas in French Canada*, the stories that are based on folklore or, better still, on life in the forest encampments where woodcutters spend the winter felling trees are excellent. Far from devoid of wit or irony, he understood and enjoyed the mentality of his characters, and he had an excellent ear for the language which expressed it.

Fréchette died in 1908 at the age of sixty-eight. His mind was alert; his wit was as quick as ever. His presence in Montreal, where he spent his last years, seemed like the continuation of an era which, in fact, had already vanished.

In some ways French Canadian literature of the first thirty years of the twentieth century was a continuation of the literature of the nineteenth. This is true of the novel, insofar as novelists remained faithful to the rural setting that writers like Chauveau had made popular, although there is a difference as will be seen. It is less true of poetry, notably the poetry of the early years of L'Ecole littéraire de Montréal, founded in the 1890s by a group of young intellectuals, poets, and would-be poets. Its members greatly admired Fréchette, but in their own poetry they rejected the national themes which had informed his works and those of Crémazie. They were followers of the French and Belgian symbolists: Verlaine, Baudelaire, Rollinat, Rodenbach, and Verhaeren. Among these Montreal poets, Emile Nelligan was the first authentic French Canadian poet. Much has been said, and with good reason, of a sense of premonition which haunts his poetry, a premonition which was soon to be justified. At the age of seventeen he had already made his reputation as a poet. Three years later his mind gave way. He was to spend the rest of his life in a mental institution where he died in 1941 at the age of sixty-two.

In 1908 a number of the members of l'Ecole littéraire de Montréal felt drawn again to the national traditions as a source of inspiration, and they began to publish a review appropriately named *Le Terroir* [The soil]. L'Ecole littéraire de Montréal lasted until 1935; some twenty years later, one of its youngest members, Victor Barbeau, a distinguished critic, founded l'Académie Canadienne-française.

A startling aspect of the literature of the first thirty years of this century is the contrast it offers between the novel and poetry. The latter, irrespective of its French or French Canadian sources of inspiration, was essentially artistic in intention and generally free from national preoccupations. The novel, on the contrary, reflected the new nationalism aroused by dissatisfaction with the results of confederation and by the lack of interest the federal government showed toward French Canadians everywhere in Canada. This dissatisfaction had been aroused first in the 1890s by the decision of the Manitoba government to rescind the laws passed in 1875 according to which the provincial government supported the French Catholic schools. These anti-Catholic and anti-French measures were also adopted by Saskatchewan and Alberta some years later. Finally, in 1917 the Ontario legislature passed Regulation 17, which deprived the large French Canadian population in that province of French schools which the provincial government had supported since confederation. That this measure was not anti-Catholic but anti-French was amply proved by the support it received from the Irish bishops in Ontario.

The new nationalism in Quebec, for many of those who embraced it, was welded to the Catholic faith. As Jean Charles Falardeau observed, the French language, which heretofore had been considered as a national value as well as a value in itself, was now looked upon and defined as a means of protecting one's religion. "La langue gardienne de la foi" became a popular slogan. Return to the land was advocated by the clergy and others. As a result, rural novels proliferated, all of them less than mediocre. They portrayed artificially rather than naively the serenity, the virtuous happiness of life on a farm, far away from harm. As this period was drawing to an end, however, two rural novels appeared, both of which depicted the seamy side of this supposedly idyllic life. If the maturity of a national literature is judged by the lack of self-consciousness which distinguishes professional writers from amateurs, French Canada attained that state in the 1930s with the appearance of two novels: *Un Homme et son péché* [A man and his sin] by Claude-Henri Grignon (writing under the name Valdombre) was published in 1933, and *Trente Arpents* (published in English as *Thirty Acres*) by Philippe Panneton (whose pseudonym was Ringuet) was published in 1938. Although both novels are set in the traditional rural environment, neither is edifying, much less hortatory.

The sin of Séraphin Poudrier, the anti-hero of *Un*

Homme et son péché, is Avarice with a capital *A.* The scene of his tireless efforts to get, to save, and never, or almost never, to spend is one of the Laurentian villages north of Montreal, Sainte-Adèle, a village known to generations of vacationers and, more recently, to skiers. *Un Homme et son péché* was an instant and huge success. A dramatic version soon went on the air on Radio Canada where it was even more successful; for years, at seven in the evening, throughout the Province of Quebec, families stopped whatever they were doing and listened. When television came, Séraphin continued his career unperturbed, ever devising new ways to acquire "de l'argent" which he pronounced with a nasal twang that somehow emphasized his stinginess.

Trente Arpents is a somber and, at times, moving book. Euchariste Moisan and his family live on a farm close to Montreal in a flat landscape which is no flatter than their minds and their lives. Euchariste does not love the land, he loves *his* land. At the end of the novel, after his dull wife's death and the loss of his money through the dishonesty of the village *notaire,* he leaves for a New England factory town where one of his sons, like thousands and thousands of other French Canadians, had settled. Here, he ends his days as a night watchman in one of the factories. Dreary though its characters and the lives they lead are, the novel is absorbing. Its high quality was immediately recognized in Paris, where it was first published, as well as in Quebec; it has been translated into a number of languages.

Contemporary French Canadian literature began when two novels, both of them set in cities, appeared. At the end of 1944 Roger Lemelin's *Au pied de la pente douce* came out; it is set in one of Quebec City's poorer quarters, Saint-Sauveur. Early in 1945 Gabrielle Roy's *Bonheur d'occasion* was published; its setting is Saint-Henri, one of Montreal's most underprivileged sections. Although they appeared almost simultaneously, these two urban novels are completely different from each other.

Roger Lemelin, a caricaturist at heart and a fine and kindly one, describes the milieu in which he grew up. Saint-Sauveur in the lower town is connected physically, and physically only, with Quebec's aristocratic Haute-Ville by an easy slope, *la pente douce*. While the citizenry of the upper town live in an atmosphere of serene dignity, the town below teems with incessant and picturesque activity. Although the novel has moments of deep sadness, admirably described by the author, the general atmosphere is unquestionably one of gaiety. In 1948 Lemelin brought out *Les Plouffes* (*The Plouffe Family*), a fine novel of a working-class family in the city of Quebec; the reduced number of characters enabled him to go deeper in the study of their individual tricks and manners. *Pierre le magnifique* (1952), published in English as *In Quest of Splendour*, is Lemelin's last novel, a very uneven one. After it, Lemelin gave up writing and has become a most successful publisher and businessman.

Unlike Lemelin, Gabrielle Roy does not belong to the locality or to the milieu in which her *Bonheur d'occasion* is set. Although her family came from the Province of Quebec, they moved to Saint-Boniface, Manitoba, where she was born, grew up, and taught school briefly before going to France. In 1939, at the outbreak of the war, she returned to Canada and obtained a job in Montreal as a journalist. It was not in this capacity, however, that she discovered Saint-Henri and the characters of her first novel, but on the solitary walks she took, to while away the loneliness she felt away from her family out West. *Bonheur d'occasion* is the result of her observations and of the sympathy they awoke in her. But nowhere in this remarkable book does the sympathy degenerate into sentimentality. The sympathy was too deep, and Gabrielle Roy is far too intelligent for this to happen. On the contrary, her quick understanding and her quiet sense of humor are ever-present.

Bonheur d'occasion is a profoundly human book. Its characters, even the minor ones, live on with the reader as do those of great novelists. Like great novelists also, Gabrielle Roy tells her story so well that her readers are unaware of the telling; her style never intrudes. Since the publication of *Bonheur d'occasion*, Roy has lived in Quebec City. She has published nearly a dozen books, and most of them have been very successful, notably *La Petite Poule d'eau* (*Where Nests the Water Hen*) and *Rue Deschambault* (*Street of Riches*), her autobiography. The number of good and very good novels published in Quebec is impressive, but in the eyes of many in the ever-growing circle of their readers, *Bonheur d'occasion* remains the best.

"Quiet Revolution" describes perfectly the atmosphere in which the Province of Quebec was transformed during the 1960s. The changes it underwent were revolutionary and they were effected quietly.

The immediate cause of the Quiet Revolution was the sudden death of the premier, Maurice Duplessis, on September 1, 1959. Its remote cause was his long and repressive administration. For twenty-six years, except for one brief interruption, Duplessis ruled Quebec and imposed upon it his reactionary views. These coincided with the views of the rural population upon which he showered his bounties: bridges, hospitals, patronage, and so on. His views also coincided with those of some rural bishops and of a considerable part of the Quebec clergy. He looked upon cities, especially Montreal, as his natural enemies. He was suspicious of the universities, whether French or English, and he detested the labor unions.

In 1960, less than a year after Duplessis's death, the Liberals came to power under the leadership of Jean Lesage. As premier, Lesage chose a number of able men for his cabinet. Among them, the best known was René Lévesque, a brilliant radio and television commentator on public affairs. He was to leave the Liberal party and found the Parti Québécois, which came into power on November 15, 1976. One of the ablest and certainly the most effective member of the Lesage cabinet was Paul Gérin-Lajoie, scion of a distinguished Montreal family and an authority on constitutional law. In 1963, after resuscitating the Ministry of Education established by Chauveau in 1867 and abolished eight years later by an ultraconservative premier, Gérin-Lajoie became minister of education and immediately set about reorganizing the educational system along democratic and modern lines. He established throughout the province a system of public junior colleges, not unlike American junior colleges, called CEGEPs (Collèges d'Enseignement Général et Professionel). These colleges replaced the private *collèges classiques* which had been from time immemorial in the hands of priests. In these schools, as was true in France until the 1930s and in Latin American countries until even more recently, the curriculum was based on a hierarchy of knowledge according to which the classics were at the top and the sciences at the bottom. The *collèges classiques* produced a remarkable number of cultivated men and, more recently, women. On the other hand, the classical education reduced the choice of a career to three possibilities: law, medicine, or theology, the last closed, of course, to women. Students who wished to pursue scientific studies when they reached university were too often precluded from doing so by their lack of preparation. Moreover, students in the *collèges classiques* paid tuition; the CEGEPs are free. In short, the revolution that resulted from Gérin-Lajoie's administration was the inevitable closing of most of the *collèges classiques* and the "democratizing" and secularization of education. The last processes were furthered by the founding of a provincial university, l'Université du Québec, which is also free from all sectarian ties. Its main campus is in Montreal, and like other provincial universities in Canada and state universities in the United States, l'Université du Québec has campuses in several localities.

The new educational system has not been free from serious problems, some of which were not present in the old educational system. Such problems are part of the modern world. For one thing, Gérin-Lajoie's revolutionary measures failed to satisfy the wishes of some students at the University of Montreal. In 1963 a few of them founded a review whose name, *Parti-Pris* [Inflexible decision], indicated clearly that their minds were made up and that they supported ideas and changes which went far beyond what older "progressives," including Gérin-Lajoie, considered advanced. They rejected the slogan "Notre maître, le passé" [Our teacher, the past], which had been made popular by the historian Abbé Groulx, and replaced it by the slogan "Notre maître, le présent." Furthermore, many of the founders of *Parti-Pris* came from modest homes and were resentful of the bourgeoisie, the capitalists, the elite. They proclaimed themselves champions of the underprivileged. In their desire to right one of the wrongs which deprived the poor of their dignity, the ignorance of correct French, the young members of *Parti-Pris* proposed that henceforth all Quebec literature should be written in *joual* (a debased pronunciation of *cheval*), the language spoken in the slums.

The members of *Parti-Pris* were, needless to say, separatists. However, although separatist activities came out openly and grew during the Quiet Revolution, they did not stem from it. One source of this movement is to be found in Africa, where in the early 1960s colonies long held by European nations became independent. Moreover, in 1962 Jacques Berque, a professor at the Collège de France and the foremost authority on Algeria, came as a visiting professor to the University of Montreal, where he lectured in his special field, the colonization and decolonization of the Arabs. His role in encouraging French Canadian students to "decolonize themselves" is unquestionable. Although much space has been given here to *Parti-Pris* as a lively example of intellectual activity in French Canada, it must be emphasized that several other groups in other fields were and are active. Quebec is not today, nor has it ever been, a monolithic society.

The sweeping changes brought by the Quiet Revolution produced a sense of freedom, especially from the clergy's traditional authority, which Quebec had never known. This new freedom was not received with euphoria; it was taken for granted from the first. It produced and continues to produce undreamed-of successes in the arts, most striking of all, in the theater and cinema.

Regardless of their individual vision of reality, the poets, novelists, and playwrights of French Canada have a fundamental characteristic in common: all appear free from other contemporary literatures. While the intellectual influence of France on Quebec is still considerable and beneficent, its literary influence diminished after the Second World War. As for the influence of the literature of the United States, it is so faint as to be practically invisible. The same is true of the reciprocal influences one might expect of two literatures belonging to the same country. This assumption, however, has been proved false with respect to all bicultural and tricultural European countries: Belgium, Switzerland, and Spain, to name a few. It is also false in Canada's case. So far, English and French Canadian literatures have exerted no influence on each other although literary works in each language have been translated into the other. Regarding this situation it should be borne in mind that they stem from two great European literatures and that, culturally speaking, they reflect two Canadian societies. Finally, notwithstanding the lively cultural relations which exist between Latin America and Quebec, it is clear that these relations have not had the slightest impact on Quebec's literature. Quebec writers are going it alone, and, to all appearances, deliberately so. They are not only fully aware of the wealth and variety of material which their own society presents, but they are also discovering and developing the techniques needed to transform this material into literature. In short, considered in its American context, in the context of young literatures, Quebec literature is far more than promising; it is stimulating. It has come into its own.

VIII

Canada:
The Borderline Case

Marshall McLuhan

The boundary between Canada and the United States is a typically human creation; it is physically invisible, geographically illogical, militarily indefensible, and emotionally inescapable.

Hugh L. Keenleyside, Canadian diplomat

In the United States there is more space where nobody is than where anybody is. That is what makes America what it is.

Gertrude Stein[1]

A border is not a connection but an interval of resonance, and such gaps abound in the Land of the DEW Line. The DEW Line itself, the Distant Early Warning radar system installed by the United States in the Canadian North to keep this continent in touch with Russia, points up a major Canadian role in the twentieth

---

1. Both epigraphs are quoted in the official Canadian bicentennial gift to the people of the United States, *Between Friends/ Entre Amis* (Toronto: McClelland and Stewart, 1976), pp. 4, 24.

century, the role of hidden *ground* for big powers. Since the United States has become a world environment, Canada has become the anti-environment that renders the United States more acceptable and intelligible to many small countries of the world; anti-environments are indispensable for making an environment understandable. Canada has no goals or directions, yet shares so much of the American character and experience that the role of dialogue and liaison has become entirely natural to Canadians wherever they are. Sharing the American way, without commitment to American goals or responsibilities, makes the Canadian intellectually detached and observant as an interpreter of the American destiny. In the age of the electric information environment the big nations of the First World are losing both identity and goals. France, Germany, England, and the United States are nations whose identity and goals were shaped by the rise of the self-regulating markets of the nineteenth century, markets whose quantitative equilibrium has been obsolesced by the dominance of the new world of instant information. As software information becomes the prime factor in politics and industry, the First World inevitably is minus the situation which has given meaning and relevance to its drive for mere quantity. New images of identity based on quality of life are forming in a world where suddenly "small is beautiful" and centralism is felt to be a disease. In this new world the decentralized and soft-focus image of the flexible Canadian identity appears to great advantage. Canadians never got "delivery" on their first national identity image in the nineteenth century and are the people who learned how to live without the bold accents of the national ego-trippers of other lands. Today they are even more suited to the Third World tone and temper as the Third World takes over the abandoned goals of the First World. Sharing many characteristics of the Third World, Canada mediates easily between the First and Third worlds.

No one better understood the advantages of being nationally a "nobody" than George Bernard Shaw, whose borderline frontiersmanship created his great career on the stage. In the preface to *John Bull's Other Island,* Shaw explained:

> When I say that I am an Irishman I mean that I was born in Ireland, and that my native language is the English of Swift and not the unspeakable jargon of the mid-XIX century London newspapers. My extraction is the extraction of most Englishmen: that is, I have no trace in me of the commercially imported North Spanish strain which passes for aboriginal Irish: I am a genuine typical Irishman of the Danish, Norman, Cromwellian, and (of course) Scotch invasions. I am violently and arrogantly Protestant by family tradition; but let no English Government therefore count on my allegiance: I am English enough to be an inveterate Republican and Home Ruler. It is true that one of my grandfathers was an Orangeman; but then his sister was an abbess; and his uncle, I am proud to say, was hanged as a rebel. When I look round me on the hybrid cosmopolitans, slum poisoned or square pampered, who call themselves Englishmen today, and see them bullied by the Irish Protestant garrison as no Bengalee now lets himself be bullied by an Englishman; when I see the Irishman everywhere standing clear-headed, sane, hardily callous to the boyish sentimentalities, susceptibilities, and credulities that make the Englishman the dupe of every charlatan and the idolater of every numbskull, I perceive that Ireland is the only spot on earth which still produces the ideal Englishman of history.[2]

Like Shaw, the Canadian "nobody" can have the best of two worlds: on the one hand, the human scale of the small country and, on the other hand, the immediate advantages of proximity to massive power. Knowing the

2. *Prefaces by George Bernard Shaw* (London: Constable, 1934), p. 440.

United States like the back of his hand, the Canadian can be playful in discussing America. He is happy to invite "the ugly American" to enjoy the idyllic playgrounds of our largely unoccupied land of lakes and forests, whether of Quebec or Ontario or British Columbia.

If there are 250,000 unnamed lakes in Ontario alone, there is an even larger problem of toponymy in naming the Canadian language. Morton Bloomfield, a professor of English at Harvard University and a Canadian by birth, surfaced one of the many hidden borderlines that interlace the Canadian psyche when he explored the character of Canadian English, a subject neglected by both Canadian and American scholars. In "Canadian English and Its Relation to Eighteenth-Century American Speech," he notes: "The probable explanation for this neglect lies in the fact that most American investigators, ignorant of Canadian history, are under the impression that Canadian English, as undoubtedly is the case with Australian, South African, and Newfoundland English, is a direct offshoot of British English and therefore does not belong to their field of inquiry. It is, however, necessary to know the history of a country before one can know the history of its language."[3] Bloomfield points out that in *The American Language* H. L. Mencken shared the widespread illusion that American English conquered the British English of Canada, whereas Canadian English had been American from the time of the American Revolution: "After 1776, however, the situation changed and a large increase in population occurred, entirely owing to the movement north of many Tories or Loyalists who wished, or were forced, to leave the United States because of the American Revolutionary War. They carried with them, as a matter of course, the language spoken in the Thirteen Colonies at the time."[4]

3. *Journal of English and Germanic Philology*, 47 (1948): 59.
4. Ibid., 60.

Without any self-consciousness English Canadians enjoy the advantages of a dual language. Canada is linguistically in the same relation to the United States as America is to England. Stephen Leacock humorously varied the theme: "In Canada we have enough to do keeping up with the two spoken languages without trying to invent slang, so we just go right ahead and use English for literature, Scotch for sermons and American for conversation."[5]

Another psychological borderline shared by Canadians and Americans is a legacy of their nineteenth-century war on the empty wilderness, as indicated in Lord Durham's *Report on the Affairs of British North America* (1839):

> The provision which in Europe, the State makes for the protection of its citizens against foreign enemies, is in America required for what a French writer has beautifully and accurately called, the "war with the wilderness." The defence of an important fortress, or the maintenance of a sufficient army or navy in exposed posts, is not more a matter of common concern to the European, than is the construction of the great communications to the American settler; and the State, very naturally, takes on itself the making of the works, which are matters of concern to all alike.[6]

It would be strange indeed if the population of North America had not developed characteristic attitudes to the spaces experienced here. A century of war on the wilderness made customary the habit of going outside to confront and explore the wilderness and of going inside to be social and secure. Going outside involved energy and effort and struggle in frontier conditions that called for initiative amid solitude. Thus Margaret Atwood notes in her critical study *Survival:* "The war against Nature assumed that Nature was hostile to begin with;

5. *How to Write* (New York: Dodd, Mead, 1943), p. 119.
6. Lord Durham, *Report on the Affairs of British North America* (Oxford: Clarendon Press, 1912), II, 91.

man could fight and lose, or he could fight and win. If he won he would be rewarded: he could conquer and enslave Nature, and, in practical terms, exploit her resources."[7]

Atwood's study of Canadian writers reveals the frontier trauma, yet one that is not uniquely Canadian. Twain's *The Adventures of Huckleberry Finn*, Whitman's *Leaves of Grass*, Thoreau's *Walden*, and Melville's *Moby-Dick* record new attitudes to both inner and outer space, spaces that had to be explored rather than inhabited. Here, then, is the immediate effect of our continental space: to seem to be a land that has been explored but never lived in. The oriental comment is not without good grounds: "You Westerners are always getting ready to live." Between Whitman's "Song of the Broad-Axe" and Clement Clarke Moore's "A Visit from St. Nicholas" ("The stockings were hung by the chimney with care") lie the two psychic poles of the special North American feeling for space—the outer space for aggressive extroversion and the inner space for cozy sociability and security amid dangers. On the borderline between these areas of aggression and hospitality Hawthorne and Henry James etched their psychic adventures and "the complex fate" of being a North American. "It's a complex fate, being an American," James wrote, "and one of the responsibilities it entails is fighting against a superstitious valuation of Europe." To become cultured in America while resisting European values became a major theme in Hawthorne and James. Neither thought to consider the hidden physical polarities of this continuing conflict. In Canada and the United States the shared feeling for space is totally different from that of any other part of the world. In England or France or India people go outside to be social and go inside to be private or alone. By contrast, even at our picnics and camping holidays and

7. (Toronto: House of Anansi Press, 1972), p. 60.

barbecues we carry the frontier with us, just as our motor cars, our most cherished form of privacy, are designed for special effects of quiet enclosure. Where a European thinks of "a room of one's own," the North American depends upon the car to provide the private space for work and thought. Typically, you can see *through* an American car when driving, but you cannot see *into* the car when standing. The reverse is true of a European car; you can see into it but not through it when on the road.

Since we are seeking to delineate some of the Canadian borderlines, it is natural that those psychologically shared with the United States are the areas of maximal interplay and subtle interpenetration. One mythic borderline Canada shares with the United States springs from the heroic deeds of Paul Bunyan and Babe the Blue Ox. It is generally accepted that Paul Bunyan was a French Canadian logger of the 1840s and 1850s. The folk art of the tall story is dear to the frontier, that world of the resonant interval where public amplification proliferates. These tall stories are often called in to calm the ardor of those who delight in exaggeration. The Paul Bunyan man can retort with a story of the huge pines in his territory which he began to notch with Paul. After notching for an hour or more, they went round the tree and found two Irishmen who had been chopping at the same tree for three years, including Sundays. Paul is a frontier or borderline figure who is a continent-striding image to be met in the Midwest or the Far West. Newfoundland poet E. J. Pratt had a special gift for the gigantic in verse as in his *Witches' Brew* and *The Cachalot*. The frontier poet or novelist will feel "the call of the wild" rather than the lure of the parlor or even the pub. As Thoreau wrote in *Walden:* "I have never found the companion that was so companionable as solitude."

The frontier is naturally an abrasive and rebarbative area which generates irritation and grievance, the formula for humor. Thus the first major Canadian literary character was Sam Slick, the Yankee clockmaker. The frontier abounds in figures of fun-writing like Stephen Leacock, the Canadian Mark Twain.

Hugh Kenner looks into the borderline matter in his essay "The Case of the Missing Face."[8] He begins his quest for the missing face of Canadian culture with an observation of Chester Duncan: "Our well-known Canadian laconicism is not always concealed wisdom, but a kind of . . . between-ness. We are continually on the verge of something but we don't quite get there. We haven't discovered what we are or where we're going and therefore we haven't much to say." Duncan found the key with "between-ness," the world of the interval, the borderline, the interface of worlds and situations. It may well be that Canadians misconceive their role and opportunities and feel the misguided urge to follow the trendy ways of those less fortunately placed. The interface is where the action is. No need to move or follow, but only to tune the perceptions on the spot.

Harold Innis, the Canadian pioneer historian of economics and communication, imaginatively used the interface, or borderline situation, to present a new world of economic and cultural change by studying the interplay between man's artifacts and the environments created by old and new technologies. By investigating social effects as contours of changing technology, Innis did what Plato and Aristotle failed to do. He discovered from the alphabet onward the great vortices of power at the interface of cultural frontiers. He recovered for the West the world of entelechies and *formal* causality long buried by the logicians and teachers of *applied* knowledge; and he did this by looking carefully at the immediate situation created by staples and the action of the Canadian cultural borderline on which he was located.

8. In Malcolm Ross, ed., *Our Sense of Identity* (Toronto: The Ryerson Press, 1954), pp. 203–208.

Looking for the missing face of Canada, Kenner feels we have been beguiled into nonentity by the appeal of the big, tough wilderness-tamers and our urge to identify with "rock, rapids, wilderness and virgin (but exploitable) forest." But Kenner gives up just when the trail is promising. Yes, the Canadian, as North American, answers the call of the wild and goes out into the wilderness to "invite his soul," but unlike the rest of mankind, he goes out with a merely private face (and also a private voice). Whereas the Frenchman or the Russian or the Irishman records the defeats and miseries (as well as the joys and successes) of his life on his countenance, the North American keeps his face to himself and "scrubs" it daily. Somewhat in the manner of Dorian Gray, the real picture of the individual life is hidden away for private judgment rather than public inspection. On the other hand, the extrovert who goes outside to be a lonely fighter and explorer is not an extrovert at home. Charlie Chaplin's pictures of the lonely tramp never take us *inside* an American home, thereby ignoring the hidden *ground* of his lonely *figure* of the little tramp. Chaplin was an Englishman who never understood America, but he gave Europeans what they still view as American documentaries.

Equally as fascinated and confused as Chaplin, W. H. Auden shared the bafflement of Henry James about the missing face in North America:

> *So much countenance and so little face.* (*Henry James*)
> Every European visitor to the United States is struck by the comparative rarity of what he would call a face, by the frequency of men and women who look like elderly babies. If he stays in the States for any length of time, he will learn that this cannot be put down to a lack of sensibility—the American feels the joys and sufferings of human life as keenly as anybody else. The only plausible explanation I can find lies in his different attitude to the past. To have a face, in the European

sense of the word, it would seem that one must not only enjoy and suffer but also desire to preserve the memory of even the most humiliating and unpleasant experiences of the past.

More than any other people, perhaps, the Americans obey the scriptural injunction: "Let the dead bury their dead."

When I consider others I can easily believe that their bodies express their personalities and that the two are inseparable. But it is impossible for me not to feel that my body is other than I, that I inhabit it like a house, and that my face is a mask which, with or without my consent, conceals my real nature from others.

It is impossible consciously to approach a mirror without composing or "making" a special face, and if we catch sight of our reflection unawares we rarely recognize ourselves. I cannot read my face in the mirror because I am already obvious to myself.

The image of myself which I try to create in my own mind in order that I may love myself is very different from the image which I try to create in the minds of others in order that they may love me.[9]

Auden is here speaking of a psychic dichotomy alien to North Americans. "The case of the missing face," however, has a simple solution from one point of view, since the North American, in poetry, art, and life, tends to substitute the face of nature for the human countenance. Like Wordsworth and Thoreau we spend our time scanning the environmental mystery, taking spins in the country instead of spinning thoughts at home. The North American goes to the movie or theater to be alone with his date, whereas Europeans go to enjoy the audience. The North American excludes advertisements from his cinema and theater, while Europeans find no violation of their privacy from ads in places of public

---

9. *The Dyer's Hand* (New York: Random House, 1962), pp. 103–104.

entertainment. Europeans, on the other hand, exclude ads from radio and television in their homes, but since there is little or no privacy in the North American home, ads are tolerated, if only because we go elsewhere for privacy.

Earlier I noted that the entire paradox of the "reversed space" of the North American frustrated Henry James who made it a psychological crux in his novels, regarding it as "the complex fate" of being American. In *Daisy Miller*, a story of an American girl in Europe, he noted:

> "She has that charming look that they all have," his aunt resumed. "I can't think where they pick it up; and she dresses in perfection—no, you don't know how well she dresses. I can't think where they get their taste."
>
> "But, my dear aunt, she is not, after all, a Comanche savage."
>
> "She is a young lady," said Mrs. Costello, "who has an intimacy with her mamma's courier."[10]

Far from being accepted into the space of European society, Daisy is considered a kind of "noble savage":

> Winterbourne stood looking after them; he was indeed puzzled. He lingered beside the lake for a quarter of an hour, turning over the mystery of the young girl's sudden familiarities and caprices. But the very definite conclusion he came to was that he should enjoy deucedly "going off" with her somewhere.

They do indeed go off to the Castle of Chillon, and this also increases his puzzlement:

10. All quotations from *Daisy Miller* are taken from *The Novels and Tales of Henry James* (New York: Charles Scribner's Sons, 1909), vol. 18.

The sail was not long, but Winterbourne's companion found time to say a great many things. To the young man himself their little excursion was so much of an escapade—and adventure—that, even allowing for her habitual sense of freedom, he had some expectation of seeing her regard it in the same way. But it must be confessed that, in this particular, he was disappointed.

Going out with her date to be alone was in fact the most natural thing in the world for Daisy Miller, whereas for her European friend Winterbourne it was a bizarre event:

> Daisy Miller was extremely animated, she was in charming spirits; but she was apparently not at all excited; she was not fluttered; she avoided neither his eyes nor those of any one else; she blushed neither when she looked at him nor when she felt that people were looking at her. People continued to look at her a great deal, and Winterbourne took much satisfaction in his pretty companion's distinguished air. He had been a little afraid that she would talk loud, laugh over-much, and even, perhaps, desire to move about the boat a good deal. But he quite forgot his fears; he sat smiling, with his eyes upon her face, while, without moving from her place, she delivered herself of a great number of original reflections. It was the most charming garrulity he had ever heard. He had assented to the idea that she was "common"; but was she so, after all, or was he simply getting used to her commonness?

Henry James's delight in presenting his American personae to European bewilderment is a very rich subject indeed, but one which depends entirely on understanding the peculiar American quest for solitude in the wilderness, and discovering thereby a privacy and a psychic dimension which Europeans cannot encompass or understand. The conflict in the mind of Henry James had occurred earlier in the life and work of Hawthorne.

The latter had also confused the North American quest for privacy out-of-doors with a weak concession to autocratic values and thereby a betrayal of democratic values. In going outside to be social, the European seemed more democratic than the North American going outside to be alone:

> To state the case succinctly: Hawthorne's compulsive affirmation of American positives, particularly in the political sense, led to a rejection of the idea of solitude; and solitude as an expression of aristocratic withdrawal sided with Europe rather than America when the two traditions stated their respective claims.[11]

Henry James finally clarified the conflict by a confession about his personal life which Hamlin Garland reported:

> He became very much in earnest at last and said something which surprised and gratified me. It was an admission I had not expected him to make. "If I were to live my life over again," he said in a low voice, and fixing upon me a somber glance, "I would be an American. I would steep myself in America, I would know no other land. I would study its beautiful side. The mixture of Europe and America which you see in me has proved disastrous. It has made of me a man who is neither American nor European. I have lost touch with my own people, and I live here alone. My neighbors are friendly, but they are not of my blood, except remotely. As a man grows old he feels these conditions more than when he is young. I shall never return to the United States, but I wish I could."[12]

Refusing to accept the European past he had not earned or made, Henry James is here telling Canadians that the American sense of identity was as much a question mark

11. Marius Bewley, *The Complex Fate* (London: Chatto and Windus, 1952), p. 57.
12. Hamlin Garland, *Roadside Meetings* (New York: Macmillan, 1930), p. 461.

in the late nineteenth century as the Canadian sense of identity is today, and James serves to stress for us the crucial role of the imaginative native artist in creating the uncreated consciousness of a people.

It is by our encounter with the hidden contours of our own psyches and society that we gradually develop group identity. That Canada has had no great blood-letting such as the American Civil War may have retarded the growth of a strong national identity, reminding us that only the bloody-minded could seriously wish to obtain a group identity by such violence.

The strike of the airline pilots and controllers over the bilingual issue at Canadian airports clearly marks another of the vivid borderlines of Canadian interface and abrasion. The French language is a cultural border and vortex of energy that has roots in the beginnings of Canada as a territory cherished by both French and English settlers. The new technology of air travel projects an ancient quarrel in a new dramatic medium. The drama of the civilian air controllers resonates with the events of 1759 and the fall of Quebec City. The repercussions of that event affect all of North America today. Donald Creighton discerns the action on both sides of the border in the opening sentence of his *The Empire of the St. Lawrence:*

> When, in the course of a September day in 1759, the British made themselves the real masters of the rock of Quebec, an event of apparently unique importance occurred in the history of Canada. There followed rapidly the collapse of French power in North America and the transference of the sovereignty of Canada to Great Britain; and these acts in the history of the northern half of the continent may well appear decisive and definitive above all others. In fact, for France and England, the crisis of 1759 and 1760 was a climax of conclusive finality. But colonial America, as well as imperial Europe, had been deeply concerned in the

long struggle in the new continent; and for colonial America the conquest of New France had another and a more uncertain meaning. For Europe the conquest was the conclusion of a drama; for America it was merely the curtain of an act. On the one hand, it meant the final retirement of France from the politics of northern North America; on the other, it meant the regrouping of Americans and the reorganization of American economies.[13]

The fall of Quebec (1759) and the Peace of Paris (1763) created the same psychic border for French Canada as the Civil War defeat did in the mind of the American South. The defeat stimulated the feeling of an historical present that was absent in the victors. "For many French Canadians," writes Ramsay Cook in *The Maple Leaf Forever*, "the past, and especially the conquest, has always been part of the present." He continues with the words of Abbé Groulx:

"History, dare I say it, and with no intention of paradox, is that which is most alive; the past, is that which is most present." Or in Esdras Minville's revealing remark about "we who continue history, who are history itself." This attitude toward history which makes the past part of the present is not, of course, uniquely French Canadian. It bears a marked similarity to the comment of a distinguished Mexican philosopher concerning Hispanic America. "The past, if it is not completely assimilated, always makes itself felt in the present," Leopoldo Zea has written. "Hispanic America continued to be a continent without a history because the past was always present. And if it had a history, it was not a conscious history. Hispanic America refused to consider as part of its history a past which it had not made." Is it not the failure to "assimilate" the Conquest, to make it part of French-Canadian history, that explains the endless attempts to interpret it?[14]

13. (Toronto: Macmillan, 1956), p. 1.
14. (Toronto: Macmillan, 1971), pp. 111–112.

These hidden borders in men's minds are the great vortices of energy and power that can spiral and erupt anywhere, and it is not for lack of such vortices that the Canadian identity is obscure. Rather, there are so many that Canadians have dissipated and smothered them in consumerism and affluence. The vast new borders of electric energy and information created by radio and television have set up world frontiers and interfaces among all countries on a new scale that alter all preexisting forms of culture and nationalism. The superhuman scale of these electric software vortices has created the Third World with its threat to the old industrial world of "hardware."

On the occasion of Queen Elizabeth's visit to the White House to congratulate the United States on its bicentennial, the President proposed that the dignity of the occasion might be enhanced by reading aloud the Declaration of Independence. So much for subliminal wisdom, even though a G. K. Chesterton might well have found in this much food for transcendental meditation. The historian Kenneth McNaught observes: "It is sometimes said that Americans are benevolently uninformed about Canada while Canadians are malevolently well-informed about the U.S."[15] McNaught is here pointing to one of the great borderline features of the Canadian, namely his opportunities to "take over" the United States intellectually in the same way Alexis de Tocqueville did earlier. Is it not significant that Tocqueville was unable to see the French situation with the same clarity that he brought to the United States? France was driving to the extremes of specialism and centralism under the fragmenting pressure of print technology, creating the matrix for Napoleon while Tocqueville was enjoying the naiveté of Americans

15. "Canadian Independence, Too, Was Won in 1770s," *Toronto Star*, July 1, 1976, p. C3.

whose politics were the first to be founded on the printed word.

In the same way, Canadians repine in the shadow of the American quest for identity, saying "Me too!," while ignoring the anguish of the American struggle to find out "Who are we?" Kenneth McNaught cites the American historian C. Vann Woodward to underline the plight of Canada's fellow borderliners: "Lacking a common racial, religious, linguistic, or political heritage, they had to look elsewhere for the bases of nationality. Their anxiety over this quest for national identity helps explain . . . 'a somewhat compulsive preoccupation with the question of their Americanism.'" McNaught himself concludes: "How many of us have experienced a feeling of being really Canadian only during our first trip abroad? I suspect that this feeling flows from the fact that we have always been self-confident without really understanding it."[16]

Many Canadians had their first vivid experience of national identity while watching the Russian teams play the Canadians at Canada's own game of hockey. The Russians gave Canada a very bad time by playing a close style of hockey that Canadians had developed in the 1930s and forgotten in the 1940s. It was in the earlier period that Canada sent its coaches to Russia to teach the game. Here was surely an admirable example of the borderline case in full interface. Canadian participation in past wars, whether in 1812 or 1914 or after, has never been on a scale to enable Canadians to identify with the total operation. With hockey the scale is right but the personnel are confusing. In professional hockey American teams consist mostly of Canadians. The jet plane knows no geographic borders with the result that hockey is played by Canadians in American arenas as an American sport. There is enough psychic and social overlap to make both American baseball and Canadian

16. Ibid.

hockey acceptable dramatizations of the competitive drives and skills of both countries.

Related and comparable in scope to the gap of the missing face of North America is the case of the missing voice. If going outside to be alone forbids the assuming of a culturally acquired countenance, the same inhibition extends to "putting on" the North American voice. When we go outside, we use only a private voice and avoid the cultivation of an educated or modulated tone. One might even suggest that the absence of class barriers in North America owes more to North Americans' refusal to assume a group or class speech than to their political convictions or institutions. When a William F. Buckley tilts his head and intones on television, he is clowning. Any American who tried to do seriously what the British public-school boy is taught to do publicly would be run out of town on a rail. The North American hesitation to "put on" a public voice or a face is also a block to the artist and writer in "putting on" an audience for his work. Going out to be alone is antithetical to the role of the artist who must invent an image that will sting or intrigue a public to encounter his challenge. The artist has to upset his audience by making them aware of their automatism or their own inadequacy to their daily lives. Where mere survival exhausts the creative energies as on our borderline, few have the daring to confront their public with an aesthetic vision.

There is a great new television borderline in North America which endangers many established features of our lives, including our assumed right to use only the private voice out-of-doors. The TV generation has begun to "put on" a peer-group or tribal dialect which could send us Upstairs *or* Downstairs in our sleep. The fact that the great vortex of interface between inside and outside in North America has gone unnoted by historians and psychologists for two centuries and more is testimony to the vast subliminal energies that are outside our consciousness.

Canada is a land of multiple borderlines, psychic, social, and geographic. In addition to the ones already noted, the student would be interested to know some of the many others. Canada has the longest coastline in the world, a coastline which represents the frontier for Europe on one side and the Orient on the other.

T. S. Eliot was very conscious of the "up-dating" power of frontiers. Commenting on this in regard to Mark Twain and the Mississippi, on whose shores he was born, Eliot states: "I am very well satisfied with having been born in St. Louis: in fact I think I was fortunate to have been born here, rather than in Boston, or New York, or London."[17] Within the city itself, he was conscious of borderlines. Mentioning the boundaries of the city, he says: "The utmost outskirts . . . touched on Forest Park, terminus of the Olive Street streetcars, and [were] to me, as a child, the beginning of the Wild West."[18]

Eliot is especially concerned with the effects of borderlines on language and literature, seeing in Mark Twain "one of those writers, of whom there are not a great many in any literature, who have discovered a new way of writing, valid not only for themselves but for others. I should place him, in this respect, even with Dryden and Swift, as one of those rare writers who have brought their language up to date, and in so doing, 'purified the dialect of the tribe.' "[19] Eliot sees the frontier as an area of transformation and purgation, a character which belongs to frontiers and borderlines in many other places.

17. "American Literature and the American Language," in Eliot, *To Criticize the Critic and Other Writings* (New York: Farrar, Straus & Giroux, 1965), p. 45.
18. Ibid., p. 44.
19. Ibid., p. 54.

Frederick J. Turner wrote a celebrated piece on the significance of the frontier in American history, noting that "American social development has been continually beginning over again on the frontier. This perennial rebirth, this fluidity of American life, this expansion westward with its new opportunities, its continuous touch with the simplicity of primitive society, furnish the forces dominating American character."[20] The Canadian borderline, as well as the numerous frontiers *within* Canada's borders, shares many of the features that Turner observes concerning the frontier in American history. He sees it as reacting on Europe as well as being the door for the entry of Europeans. In saying that the frontier is "the line of most rapid and effective Americanization" he is pointing to one of the major features of the Canadian borderline where the process of Canadianization also takes place. A frontier, or borderline, is the space between two worlds, constituting a kind of double plot or action that the poet W. B. Yeats discovered to be the archetypal formula for producing the "emotion of multitude" or the sense of universality. In his essay "Emotion of Multitude" Yeats explains and illustrates how in poetry and in art the alignment of two actions without interconnection performs a kind of magical change in the interacting components.[21] What may be banal and commonplace situations, merely by their confrontation and interface, are changed into something very important. The borderline of interface between cowboys and Indians captured the imagination not only of Europeans but of Asians as well. Even today affluent Japanese and Germans dress up in the costumes of cowboys and Indians and mount their horses to play the games of the Wild West. This frontier, to them exotic, has always been a major part of the Canadian

20. *The Frontier in American History* (New York: Henry Holt, 1920), pp. 2–3.
21. In Yeats, *Ideas of Good and Evil* (New York: Macmillan, 1903).

experience. The old frontier had been the melting pot for the immigrant, while today it continues as the melting pot of the affluent. Suburban Canada has its camps and cottages in the North.

Borderlines, as such, are a form of political ecumenism, the meeting place of diverse worlds and conditions. One of the most important manifestations of Canadian ecumenism on the Canadian borderline is the interface between the common-law tradition (oral) and the American Roman law (written). There have been no studies of this very rich situation, but then there have been no studies of how the oral traditions of the Southern states are the creative foundations of American jazz and rock music. Borderlines maintain an attitude of alertness and mutual study which gives a cosmopolitan character to Canada. One of the more picturesque borderlines in Canadian life is its royal commissions, which serve as mobile interdisciplinary and intercultural seminars, constituting a kind of grass-roots tradition in Canada. In search of hyperbole, only a Canadian can say, "As Canadian as a royal commission." There is an *outré* hyperbole of even more local significance: "As Canadian as Diefenbaker's French." John Diefenbaker would be delighted to know that he had become a cultural frontier.

Yes, Canada is a land of multiple borderlines, of which we have probed very few. It is these multiple borderlines that constitute Canada's low-profile identity, which, like its territory, has to cover a lot of ground. The positive advantage of a low profile in the electric age would be difficult to exaggerate. Electric information now encompasses the entire planet, forming another hidden borderline or frontier whose action has been to rob many countries of their former identities. In the case of the First World, the Fourth World of electric information dims down nationalism and private identities, whereas in its encounter with the Third World of India, China, and Africa, the new electric information environment has the effect of depriving people of their group identities. The borderline is an area of spiraling repetition and replay, of both inputs and feedback, of both interlace and interface, an area of "double ends joined," of rebirth and metamorphosis. Canada's five-thousand-mile borderline is unfortified and has the effect of keeping Canadians in a perpetual philosophic mood which nourishes flexibility in the absence of strong commitments or definite goals. By contrast, the United States, with heavy commitments and sharply defined objectives, is not in a good position to be philosophic, or cool, or flexible. Canada's borderline encourages the expenditure on communication of what might otherwise be spent on armament and fortification. The Canadian Broadcasting Corporation and the National Film Board are examples of federally sponsored communication rather than fortification. At the same time, Canadians have instant access to all American radio and television which, experienced in the alien milieu of Canada, feeds the philosophic attitude of comparison and contrast and critical judgment. The majority of Canadians are very grateful for the free use of American news and entertainment on the air and for the princely hospitality and neighborly dialogue on the ground.

Canada's advantages of having no sharply defined national or private identity appear in the general situation where lands long blessed by strong identities are now bewildered by the growing perforation and porousness of their identity image in this electronic age. The low-profile Canadian, having learned to live without such strongly marked characteristics, begins to experience a security and self-confidence that are absent from the big-power situation. In the electric age centralism becomes impossible when all services are available everywhere. Canada has never been able to centralize because of its size and small population. The national unity which Canadians sought by the railway "hardware" now proves to be irrelevant under electric conditions which yet create an inclusive consciousness. For Canada a federal or inclusive consciousness is an inevitable condition of size and speed of intercommunication. This inclusiveness, however, is not the same as the nineteenth-century idea of national unity; rather, it is that state of political ecumenism that has already been mentioned as the result of our multiple borderlines.

In order to have a high-profile identity nationally and politically, it is necessary to have sharp and few political and cultural borders. From 1870 onward Germany strove for a high-profile identity amid its multiple borders. In the industrial age this drive toward centralized and intense identity imagery seemed to be part of competitive commerce. Today, when the old industrial hardware is obsolescent, we can see that the Canadian condition of low-profile identity and multiple borders approaches the ideal pattern of electronic living.

The Authors

MARGARET ATWOOD was born in Ottawa, Ontario, in 1939. She received her B.A. (1961) from the University of Toronto, her M.A. (1962) from Radcliffe College, and pursued doctoral studies at Harvard University. She has published seven volumes of poetry: *Double Persephone* (1961), *The Circle Game* (1966), *The Animals in That Country* (1968), *The Journals of Susanna Moodie* (1970), *Procedures for Underground* (1970), *Power Politics* (1971), and *You Are Happy* (1974); *Margaret Atwood: Selected Poems* was published in 1976. She has also written three novels, *The Edible Woman* (1969), *Surfacing* (1972), and *Lady Oracle* (1976), nearly two dozen short stories published in a variety of Canadian and American journals, and a volume of literary criticism, *Survival: A Thematic Guide to Canadian Literature* (1972).

PETER BUITENHUIS, Professor of English, Simon Fraser University, was born in London, England, in 1925. He received his B.A. (1949) and M.A. (1953) from Oxford University and his Ph.D (1955) from Yale University, where he took his degree in American studies. He is the editor of Henry James's *French Writers and American Women* (1960) and the author of *Hugh MacLennan* (1969) and *The Grasping Imagination: The American Writings of*

Henry James (1970). In 1968 he edited *Selected Poems of E. J. Pratt.*

DOUGLAS BUSH, Gurney Professor of English Literature Emeritus, Harvard University, was born in Morrisburg, Ontario, in 1896. He received both his B.A. (1920), in Classics, and M.A. (1921), in English from the University of Toronto and his Ph.D. (1923) from Harvard University. He has written extensively on English literature and the classical tradition. Among his many works are *Mythology and the Renaissance Tradition in English Poetry* (1932), *Mythology and the Romantic Tradition in English Poetry* (1937), *The Renaissance and English Humanism* (1939), *English Literature in the Earlier Seventeenth Century* (1943), *Paradise Lost in Our Time* (1945), *Science and English Poetry* (1952), *John Milton* (1964), *Prefaces to Renaissance Literature* (1965), *Engaged and Disengaged* (1966), *John Keats* (1966), *Pagan Myth and Christian Tradition in English Poetry* (1968), *Matthew Arnold* (1971), and *Jane Austen* (1974). During the twenties he wrote a series of witty and penetrating commentaries on the Canadian scene for Canadian and American journals.

NORTHROP FRYE, University Professor, University of Toronto, was born in Sherbrooke, Quebec, in 1912. He received his B.A. (1933) from the University of Toronto, studied theology at Emmanuel College, Toronto, and was ordained in the ministry of the United Church of Canada in 1936. He returned to literary studies at Merton College, Oxford, where he received his M.A. (1940). He has published influential studies of almost every aspect of English literature and literary criticism. Among his many books are *Fearful Symmetry: A Study of William Blake* (1947), *Anatomy of Criticism* (1957), *The Well-Tempered Critic* (1963), *The Educated Imagination* (1963), *T. S. Eliot* (1963), *Fables of Identity* (1963), *A Natural Perspective: The Development of Shakespearean Comedy and Romance* (1965), *The Return of Eden: Five Essays on Milton's Epics* (1965), *Fools of Time: Studies in Shakespearean Tragedy* (1967), *The Modern Century* (1967), *A Study of English Romanticism* (1968), *The Stubborn Structure* (1970), *The*

Critical Path (1971), *The Secular Scripture: A Study of the Structure of Romance* (1976), and *Spiritus Mundi: Essays on Literature, Myth, and Society* (1976). He has been a frequent contributor of essays on all aspects of Canadian literature and culture; for ten years (1950–1959) he compiled the annual survey of English Canadian poetry that appeared in the *University of Toronto Quarterly;* some of his Canadian studies have been gathered together in *The Bush Garden: Essays on the Canadian Imagination* (1971).

MARINE LELAND, Professor of French Literature and French Canadian Civilization Emeritus, Smith College, was born in Quebec City, Quebec, in 1899. She attended Radcliffe College where she received the degrees of A.B. (1923), A.M. (1925), and Ph.D. (1928). From 1924 until her retirement in 1965 she was a member of the French department of Smith College; in the forties she established a course on French Canadian civilization. One of the pioneers in the study of French Canada, she has published many articles and studies in American and Canadian reviews, and she has lectured widely in both countries. In 1950 the Ministère des Affaires Etrangères in Paris awarded her its silver Médaille d'Honneur for her work in furthering knowledge of French Canadian culture in the United States; she has also received honorary degrees from Laval University (1952), the University of Montreal (1962), and the University of Vermont (1967). In 1967–68 she occupied the chair of French Canadian literature at McGill University.

MARSHALL MCLUHAN, Professor of English and Director of the Centre for Culture and Technology, University of Toronto, was born in Edmonton, Alberta, in 1911. He received his B.A. (1932) and his M.A. (1934) from the University of Manitoba; he pursued further literary studies at Cambridge University where he received the degrees of B.A. (1936), M.A. (1939), and Ph.D. (1942). His literary interests are reflected in his master's thesis, "George Meredith as a Poet and Dramatic Parodist," his doctoral dissertation, "The Place of Thomas Nashe in the Learning of His Time," and *The Literary Criticism of Marshall McLuhan 1943–1962* (1969). Among his many books are *The Me-*

chanical Bride: Folklore of Industrial Man (1951), *The Gutenberg Galaxy* (1962), *Understanding Media: The Extensions of Man* (1964), *The Medium Is the Massage* (1967), *War and Peace in the Global Village* (1968), *Counterblast* (1969), and *Culture Is Our Business* (1970). He has co-authored *Explorations in Communications* (1960) with E. S. Carpenter, *Through the Vanishing Point: Space in Poetry and Painting* (1968) with Harley Parker, *From Cliché to Archetype* (1970) with Wilfred Watson, *Take Today: The Executive as Dropout* (1972) with Barrington Nevitt, and *City As Classroom* (1977) with Kathryn Hutchon and Eric McLuhan.

BRIAN PARKER, Professor of English, University of Toronto, was born in Bunbury, Cheshire, in 1931. He received his B.A. (1953) and his M.A. (1955) from the University of Liverpool and his Ph.D. (1957) from the Shakespeare Institute, University of Birmingham. As an editor and critic, he has published numerous articles on the Jacobean theater as well as on the modern theater. Formerly Director of the Graduate Centre for the Study of Drama, University of Toronto, he was general editor of the New Press Canadian Drama Series. He has edited collections of plays by George Ryga and James Reaney.

DAVID STAINES, Assistant Professor of English, Harvard University, was born in Toronto, Ontario, in 1946. He received his B.A. (1967) from the University of Toronto and his A.M. (1968) and Ph.D. (1973) from Harvard University. He has published many articles on romance, medieval drama, and Arthurian literature. In addition to his teaching in the medieval field, he introduced Canadian literature courses at Harvard University. For the New Canadian Library he has written introductions to Sylvia Fraser's *Pandora* and Margaret Laurence's *The Diviners;* he compiled and edited *Responses and Evaluations: Essays on Canada by E. K. Brown,* the first collection of the late critic's Canadian studies.

GEORGE WOODCOCK was born in Winnipeg, Manitoba, in 1912, but lived in England until 1949. His formal education, apart from a few evening classes at Morley College, London, never extended beyond Sir William Borlase's School at Marlow in the Thames Valley. Since 1949 he has been living in British Columbia. In 1956 he became Associate Professor of English and Lecturer in Asian Studies at the University of British Columbia; in 1963 he abandoned regular teaching to devote his time to editing and writing. Among his many books are *The White Island* (1940), *William Godwin: A Biography* (1946), *Imagine the South* (1947), *The Writer and Politics* (1948), *The Paradox of Oscar Wilde* (1950), *Ravens and Prophets: Travels in Western Canada* (1952), *Pierre-Joseph Proudhon* (1956), *Anarchism: A History of Libertarian Ideas and Movements* (1962), *Asia, Gods and Cities: Aden to Tokyo* (1966), *The Crystal Spirit* (1966), *The British in the Far East* (1969), *Hugh MacLennan* (1969), *Canada and the Canadians* (1970), *Odysseus Ever Returning: Essays on Canadian Writers and Writing* (1970), *Mordecai Richler* (1971), *Dawn and the Darkest Hour: A Study of Aldous Huxley* (1972), *Gandhi* (1972), *Herbert Read: The Stream and the Source* (1972), *Who Killed the British Empire?* (1974), and *Gabriel Dumont* (1975). In 1959 he founded *Canadian Literature: A Quarterly of Criticism and Review*, which he has edited since its inception.

Index

H